REVOLUTIONS
AND PEACE TREATIES
1917–1920

REVOLUTIONS
AND PEACE TREATIES
1917–1920

Gerhard Schulz

TRANSLATED BY MARIAN JACKSON

METHUEN & CO LTD
LONDON

First published in 1967 by
Deutscher Taschenbuch Verlag, Munich as
'Revolutionen und Friedensschlusse, 1917–1920'
Copyright © 1967 Gerhard Schulz
This edition first published in Great Britain in 1972 by
Methuen & Co Ltd, 11 New Fetter Lane, London EC4
English translation © 1972 Methuen & Co Ltd
Printed in Great Britain by
Butler & Tanner Ltd
Frome and London

SBN 416 15940 0

Distributed in the U.S.A.
by Barnes & Noble Inc.

Contents

Introduction: World War and World Crisis

The First World War breaks the continuity of modern history. The upheaval which it created was caused by the use of the arms and the economic potential at the disposal of the Great Powers. But the extent and the lasting effects of the upheaval were not determined by the use of these resources. What happened was something more than could be decided by arms and armies. If the historian wants to appreciate this fact fully he must leave military history aside and look at the world-shaking event of the war as part of the history of the world.

The war was the manifestation of an historic crisis which affected every aspect of the political life of the preceding period: the system of states and alliances, international relations, economic interests, economic, social and political structures, constitutional arrangements, internal and international power constellations, social conditions, the attempts to reform them, the revolutionary movements created by these conditions and the interpretations put on them, the ideologies.

In origin the war was a conflict between the two great European systems of alliances; but inevitably almost all the problems of the age came in one way or another to be affected by this momentous event. Into this category fell the military and political rivalry between Germany and France, aggravated as it was by the Alsace-Lorraine question, the maritime rivalry between Germany and Britain and the traditional causes for friction on issues of colonial and overseas policy in the Near East, the Far East and in Africa. The fate of the Danube monarchy and of the peoples of South East Europe, so significant in the history of Europe, was at stake; so was that of the Ottoman Empire chronically sick after two centuries of inadequate reforms and general decline; and so too was the political future of Turkey and of the Arabian peninsula .Big structural flaws were revealed in the British Empire, and its relationship with the emergent Great Powers, particularly the United States but also Japan, underwent a fundamental change. In most of the belligerent countries new political trends assumed shape and significance as a result of the war and existing movements were given new impetus.

The reverberations of the war were felt for years and even today their ultimate effects are still present. Looking at these effects from a political and historical viewpoint we find that at least four conflicts which reached an acute stage as a result of the war are still basically as acute today despite the changed situation:

(1) The conflict between imperialism and anti-imperialism in all nations with overseas interests.

(2) The conflict between the democratic ideals of Western Europe and the authoritarian systems and movements, both the old monarchical and traditional ones and the new dictatorial and revolutionary kind.

(3) The conflict between social revolutionary elements and the forces of the established order.

(4) The conflict between on the one hand the un-free or dependent peoples of Europe who were becoming nationally conscious and the colonial peoples under the tutelage of the great European powers, and on the other the ruling nations of the imperialist age.

The great historical turning point can be pinpointed with some degree of precision by examining the internal development of the Great Powers as effected by the war. From the summer of 1916 onwards several of the nations involved in the war experienced changes which basically altered the established order of things. Not one of the great European peoples was spared completely. There was ample confirmation of the observation made during the July crisis of 1914 by the British Foreign Secretary, Sir Edward Grey, to the Austrian ambassador: 'A great war would mean a state of things worse than in 1848 . . . many things might be completely swept away.' Almost from the start the war tested the nations' constitutions and proved a particularly severe strain on the relationship between the rulers and their subjects who were continuously called upon to make sacrifices of a magnitude unknown for generations. In some states the crisis occurred more quickly and was more fateful than in others; some survived it, others did not or only just. In the last resort there was no quarter given anywhere in Europe, and no complete victory and success gained. But it is a fact that the great countries with liberal constitutions and firmly rooted democratic traditions and institutions encountered the wartime crises with more strength, perseverance and resilience than the autocratically, oligarchically and bureaucratically governed states.

It has become customary to date the start of the upheavals in the old European order from the Russian revolution of 1917 and the overthrow of Tsarist rule. Because of the succession of overwhelming events in 1917 historians have come to look upon this date as the beginning of the latest epoch in history and to see the happenings of that year as a complete break in the continuity of events since the French revolution. The experiences of 1914 – the July crisis, the outbreak of war, Germany's offensive in the West and Russia's campaign in the East – were the last links in an unbroken chain of events. After the growing destruction of the first war years the epoch-making happenings of 1917 marked a turn towards something new. In the summer of 1914 it was possible to see the preliminary results of post-Bismarckian *Weltpolitik* as the sum of a 'conspiracy of the diplomats', that is of the old generation of diplomats who were accustomed to a positivist approach and who, without false optimism or emotion, weighed up the possibilities so as to prepare what their own country's interests appeared to demand.

In the vital decisions and also in the many terrible consequences of this diplomacy Europe demonstrated once more its basic unity. As late as the spring of 1915 one of the makers of British foreign policy, the Permanent Under-Secretary at the Foreign Office, Sir Arthur Nicolson, perceiving the magnitude of what lay ahead wrote that he was thinking anxiously of the time when peace conditions would be negotiated; that he had always favoured Bismarck's policy of not making conditions that would force the one-time enemy to wait for the day of revenge. But soon such observations were lost in a reality of other values and conditions. Because of the great nations' increasing efforts and sacrifices, and because of propaganda activity designed to mobilise all national resources, the dividing lines became progressively clearer as the struggle continued and uncompromising alternatives divided friend and foe. It was as though people could bear the sacrifice and burdens only by extreme partisanship. Special qualities were needed indeed to escape from this fateful progress towards emotional and intellectual radicalism and to remain calm and detached in the midst of the universal excitement.

The magnitude of the effort and the scale of the world-wide war coalitions were soon matched on both sides by grandiose ideas about war aims and victory. *La victoire intégrale* became a slogan which even calm minds could not question openly. Correspondingly extreme was the extent of the reaction against the old order and the old policies, against the supremacy of the national idea and the national preoccupation with power which flowed from this.

The number of states involved in the war continued to grow until it finally included almost the whole world. In Europe it was only the North European countries, Sweden, Norway and Denmark, that remained neutral, apart from the Netherlands, Switzerland and Spain.

The growth of hostilities into a 'world war' produced domestic repercussions among the European nations involved. The extension of the war into every sphere, the 'total mobilisation' of their countries' economic and military resources presented the leaders of the belligerent countries with domestic problems of totally new dimensions. No nation, no state and no form of government was spared altogether.

The intellectual atmosphere of the age was also deeply affected by this fateful event. The national traditions of the German philosophical schools, and the branches of learning which they came to influence in the nineteenth century, made it seem natural that at the outbreak of the war philosophers and scholars should place themselves at the service of the nation and defend its cause. The French, the Italians and the British did the same and in their enthusiastic activity on behalf of the national cause often adopted a tone that seems regrettable rather than praiseworthy to a less committed generation. The chauvinist exaltation of those who claimed to base their arguments on philosophical or scientific principles reached a degree unknown in the modern state. It was their self-chosen task to make their own nation believe in the importance of the struggle that must be won in order to protect and preserve the world. There were many variations on the same theme. But common to them all was a missionary idealism and a loudly proclaimed belief in the divine right of the national cause in the merciless struggle of mighty powers. What they ignored were the vital issues of the great historical crisis that were brought to the fore by the war.

The French were the first to see signs of barbarism and brutality in German civilisation. Distinguished men of letters familiar with Germany's intellectual life spoke of the threat to the civilisations of the European nations. The barbarism theme was retained by the belligerent nations even after the war had ended. It became one of the main features of the Germanophobia which for a long time caused great indignation in Germany. But there were similar manifestations in Germany itself.

Under the influence of the neo-idealists the start of the war was seen in Germany as the beginning of an age which was at last rejecting the materialist way of life. The German people, the argument ran, were acting for the whole of humanity. A divine 'inner quality' and 'spirituality' were upheld against the known facts and stressed out of all proportion. This idealistic extravaganza gave the impression of a rapidly growing feeling of national awareness which was creating a 'new German state', although this was in fact nothing more than an organisation which controlled every aspect of economic, political and military life. These German 'Ideas of 1914' would triumph over the ideas of 1789. At the same time there were also cool-headed men like the religious philosopher Ernst Troeltsch who looked, with much less success, for the real causes of the tension between the 'German mind and Western Europe'.

A great number of people were led by the exuberance of their own ideals to biased and emotional judgments. The effects of these emotions are seen best by taking as illustrations not the extreme examples but the borderline cases. Even a moderate historian like Karl Lamprecht could wax emotional over the 'ignominious and despicable military crimes' of the Belgian and French populations, condemning them with great passion as a 'disgrace to the nationalist movement in European history', without so much as mentioning Germany's illegal entry into neutral Belgium. Like many others he considered it was common sense to speak of the 'final struggle of Teutonism . . . against the advancing eastern barbarism', a struggle that was the logical historical continuation of the battles 'against the Huns and the Magyars and the Turks'.

The frequent manifestation of exaggerated nationalism can in the last resort be seen as an exogenous part of a war propaganda that grew unplanned out of the traditional world of learning and was directed towards the same end as the organised propaganda. The Central Powers possessed the most developed and best organised machinery for influencing public opinion, centrally controlled and purposeful. In Germany the entire press system depended on being fed information by the Military Press Office of the Prussian Ministry of War which was under military orders and interested only in military objectives. Apart from Russia there was no country in which negative and positive press censorship – which everywhere of course was governed by the same laws of secrecy – went as far as in Germany. In Britain the press remained far freer and subject to its own rules; but for the duration of the war, under the influence of the great papers owned by Lord Northcliffe, almost the entire press steered a nationalist course which proved a most effective factor in moulding public opinion and which the government had to respect but could not control. The symptoms of an all-out war policy, the hysteria of extravagant patriotism and the excesses of unrestrained propaganda characterised the domestic scene in Britain as much as in Germany, Austria–Hungary, France, Russia and Italy.

The most important factor in the history of the war, until the United States joined in and until the military and political collapse of Russia, was the surprising strength and unity of the British Empire then faced with its greatest test. The soldiers and politicians of the Central Powers had never fully allowed for the possible consequences of such a situation. As a result the struggle was substantially prolonged and extended and a victory of the Central Powers became less and less likely. While propaganda and public opinion in the nations at war had at first encouraged the prevailing view that the conflict was a surprise adventure of short duration, the British government at once, with great energy and without vacillation, prepared for a long, hard struggle. It never underestimated its German adversary, his military power, the strength of his organisation and his patriotism. Although the British government did not introduce general conscription until 1916, Lord Kitchener from the very start took steps to prepare for a war of at least three year's duration, a time span on which the War Office counted from the outset. To make these preparations without illusions and without wasting time was one of the most important decisions taken at the beginning of the war. As a result Britain immediately became subject to a form of military planning that took the country into the ranks of the great military powers of the world.

The major part of the German navy on which Germany had lavished great expenditure before the war and for which it had sacrificed important diplomatic opportunities remained inactive and inglorious at its bases; it became finally the most vulnerable point of the old order and the focus of growing, desperate discontent about the war, and of revolt. The British army on the other hand, which did not even figure in the plans of the German General Staff, on the outbreak of war rapidly emerged as an instrument of great strength and importance.

From 1914–15 onwards Dominion troops appeared in growing numbers at the fronts, primarily in the colonial fighting – which did not, however, continue after the first year of the war except in East Africa – but also in the Near East, the Balkans and finally in France. After the failure of the French offensive in April 1917, when parts of the French army mutinied and had to be withdrawn from the front line and reformed, large sections of the most important front depended, before the arrival of American military assistance, on the British contingent, among which there were at that time approximately 100,000 Canadians, 150,000 Australians and New Zealanders, 10,000 Indians and several thousand South Africans. During this military crisis in France, which was one of the greatest tests in its history, the British army showed itself fully equal to its task and proved completely a match for its German adversary.

At this stage in the war it seemed as though the British Empire had dealt successfully with its first crisis. Even India, which was its most vulnerable member, sent valuable troops with great fighting potential to Europe. In 1918 at the time of the armistice there were almost 270,000 Indians, Muslims and Hindus in the battleline.

India's internal unity and involvement in the war, her representational national movements, the All India Congress and the All India Muslim League, seemed brilliant proof of the theory formulated half a century earlier by the Liberal exponent of the concept of the Empire, Sir Charles Wentworth Dilke, who had argued that the 'English race' provided the dominating element and the unifying cultural and political link in the British Empire. It must be said that this argument was valid only to a qualified extent and for a limited time. But at first the political unity of the Empire proved stronger than India's internal religious conflicts and stronger also than the ties of the Islamic religion.

When Turkey became a belligerent and the Caliph called for a Holy War, a *jihad*, the Mohammedan population of India showed signs of wanting to escape from the war and from military service with the British. This situation the Central Powers sought to exploit. But the Hindus from the start proved receptive to the ideas of Gandhi, a high-caste Indian who in the clashes between Indian immigrants and the Boers in South Africa had organised a campaign of passive resistance. Gandhi returned home determined to keep his country-men on the side of Britain and with them hoped for the hour when India could expect a political reward for its loyal support of the British war against Germany and Turkey. It was largely his doing that both national parties adopted this attitude which led to the Lucknow Treaty, the first joint national Indian programme drawn up by the two great organisations, Congress and the Muslim League. The two parties then jointly called upon the viceroy to set up a constituent assembly based on elections. Only a few radical groups and spokesmen publicly demanded home rule, taking the road followed for years by the Irish independence movement which after the brutal suppression of the Easter Rebellion in Dublin in 1916 entered upon a new and, for Britain, dangerous stage.

In the immediate future, however, the situation in India took a much less dramatic turn than in Ireland, the small, restless country which was so close to the European theatre of war. In 1917 the India Office in London decided to publish proposals for Indian self-administration, a plan whose subsequent development produced violent reactions on the part of the Indian national movement. But in the first years of the war it could not be said that the Indian problem was becoming in any way acute. Generally speaking, none of the problems that came as the war dragged on was apparent at the start, in India or in any other part of the Empire. There were almost no difficulties in bringing the whole British Empire into the war, except for some minor incidents in South Africa, where differences between the Boer nationalists and loyal citizens of Anglo-Saxon stock came briefly to a head again.

The unity of the Empire in the war made the conflict into a world war in which the Allies – Britain, France and Russia – had at their disposal the resources of the entire world, whereas the Central Powers suffered greatly as a result of the blockade and had to struggle to maintain their supplies. German war propaganda interpreted the situation subjectively, stressing only the heroic aspects. It was claimed that Germany was fighting for its existence against a 'world of enemies' whose aim it was to defeat the German people with the use of vast material resources. A tale in the same vein was that of 'Germany's encirclement' and of the enemy's sudden attack. Psychologically German war propaganda followed the simplest rules by impressing on its audience the size and world-wide presence of the enemy and by accusing him in seemingly plausible fashion of wanting to do wrong.

This approach made it easy to interpret Germany's early military successes in Belgium and France up to the Battle of the Marne, and later in the East – victories which did not really yet justify any great hopes – as manifestations of a divine force. As the Germans, and not only middle-class Germans, firmly believed in the immutable difference between a materialistic world and the force of idealism, such propaganda found a ready audience. German war propaganda was therefore able to count on the political journalists with their links with the neo-idealistic philosophy in its own way to strengthen their activities.

The bitter experiences and sacrifices of 1916 and the desperate food situation in Germany and in much of the Austrian half of the Danube monarchy imposed a severe strain on the Central Powers. Such groping attempts as were made by the Austrians and the Germans in the first years of the war to come to separate peace agreements remained in the sphere of historical happenings of secondary importance. But some of these efforts show a vague premonition of the unforeseeable consequences which the great struggle would have. To begin with, it was a few military who viewed with dark forebodings the continued strengthening of the enemy front, after fruitless campaigns had been acclaimed as victories. Gradually Germany was forced to realise the devastating scale of a 'peoples' war' between the great powers, a danger to which Caprivi had warningly referred as Chancellor in the Reichstag as long ago as 1891 when he had observed that such a war would be quite unlike the 'cabinet wars' of the past.

PART ONE

Crises and Revolutions

1. Peace feelers and war aims before the United States entry into the war

Once the Central Powers made up their minds that there would be no compromise, the story of their domestic affairs becomes a tragedy. The commitment to 'positive' aims which could only be achieved after a military victory made all out war inevitable and put a stop to any move to limit the war. Some of the attempts which had already been made to do so resulted from gloomy but not necessarily unrealistic estimates of the Central Powers' real chances.

General von Falkenhayn, Moltke's successor as Chief of the General Staff and therefore as Germany's military leader, had taken a pessimistic view of the consequences of Italy's entry into the war, displaying only a little less gloom than his Austrian colleague, Conrad von Hötzendorff, who painted the prospects in the blackest colours. Conrad advised the Foreign Minister, Burián, to make immediate peace with Russia, even to offer it, at the expense of Germany's ally Turkey, complete possession of the territory on the Dardanelles and the Bosphorus. Almost simultaneously Britain and France actually made the same offer to their Eastern ally so as to keep him on their side. In addition Conrad even wanted to give the Tsar parts of Austrian Galicia and to let Austria recoup its losses in Serbia and Montenegro. With a remarkable lack of political perceptiveness Conrad wanted to end the war against Russia. This explains some aspects of the July crisis and Austria's hesitation in preparing for war against Russia due to gaps in Conrad's plans which counted on Rumanian and Italian divisions. When the military arrangements of the most enthusiastic advocate of a preventive war against Serbia were upset by the situation of 1914 and in 1915 were about to collapse, Conrad became as determined to get out of the war against Russia as he had been to have a war against Serbia.

Burián was not prepared to go as far as Conrad wished. Nevertheless he decided to suggest to Bethmann Hollweg that Germany should make peace with Britain and withdraw from Belgium so as to have troops available for the Italian front, although the moment when Italy decided to join the Entente powers was probably the least auspicious occasion on which to tempt Britain with a separate peace.

But Italy's entry into the war did not affect the position of the Central Powers as adversely as the military and the diplomats had feared. From a military point of view the situation looked much more favourable than expected after the spring of 1915. Yet Conrad's peace proposals did not remain the only ones. Earlier the German Foreign Ministry had responded to peace feelers put out by the Japanese Ambassador in Stockholm and by personalities in St Petersburg. But when in May 1916 these activities came to light the diplomat was disowned completely by his government. What was of interest to Germany in these proposals was the possibility, which was also being explored through other channels, of making a separate peace with Russia. In spite of contacts with the Tsar's entourage and with Russian policy makers nothing came of the idea. Equally unsuccessful were the peace feelers that were put out via the German Embassy in the spring of 1916 to King Albert of the Belgians and to opposition groups in the French Chamber. In all these activities the war aims problem played a part. Historians remain divided in their opinion on these peace moves. But to the Central Powers they held out no prospect of change or of relief, so that until the end the only way out of the war remained military victory on all fronts.

In the spring and summer of 1915, under the pressure of Falkenhayn's great offensives in the East, the whole of Galicia was won back and Poland, Lithuania and Courland conquered in a little over four weeks. In the next few months almost the whole of Serbia and Montenegro was occupied, so that at the beginning of 1916 Central Europe formed one great German–Austrian power complex. In spite of a few crises the favourable position of the Central Powers remained unshaken by the renewed heavy and costly fighting in the West. This was followed in the East by the last great Russian offensive under Brusilov and – in connection with this – by Rumania's entry into the war and its brief victorious campaign. But these battles affected the situation in other ways; above all in that the army came to play a greater role in political decision making. Because these tangible successes had not been won by diplomacy but by the strength of the nation in arms, military confidence in the army now grew to almost limitless dimensions. But as the power of the military increased for all

14

to see, the expectations and aims became correspondingly more ambitious.

In many ways the political system of the parliamentary democracies was more suited to the growing demands of the war than that of the semi-parliamentary, essentially autocratic monarchies of Germany, Russia and Austria-Hungary. Since Bismarck no efforts had been made to liberalise Germany's constitution by the introduction of a greater degree of parliamentary government and democracy. As the Chancellor had to dispense with parliamentary support, his position depended in the last resort on the Kaiser and he sought to do his duty as the Kaiser's trusted adviser within the framework of the possibilities as he saw them. But after the start of the war the monarch had not been able to increase his authority. Whereas in 1870–71 William I towered above the military in reputation and was assured of lasting devotion, in 1914–18 the autocratic system lost its autocratic point of reference. William II never became a popular leader. He was temperamentally unsuited to be commander in chief because he lacked perseverance and energy and often also the ability to make objective judgments. He remained 'supreme commander' in name and tradition only. As the war went on other forces were quick to move to the fore. Nor was the Chancellor able to have his way as the Kaiser's mouthpiece when the all-powerful military insisted on a point. In the first years of the war, however, the army leaders did not as yet have the position and general standing which Hindenburg and Ludendorff enjoyed from the summer of 1916 onwards.

Even in the days of undisturbed parliamentary truce the Chancellor's position was not really secure. He was harassed by economic pressure groups as much as by the Admiralty and the General Staff. He frequently turned for support to the Reichsrat and to the Federal States, particularly to Prussia. But with the war the complicated relationship between Prussia and the Reich entered upon a new phase. When Count Hertling, hitherto Prime Minister of Bavaria, became Reich Chancellor and Prime Minister of Prussia the administrative links between Prussia and the Reich were strengthened because several Secretaries of State in charge of Reich ministries became at the same time Prussian ministers. In the other states the Chancellor had to look for support elsewhere so as to survive the 'first real test' of the Reich constitution, which was in reality a test of the political leadership of the country.

The German Reich had emerged in 1871 from a wartime coalition of German states; it was made up of three Hanseatic cities and twenty-two states governed by princes some of whom continued to regard themselves merely as 'allies of the German Emperor'. Some of the old glory of the princes of the Holy Roman Empire came to life once more in the war. Here again Bethmann Hollweg faced the threat of a new internal opposition if he refused to fall in with the special wishes of the great dynasties and of the Kaiser's 'noble allies'. This meant that the Chancellor was repeatedly compelled to take note of the war aims put forward by the states or by their dynasties. The foreign affairs committee of the Bundesrat, under the permanent chairmanship of Bavaria, remained unimportant until the war. During the war it was convened frequently to discuss questions of foreign policy with the Chancellor.

The states were afraid that future annexations would lead to a unilateral enlargement of Prussia and result in a further change in the balance of power in the Bundesrat in Prussia's favour. This they were not prepared to accept. The Bavarian king and Count Hertling, the Bavarian Prime Minister who had at heart remained a *grossdeutsche* federalist, insisted that in addition to Prussia other German states must share in the German booty and that the situation must be clarified in good time. Bavaria's claims were, at least initially, on the ambitious side. It demanded Alsace; then there was the question of Bavaria's access to the sea with Antwerp as the favoured port. Louis III was inclined to claim the whole of Belgium for Bavaria so as – with a few frontier rectifications and territorial changes in the Lower Main region – to bring a continuous land mass from the Alps to Antwerp under the rule of the House of Wittelsbach. But the Bavarian claims led the other states to demand compensation. Count Hertling and William II finally settled down to allocate the disputed territories and agreed that Lorraine should go to Prussia, Lower Alsace to Bavaria and Upper Alsace to Baden; Estonia, Livonia and Courland they made part of Prussia in a personal union, Lithuania an independent dukedom under a Saxon prince and Poland a kingdom under the regency of a member of the Royal House of Württemberg.

Although these war aims – like others – are of no interest taken singly, they are of symptomatic significance historically, particularly in view of the fact that it was always necessary for the Chancellor to consider the wishes of the states and that this tended to complicate his position. His difficulties increased as the war took a more eventful course, largely because it proved impossible to contain or permanently weaken the unyielding claims and persistent opposition of the *alldeutsche* chauvinists to whom every report of victory was an additional stimulus.

German *Weltpolitik* never pursued firm or logical objectives. It was vacillating, opportunist and often vaguely formulated. The same was true of the German war aims, but given the assumption of total victory, from which all demands, started any possible opposition from other powers was disregarded. The picture was thus more or less dominated by the reckless agitation of the Pan-Germans, the *Alldeutsche Verband*. The variety of influences and interests which had found expression in German pre-war world policy is also much in evidence in the German war aims, the common characteristic of which remained a lack of consideration for the needs and interests of other peoples and powers. In putting forward the official policy Chancellor Bethmann Hollweg quickly found himself defending the *Burgfriede*, the party truce, and the point of view of national policy. From the start overwhelming emphasis was thus placed on the 'primacy of domestic policy' as against foreign policy and the opportunities to put out peace feelers were reduced.

Under the impact of military success and the influence of a purposeful 'war aims movement' organised by the *Alldeutsche*, imaginary zones of interest were mapped out at any early stage. These revealed a variety of war aims, some of which were pursued side by side and simultaneously while others had no connection with one another. First there were the direct annexations, in the West the ore deposits of Longwy-Briey and Luxemburg and in the East a strip along the Polish frontier, as well as Courland and Lithuania. Then there was to be a European customs union between France, Belgium, Holland, Luxemburg but also including Denmark, Sweden, Norway, Italy, Austria-Hungary and an independent Poland under German economic hegemony. Along the German frontiers in the West and also in the East there was to be a chain of buffer states under German influence, Belgium, Poland and the Ukraine. Next Germany was to have an economic sphere of influence in the South East which would encompass Rumania, Turkey and Georgia. Finally Germany's colonial possessions would be rounded

17

off by the formation of a militarily viable German 'Central Africa' with land links with Turkey. The civil leadership of the Reich was involved in the preparation of some of these plans and representatives of most of the political parties also took an active part in these discussions.

Occasionally Bethmann Hollweg gave way. But it is difficult to find a clear line running through his policy which he himself described as a policy of the 'diagonal'. At the beginning he was anxious as far as possible to avoid annexations in Europe and to agree only to changes on the Belgian and French frontiers, primarily for reasons of military security. The only exception to this was the small but valuable ore basin of Briey. But in two other important spheres the Chancellor showed himself very receptive to certain ideas that were gradually gaining in popularity. He recognised the goal of a consolidated Central African colonial empire for Germany. Less exclusive than the great 'Central Africa' of the *Alldeutsche* the plans for this went back to the territorial objectives of the Anglo-German treaty for a division of the Portuguese colonies, which never came about because of the war. The proposal now was to unite the areas claimed in the treaty by Germany, Angola and the northern region of Mozambique, with Germany's African colonies, and to add to this the Belgian Congo, French Equatorial Africa which bordered on the German Cameroons and French Niger.

But the most important point in Bethmann Hollweg's programme was the idea of a Central European economic association. This was to take the form of a customs union of states with equal rights and in the first place to include Austria-Hungary and France, without any political constitution being envisaged. Such an arrangement would no doubt have given Germany tremendous economic advantages. But the same was also true for Austria-Hungary and perhaps even for France. The parallel with modern economic communities springs to mind, although in the first place the 1914 project extended much further to the East and the South East and secondly its loose organisation was still far removed from the permanent administration of economic communities today. Proposals of this kind were nothing new. In the days before the war there had been suggestions of a Franco–German settlement along these lines which conflicted with the ideas of the *Alldeutsche*. Such proposals now took a more definite shape while being modified so as to leave no doubt about German hegemony.

From the outset, looked at superficially, there was some measure of agreement between the demands of the *Alldeutsche* and the plans of the Chancellor. More significant and more revealing, however, are the differences and disagreements between them. Yet it is evident that even Bethmann Hollweg's programme was based on the assumption of a definite German victory; this alone would have provided the necessary degree of political superiority which Bethmann Hollweg saw as a prerequisite for the achievement of his war aims. In some respects Bethmann later even went beyond the early aims; in particular he explored the possibilities of lasting political influence by Germany on the 'tributary state' of Belgium and in the end he also toyed with plans for the annexation of Polish and Baltic territory. But the moving spirits behind these projects were not at the Imperial Chancellory.

Another idea, however, was probably conceived there. It is not surprising that, following the political practice adopted by the Germans at the peace negotiations after the Franco-German war of 1870–71 and also after earlier wars, it was again proposed that the vanquished enemy should pay war indemnities. But now the indemnity to be imposed on defeated France was to be such that for the next eighteen or twenty years it would be unable to spend sizeable sums on armaments. This idea was voiced by the Germans as soon as the war began; later it was taken up by the French Minister of Finance and finally it became part and parcel of the Allied peace conditions. Neither side, however, was definite before the end of the war on the size of the payments to be demanded. Fiscal experts and economists considered the question of war indemnities in detail; international financiers and bankers played a leading part in the reparations story, then and later.

In Bethmann Hollweg's view it was the government's duty to give way to certain interested parties. The widespread propaganda of the *Alldeutsche* made the pressure to which the Chancellor was subjected from the right more visible than any other influence on him. But we must not underestimate the importance of the army of publicists, journalists and pamphleteers who preached national enthusiasm to all classes and occupational groups and who in the 'ideas of 1914' waxed lyrical about Germany rising to a higher position among the Great Powers and lauded the daily 'plebiscites' held to demonstrate the unity of the German nation. These ideas were spread by both liberals and conservatives and with the first military victories contributed to the initial exuberance. They survived almost intact even as the war dragged on and were in part responsible for the stubborn determination without which Germany could not possibly have survived those four hard years of war and the tremendous demands it made on its people.

A similar state of affairs could be found among the other belligerent nations, Russia being no exception. During mobilisation there the feeling of the rulers was one of apprehension and uncertainty. Their anxieties about the uncertain internal situation almost overshadowed their fears about the war and forbade any thought of military defeat. Nikolai Alexeievich Maklakov, Russian Minister of the Interior during the first months of the war, is said to have remarked that the war was not popular with the mass of the people who found it easier to understand the meaning of revolution than of victory over the Germans; but Russia would not escape its fate. The conflict between national and revolutionary mobilisation which existed in Russia from the beginning was at first decided in favour of national mobilisation. Turkey's entry into the war simplified this decision because the Slavophil dream, based on an old Russian vision, of breaking up the Danube monarchy, of acquiring the Straits and access to the Black Sea, was not revived. But in Russia the war aims discussions never became popular and hardly reached the general public. They remained confined to the political leaders and to a few groups among whom the spokesmen of the political movements of the bourgeoisie were the most prominent. Milyukov for example, the leader of the liberal Kadet party, spoke of incorporating East Prussia into Russia and the Pan-Slav, Menshikov, said in the widely read semi-official *Novoye Vremya* that Russia's western frontier should be safeguarded by a number of small buffer states and that Germany and Austria should be transformed into groups of independent peoples – an almost perfect mirror image of some of the safety provisions suggested in Germany.

But by and large during the war, there was more chauvinism, which expressed itself in more extreme forms, in Central, Western and Southern Europe than in the East. Even in Britain, where political pacifism and nonconformism played historically important roles and were never completely silenced, the nationalist press generated among the population an enthusiasm for the war and feelings of hatred that were not unlike some of the manifestations of extreme nationalism in Germany. Popular slogans such as 'Hang the Kaiser' and 'Gott strafe England' reveal comparable emotions, although there is a significant difference in the address to which this invective is directed.

The anti-British outbursts of the German press found parallels in products like Kipling's poem about the Hun at the gate. Many writers distinguished themselves in the service of nationalistic war propaganda from a literary and from a political point of view. In all the imperialist literature of the period there is a noticeably religious element; this may partly be because some political writers as well as some of the politicians who were productive in the literary field came from the ranks of the clergy. But the manner in which they participated in politics differed. Whereas the German war propagandists drew upon the idealist philosophers the British war vocabulary was permeated by Christian ideas and traditions. The British, like the Germans, spoke of a 'holy war'; but in Britain the identification of national and religious values was more direct and simple than in Germany. The struggle between Britain and Germany was presented as a life-and-death struggle with Satan or as a fight between Christ and Hell. In 1916 a Nonconformist cleric published a book with the characteristic title *The Christian Ethic of War* and another wrote of the 'Christian Imperialism' of the British. The religious fervour of such avowals cannot be doubted. Nor can it be ignored.

There was, however, no popular 'war aims movement' in Britain comparable to that of the *Alldeutsche*. The preparation of territorial plans was done by the Foreign Office or by the India Office. But the thought of a further consolidation and expansion of the British Empire with its vast resources, as well as the urge to defeat the great continental enemy, gave the British a popular objective during the war. These ideas found expression in the 'new imperialism' of Lord Milner's circle and in the widespread hope of a renewal and strengthening of the links between Great Britain and the United States of America, the two countries which Sir Charles Wentworth Dilke in his vision of 'Greater Britain' had seen as self-evidently belonging together. The representatives of the British Empire, the United States and of all other English-speaking peoples would meet at an annual 'Amphictyonic Council' to discuss questions of world-wide interest and to ensure lasting collaboration. Such schemes, of which there were many, form part of the idea of a commonwealth of British nations which it was thought the war would enlarge and develop but to which it would also give a higher Christian meaning and greater moral depth. They reveal the reverse side of a spirit which manifested itself in down-to-earth war songs.

But among all nations at war men and women were determined to oppose nationalist excesses, although theirs were often voices crying in the wilderness. Their importance grew as the war went on but became significant only towards the end. In Germany there was a 'National Committee for an Honourable Peace' which advocated a negotiated peace, and also a 'People's League for Freedom and Country', founded as an antidote to the *Vaterlandspartei* of Tirpitz, Kapp, Hugenberg and other *Alldeutsche*. Several prominent personalitities who had supported 'the ideas of 1914' in the enthusiasm and the elation of the first weeks of the war became sceptical and prudent as time went on and warned against nationalistic overbearance. The influential Reichstag deputy Matthias Erzberger finally did as complete and decisive an about turn as the writer Maximilian Harden, who with his journal *Die Zukunft* became one of Germany's most determined supporters of President Wilson's ideas. By the end the critics included the entire liberal – but not the national liberal – press, politically and journalistically active scientists like Adolph von Harnack, Friedrich Meinecke and above all others Ernst Troeltsch; also Max Weber and Hans Delbrück, whose *Mittwochstafel* became the meeting point of these circles in Berlin. But these facts are worth recording only because they contribute to a full understanding of the period and complete the picture. While the military successes lasted these movements had no influence on policy.

2. The crisis of the Central Powers in the autumn of 1916 and the United States' entry into the war

Costly military failures in 1916 led to a crisis in the German military leadership. As a result the problems of the U-boat war, which had already caused one crisis, came up again. Anxious to avail itself of every opportunity to restore its dwindling reputation by maritime victories, the naval leadership had embarked upon a submarine war against merchant shipping at a time when it had hardly sufficient resources for such a venture. At that stage it had hoped to shock the British by the unexpectedness of the blows. These expectations were disappointed, as were the hopes placed in the bombing raids by German Zeppelins; they merely added fuel to the fire of anti-German indignation without achieving anything else. Gerhard Ritter has described these developments as the first 'symptoms of the degeneration of modern war into total war' in which terror is used as a weapon to destroy the economic life and the fighting morale of the civilian population of the enemy. It is a sign of the unadmitted or admitted realisation that conventional military means are insufficient to break the opponent's military power. As the German navy found itself in this position from the beginning of the war it was quick to look to these new untried means. But the effects were not what had been expected.

To begin with the British government intensified the blockade of Germany so that all imports and exports came to a halt. On 7 May 1915 off the coast of Ireland a German U-boat without warning sank the *Lusitania*, one of Britain's largest liners, with a loss of almost 1,200 lives including 120 American citizens. With that action the U-boat war became a political problem of the first order.

From the start Bethmann Hollweg had disapproved of the development which the submarine war was taking, but the German navy did not bother to consult the Foreign Ministry, let alone any international lawyers. Bethmann took the first Wilson note on the *Lusitania* incident as an occasion to impress upon the military

23

leadership that the United States of America would break off diplomatic relations with Germany over the U-boat tactics and that such a step might lead the remaining European neutrals to join the Allies.

We shall now need to say a word or two about the American President. It must be remembered that Wilson's political ideas and decisions can be understood only in the context of American history and that they grew out of American thinking and interests without always being based on adequate knowledge of the European situation. Wilson was intellectually independent, stubborn and scholarly, a man who had grown up with strict puritanical principles. His religious background cannot be ignored when we come to examine the basis of his political ideas. These were based less on empiricism than on doctrines that were difficult to apply in any extensive or binding way to the political reality of his age. But the very fact that his own personality expressed itself in all his doings shows the degree of his determination and the steadfastness with which he pursued his aims. Wilson was a man with a great sense of responsibility who was slow and thorough in making up his mind but who stuck to his final decision with stubborn determination. His lack of flexibility and of tactical agility made him inferior to Clemenceau and to Lloyd George in the eyes of some of his contemporaries. But it would be altogether wrong to judge his ideas and his policies by these criteria.

We must also remember the United States' position in the world. The country had become a great power without abandoning the policy of isolation which it had pursued until 1914 and which influenced the view which some European politicians took of America. Wilson gradually realised that the war was eventually bound to affect America's interests. But the beginnings of America's world policy were unsure and groping. From the start Wilson's concern was to provide an ideological basis for a more active American role in Europe. His own ideas and also the inclinations of the American people made it almost impossible to persuade the country to enter upon a new era of American politics except with slogans about peace and the determination once and for all to settle Europe's quarrels. Thoughts about American policy in the nation-wide struggle thus led to thoughts about the future shape of the world. Emotionally Wilson was never on the side of the Central Powers. For anyone who believed in the Anglo-Saxon traditions of law the German invasion of Belgium remained unpardonable and the military arguments which were used to justify that were seen as clear evidence of Prussian–German 'militarism'; and to the Americans, who were reacting against the imperialist impulses of their own policy around the turn of the century, this was particularly abhorrent. A personality like Wilson who lived and thought in the spiritual traditions of puritanism could never become reconciled to such a phenomenon; all the more so as the Kaiser's widely publicised pre-war oratorical outbursts had not helped to present it in a favourable light to anyone outside Germany.

But Wilson's peace efforts were absolutely genuine and fired by missionary enthusiasm. This very fact sometimes made them appear problematic in the eyes of European politicians. But they obviously impressed Bethmann Hollweg. At any rate he not merely respected the powerful position of the American President as a mediator but for a long time wanted to maintain it as a political reserve. He may even have seen it as the last and extreme intellectual support of his wartime policy. It was in line with the pessimism revealed in many of his utterances. This alone explains why Bethmann, at first determined to keep America neutral, at the beginning of 1917, succumbed to growing resignation. The Chancellor's efforts to preserve America's neutrality mark the great caesura in Germany's war history; this was the last opportunity when peace could have been achieved before the military's determination to reach a decision in the field determined the course of events.

Once before Wilson had approached the German Foreign Ministry with an offer to mediate, but only with reference to the war between Germany and France. Although with hindsight the German refusal of the President's offer seems a misfortune, at the time it was not unjustified. A little later Wilson put out feelers through his special representative, Colonel House, to the Austrian ambassador in Washington about the possibility of an international peace conference on the conditions and legal requirements for terminating the war. But Vienna apparently saw no hope for its own cause in this idea. Given the military situation and the optimistic exuberance of the war-mongering propagandists no German government would anyway then have dared to enter into peace negotiations on unfavourable or even uncertain terms. When House visited Sir Edward Grey in London early in 1915 his mediation efforts met with the same fate there. But their exchange of views on the post-war order narrowed the gap between British Liberalism and the ideas of the American President and anticipated some of the principles of the League of Nations, whereas similar ideas which House had put to the

Austrian ambassador had found no echo. House had also made suggestions about general disarmament based on international agreements and about guaranteeing the complete freedom of the seas. It was at this early stage therefore that the first proposals – which later assumed great importance – were made on how to deal once and for all with the shortcomings of pre-war international policies as revealed by the way in which the war had started. But for the moment it was Grey's doing that even before America's entry into the war the gradual rapprochement between the two Anglo-Saxon countries started off with a vision of the future world order. This vision was based on a totally new war aim which was out and out anti-imperialist and of Utopian dimensions.

The situation in Washington changed further to the disadvantage of the Central Powers when William Jennings Bryan was replaced as Secretary of State by Robert Lansing, who had been Wilson's adviser on legal questions. Meanwhile the American business world was kept busy by a rapid export boom which seemed like a miracle after the slight depression of the last pre-war years. In the course of the war American exports increased nearly threefold and initiated a prosperity which continued almost unbroken until the economic crisis. The 'golden twenties' really began in 1914. America's main exports went to the Entente countries while trade with Central Europe ceased to be a factor in American economic life.

The military crisis of 1916 which gave a foretaste of the misfortunes to come was the result of having competing theatres of war and of supreme commanders who could not agree on a central point of attack. If the splintering of resources was fateful the disaster was made complete by the last great offensive of the Russian army under Brusilov in Southern Poland and then in the Bukovina, which brought Rumania into the war. The Austrian leadership failed to master the changed situation and in the sudden crisis at the front was faced with increasing unreliability from the Austro–Slav troops, in particular the Czech and Ruthenian (Carpatho-Ukrainian) units which surrendered *en bloc* or in large groups. Within a few weeks the whole Austrian section of the Eastern front began to give way; 500,000 men were lost. German troops and finally even two Turkish divisions were brought to Galicia to restore the front; meanwhile the German losses at Verdun and the Somme during this period reached similar proportions.

The mood in Vienna was pessimistic in the extreme. In Berlin it became known that the Austrian ambassador in Bucharest, Count Czernin, who was regarded as one of Austria's most promising diplomats, predicted the defeat of the Central Powers if the war continued. Conditions in the army led the two Prime Ministers, Tisza and Stürgkh, together with Burián, to press for the appointment of one commander-in-chief for the whole of the Eastern front. At their insistence a German–Austrian supreme command in the East was set up under Hindenburg, whose responsibility it was to improve the military situation. After Rumania's entry into the war even the Kaiser and those around him seemed for a while to have regarded the war as lost. As all efforts to make a separate peace with Russia came to nought there remained only the hope of American mediation. But the United States was at that moment preoccupied with the Presidential election and continued to be so until Wilson's re-election in November.

The Germans meanwhile did everything to ensure that an all-out effort would be made to continue the war. Germany's entire resources were placed at the disposal of the war economy and the army; and not only Germany's resources but also those of foreign peoples living under German domination. But the results fell far short of the objectives and bore no relationship to the means employed. The attempt to create a Polish national army which would fight at the side of the Germans proved a total failure. No more successful was the deportation of Belgian workers to Germany, which caused tremendous bitterness among the Belgian population and called forth protests from the Catholic Church and from neutral Spain as the power which looked after Belgium's interests. In relation to the outcry the gains to the German war economy remained practically negligible. In February 1917 the deportation came more or less to a stop and the victims were gradually repatriated. But the compulsory control of Belgian labour continued. In the spring of 1917 the Germans began systematically to dismantle Belgian industrial installations and to transfer them to Germany.

While the German military leadership refused to do without means, at the time regarded as extreme, there were signs of a serious crisis among the Central Powers. Turkey, which in the late summer of 1916 had still been sending troops to the threatened Austrian front in Southern Poland, was beginning to lose its fighting spirit by the end of the year. And at the beginning of 1917 war weariness became widespread everywhere in Austria. Whereas hitherto the country had suffered little from food shortages and state control, it now felt the effects of measures by the Hungarian government which in the middle of the worst crisis temporarily imposed a total ban on the import of all agrarian produce from the Hungarian to the Austrian part of the empire.

In view of this situation the Third Army High Command under Hindenburg and Ludendorff prepared for the resumption of unrestricted submarine warfare. Meanwhile even the nationally minded middle classes had been seized by U-boat fever because they increasingly regarded this weapon – the last that remained intact and apparently not yet fully exploited – as the means of changing the fortunes of war. The Chancellor realised that his attempts to start peace talks were up against the pressure of time because unrestricted U-boat warfare could not be postponed for much longer. Bethmann Hollweg saw only two ways of remedying the military situation: either there must be peace mediation or he would authorise the ruthless use of Germany's remaining great weapon. As was often the case the Chancellor at this vital point was swayed by considerations of personalities and domestic issues and therefore he vacillated. Already on 28 September he had made the daring pronouncement in the Reichstag that a German statesman who was afraid to employ any weapon that might shorten the war deserved to be hanged. With this pronouncement he incurred the wrath of the social democrats and also of the progressives while the *Zentrum* had joined the ranks of the determined advocates of submarine warfare. The pincer movement of the Army High Command and most of the Reichstag left the Chancellor little room for manœuvre.

The confusing sequence of events whose details are difficult to unravel led in mid-October 1916 to several almost simultaneous decisions. While the German ambassador in Washington was told of the temporary postponement of submarine warfare, it was suggested to the American ambassador in Berlin that American mediation might be welcome, a move of which Austria-Hungary was not informed. Shortly afterwards Burián proposed that the Central Powers should make a joint peace offer. As a result a series of protracted negotiations started up independent of the German move. The openly proclaimed Austrian aim, to end the war 'without surrendering vital interests', so as to escape the next big Entente offensive, could be achieved only if conditions were laid down jointly.

After the Kaiser had agreed, Hindenburg and Ludendorff also consented to a peace move by the Central Powers. It has rightly been suspected that Ludendorff always expected the peace offer to be rejected but had chosen this course to dispose once and for all of the diplomats' objections to unrestricted submarine warfare. The Army High Command exploited its position according to all the rules of strategy and laid down a number of highly significant conditions. It insisted on the controversial proclamation of Poland and also on the introduction of universal compulsory war service for which a special law and the consent of the Reichstag were required. Ludendorff further demanded that the peace offer should be formulated in such a way as to preclude any impression of German weakness. We are forced to conclude that the Army High Command concentrated exclusively on new military decisions and on an intensification of the war.

Nevertheless Bethmann Hollweg announced to the Prussian government and to the Bundesrat Committee for Foreign Affairs what peace conditions he envisaged as a basis for future negotiations. They were pretty remarkable and hardly befitted the situation. Part of the ore basin of Briey was to be exchanged for a few communes in Alsace and Lorraine; Belgium was to be restored but Liège would be cut off. Russia was to give up Courland and Lithuania and recognise the independence of Poland. Bethmann Hollweg was prepared to give up Germany's colonial possessions in East Asia and the Pacific but the idea of a great central African colonial empire was not abandoned. War indemnities continued to be talked about, although there was no mention of figures.

Burián now suggested a general discussion of the peace conditions. This inevitably meant a postponement of his own peace move. But in making his proposal the Austro–Hungarian Foreign Minister had another idea in mind. He wanted to reach an understanding on German and Austro-Hungarian war aims and then come to a similar arrangement with Bulgaria and Turkey. In the light of these ideas the proposed peace move appears as an attempt to obtain lasting alliances. If Bethmann Hollweg's choice was between peace and U-boat warfare, the Austrian Foreign Minister faced the double necessity of making a peace move while at the same time consolidating the wartime alliance of the Central Powers to prevent it being weakened by future peace negotiations. Here we encounter the problem of protecting and continuing the wartime coalition once the war was over and peace negotiations had started, a problem that we shall meet again in connection with the Paris Peace Conference in 1919 and which also arose during the conferences of World War II from Teheran to Potsdam. The results of the first Balkan War and the growth of the second were frightening instances of the consequences of paying insufficient attention to these problems.

The ensuing negotiations between Vienna and Berlin took five whole weeks and had their ups and downs. But at the same time as important German–Austrian exchanges of view took place in Berlin and Wilson's re-election appeared certain in America, the German Foreign Ministry decided to put out new feelers to the United States. Bethmann Hollweg now appeared to take up some of Wilson's ideas. He suggested that the American President should invite all belligerent powers to enter into peace negotiations and when agreement had been reached to convene a congress with the participation of the United States. The Chancellor probably thought that in this way he could keep Wilson interested in the German peace efforts because the Central Powers needed to agree on their war aims before they could come to any decision on a peace note. But this double game was upset by new events.

At the end of November 1916 new submarine incidents and the compulsory deportation of unemployed Belgian workers imposed a distinct strain on the relations between Germany and the United States. Representations by the American chargé d'affaires in Berlin encouraged the Chancellor to put his faith in American mediation at the expense of the negotiations with Austria. Moreover, the autumn of 1916 had brought dramatic events in Austria-Hungary for which the monarchy was not at all prepared. On 22 October the Austrian Prime Minister, Count Stürgkh, was murdered. On 21 November the Emperor, Francis Joseph, died after a reign of sixty-eight years. A total change was now probable. It seemed that the heir to the throne, Charles, a great-nephew of the old Emperor and a weak and flexible man, might follow a course similar to that taken by his uncle, Archduke Francis Ferdinand, who had been murdered at Sarajevo. He was familiar with the latter's plans and sought out some of Francis Ferdinand's closest advisers like Count Clam-Martinitz, who after a short period of transition became Prime Minister, and Ambassador Count Czernin who was put in charge of the Foreign Ministry.

For the Austrian Emperor the first and foremost political objective was the early termination of the war as far as it involved the Danube monarchy so that he would be free to begin the internal reconstruction of the Empire. As regards the attainment of the first of these objectives, the Emperor soon revealed a certain readiness to adopt unorthodox means. And as regards the second, his advisers ceased to have any influence when it came to the first important decisions, whereas the Hungarian Prime Minister, Count Tisza, a clever tactician, did everything to ensure the continuation of Austria-Hungary's dualism and to prevent any reform at the expense of the Magyars. An opportunity of doing this offered itself with the Hungarian coronation oath, which under a Hungarian law of 1790 the new king was compelled to take within six months after the death of his predecessor. On the strength of this ancient law Tisza made the Emperor promise that in spite of wartime conditions he would at the earliest opportunity be crowned 'King of Hungary and Croatia-Slavonia and Dalmatia'. He cleverly managed to bring Charles's peace plans into all this and promised them his whole-hearted support. He tried to combine the coronation oath with a guarantee from the new ruler to maintain the Austro-Hungarian Compromise for twenty years, a proposal which in practice amounted to preserving the *status quo*, because further reform in the interest of the Slav nationalists would then have been impossible as the South Slav question affected both parts of the Empire. Even though Tisza failed to impose his twenty-year Compromise he was successful in arranging the solemn coronation of the imperial pair, Charles and Zita, on 30 December 1916 at Budapest, and in making the Emperor swear to respect the Hungarian constitution. Before the coronation the Estates elected Count Tisza Palatine of Hungary, permanent mediator between the Empire and the Crown and legal representative of the King in the Hungarian half of the Empire. Tisza held this position independent of the office of Prime Minister which he resigned in May 1917.

Because of these changes Vienna paid temporarily somewhat less attention to the German–Austrian negotiations. Meanwhile Bethmann Hollweg used the changes at the Austrian Foreign Ministry to persist in his attempts to secure American peace mediation. Lansing and House were at first reluctant to act because from the start they assumed that Britain would reject such overtures as long as there were deportations of Belgians and U-boat incidents. Bethmann took the American note on this subject as expressing a condition of Wilson's which was to be complied with before mediation would begin. Thereupon he once more abruptly changed course. Probably he believed that no further concessions could be obtained from the Army High Command and that it was impossible to countermand the Belgian deportations. But shortly before news had come from the Great Headquarters of the impending fall of the Rumanian capital, together with the information that the Kaiser and the Army High Command regarded this favourable turn of events as a suitable moment for producing the joint peace offer. The talks with Germany's allies were resumed immediately and brought to a quick end: the peace offer of the Central Powers was transmitted to the governments of the Entente states on 12 December 1916 and was announced also to the neutral nations and to the peoples of the Central Powers. The Reich government remained consistent and used the lack of time as an excuse to avoid going into the details of the peace conditions with its allies. The Austrians consented as news of American peace moves had meanwhile become known – though not of the German initiative in this matter. The step was warmly welcomed by the Austrian Emperor because it enabled him to associate the beginning of his reign in the eyes of his peoples with the idea of the peace for which they longed.

The Austrian intentions were thus by-passed but the step towards peace had been taken. In the end it achieved no more than a propaganda bombardment of the Central Powers by the Allies who questioned the sincerity of the move because no concrete proposals whatsoever were made. Bethmann Hollweg was not even half-heartedly behind the scheme. He had abandoned it, even though it is impossible to say with certainty when he finally did so. It is true, however, that in some ways the situation no longer was what it had been a few weeks previously. The fall of Bucharest removed some of the psychological pressure; and the annexationists began to hope again.

The Central Powers' peace offer made some impact on the nations which were tired of the war. This deserves to be noted in connection with the happenings in Russia in the following spring. But the unanimous and unequivocally negative attitude of the Entente showed that any peace move – even one sponsored by Wilson – would have no success whatsoever in the immediate future. This became clear when on 18 December Wilson made his own mediation offer and invited the belligerents to define their war aims for which Washington would act as a 'clearing house'. In some quarters of the Entente this suggestion was received with indignation as Wilson's move seemed to be too closely connected with the peace offer which the Central Powers had made six days previously. And the German reply of 26 December emphasised the principle that the United States must not participate in the war aims discussion. Wilson refused to be discouraged and at the beginning of January 1917, in a strictly confidential reply, took note of the German peace conditions. The answer given to this by the Secretary of State of the Foreign Ministry, Zimmermann, was approved by the Army High Command which was once more falling back on U-boat warfare and demanding its resumption in unrestricted form and without discussion with the Americans. So as to increase its effectiveness the preparations were to be made in secret and the campaign was to start without prior warning on 1 February 1917.

At the decisive meeting at the Great Headquarters at Pless on 29 December, Bethmann Hollweg and the Vice-Chancellor, Helfferich, again voiced the government's reservations but also stressed that they wished to reach complete agreement with the High Command and that the decision must lie with Kaiser. At the Crown Council on 9 January, which considered this question for the last time, the Chancellor expressed his political reservations at some length but finally, impressed by the military arguments, said that he himself could no longer oppose submarine warfare. Although this did not mean approval it meant surrender and resignation; the great decision was therefore no longer delayed and fate took its course.

While this was going on Washington still hoped that peace might be achieved. The disappointment was therefore all the greater when the German ambassador, Count Bernstorff, admitted openly that the Entente states' rejection of the Central Powers' peace offer had fundamentally altered the situation in Berlin. In his great message of 22 January 1917 to the Senate the American President tried in view of this state of affairs to put an end to the period of uncertainty and indecision. He did this in a dignified way which did credit to the United States and to himself by formulating the demand for 'peace without victory' and by appealing once more with impressive urgency to the belligerents to say that they were ready for peace. Thereupon on 29 January the Germans telegraphically presented their peace conditions. They had been drawn up at the Great Headquarters under the chairmanship of the Kaiser and were as follows: return of the French-occupied part of Upper Alsace; establishment of a frontier that protected Germany and Poland strategically and economically against Russia; colonial restitution in the form of an arrangement that assured Germany of colonial

possessions proportionate to the size of its population and the importance of its economic interests; return of the French territories occupied
by Germany subject to strategic and economic frontier rectifications
and financial compensation; restoration of Belgium subject to certain
guarantees relating to the security of Germany, to be agreed by negotiations with the Belgian government; an economic and financial
settlement based on the exchange of the territories conquered by both
sides and to be returned at the conclusion of peace; compensation for
German firms and individuals who had suffered from the war; abandonment after the conclusion of peace of all economic arrangements
and measures that constituted obstacles to normal trade and communications and the conclusion of trade agreements on those lines; protection
of the freedom of the seas.

By way of concession to the American President, Germany expressed
itself ready after the termination of hostilities to join in his proposed
international conference. But in reality the German proposal was not
a serious attempt to find a basis for peace. Three days later, without
preliminary warning, the Germans embarked on unrestricted U-boat
warfare.

Events now moved fast. The United States broke off relations with
the Central Powers on 3 February 1917. Two days later Wilson
appealed to the neutrals to follow suit. The break became final when
the British government informed Washington of the text of an incredibly stupid telegram from Zimmermann to the German ambassador in Mexico. It suggested collaboration between Germany and
Mexico in case of war and as reward offered Mexico the southern parts
of the United States.

The young Emperor Charles was particularly worried by the lack of
success of the Central Powers' peace message of December 1916 and of
the subsequent American peace message, because in their replies the
Entente powers had unreservedly called for the separation of the non-
German nationalities from the dual state Austria-Hungary and had
declared the dissolution of the Danube monarchy to be their war aim.
In these circumstances Charles decided to put out his own peace
feelers which had the support of his Foreign Minister, Count Czernin,
but which were largely made through Bourbon Parma family connections of the Empress Zita. An important role was played by the
Empress's mother and brothers, Prince Sixtus and Prince Xavier, who
established contact with Poincaré and Lloyd George between January

and April 1917. But their efforts never had serious prospects of success because of the opposition from Italy and also from France.

Count Czernin's objective was to continue and step up Burián's policy. From March 1917 on he tried to persuade Germany to make tangible concessions to the Entente so as to ensure that the appeals across the fronts continued and in retrospect to give greater emphasis to the December peace move. As a result the war aims question and the problem of agreement among the Central Powers was raised once more. In the course of renewed negotiations and discussions the Austrian Foreign Minister tried to persuade Germany to give up Alsace-Lorraine and to abandon the idea of any annexations in the West; Austria-Hungary expressed itself ready to renounce its claims in the Polish question, to give up South Tyrol in favour of Italy and to offer compensation in Austrian Galicia, although it then proposed to recoup its losses at the expense of Rumania. These ideas reflected the actual military situation but they also showed that Hungary's interests continued to have strong backers at the Foreign Ministry. The suggestions that were now put forward had little in common with the *status quo ante-bellum* idea which Czernin had advocated when he was ambassador to Rumania. The Germans of course never seriously entertained any such ideas.

Count Czernin was prepared to resort to doubtful ruses to make the Germans give way. To the *Zentrum* deputy, Erzberger, who was visiting in Vienna, Czernin painted the situation in the blackest colours, whereas he used the Prince Sixtus affair to give Bethmann Hollweg impression that there was a separate peace offer from the Entente. But Czernin merely managed to depress the Chancellor still further without shaking Germany's determination to fight on to victory.

From then on the enemies of Germany and Austro-Hungary grew in number. On 6 April 1917 the United States joined the Allies and declared war on Germany. The American example and the warnings of the President of the United States started an avalanche of new declarations of war which lined up against the Central Powers the majority of the countries which had remained neutral: half of South America, Brazil, Bolivia, Equador, Uraguay, all the states of Central America but also Portugal, China, Siam and even Liberia. Only a few states now remained neutral. Henceforth the world consisted of two camps, of which that of the enemies of the Central Powers was of vast dimensions and in possession of all the resources of the world. If before a German victory had seemed possible though perhaps doubtful, henceforth no one could say that the prospects looked bright for the Germans. Wilson's famous message to the Senate asking for peace without victory was therefore timely. But in 1917 the Germans were again mostly taking an optimistic view of the situation particularly as Russia's collapse was predictable and Germany could thus expect to be rid of its most powerful opponent on the Eastern front. Almost all Germans badly underestimated the importance and above all the military strength of the Americans. This was a serious and irreparable mistake on the part of the military and political leaders.

In Britain, which was run by Lloyd George's coalition government, the imperialist 'Round Table' demanded a central Europe free from German domination and without links with the Turkish Empire. The sword must not be returned to the scabbard until the complete restoration of Belgium, until France's frontier was safeguarded for the future, until the small nations received their political rights and until Prussia's military power was destroyed once and for all – 'no more but also no less' was the view of Philip Kerr who became one of Lloyd George's closest collaborators.

3. The promotion of revolution among the occupied peoples – imperialist policy and national emancipation movements

The effects of slogans about freeing the people from the yoke of foreign rule were powerful and lasting. Ideas of this kind were spread systematically with all the means at the disposal of the diplomats and the military and were used by Germany as much as by Britain and in the long run with no less success.

It was Britain's objective to persuade the peoples of the disintegrating Ottoman Empire to reject Turkish rule and to revolt. The intention was to reduce the threat to Russia from Turkey in the south, to eliminate the threat to Persia and thus also to India and finally to protect the Suez Canal, the lifeline of the British Empire, from Turkish and German attacks from the direction of the Arab peninsula. The British attempts to undermine Turkish rule in Arabia were therefore in the last resort designed to defend the most vulnerable regions of the British Empire and of Britain's Russian ally who was at risk in several places.

Britain's Near East policy followed the guidelines developed before the war to assist the Arab national movement in its quest for emancipation. With the help of this policy Britain permanently relieved the Suez Canal zone; later it also gained control of large stretches of the Hedjaz railway which linked Damascus and Medina and had been constructed by German engineers. Apart from the Baghdad railway which connected Mosul, Baghdad and Basra with Anatolia and Constantinople the Hedjaz railway was the most important modern link between the heart of the Turkish Empire and the southern part of the Arab peninsula; supplies to the troops stationed there went by this route.

The two-pronged British advance along the Euphrates and the Tigris and along the Hedjaz railway towards Syria and Damascus finally freed the whole Arab peninsula from Turkish rule. The orientalist and political agent Colonel T. E. Lawrence had a decisive share in the success of these operations, the military part of which alone would probably not have broken Turkish and German resistance. Lawrence was motivated not only by military and strategic considerations but by a thirst for adventure. His activity, which led many of the Arab tribes along the coast to revolt, relied on the long-standing Arab hostility to the Turks which had existed under Turkish rule since the end of the nineteenth century. At first the Arab national movement was confined to a small élite among the urban Arab population. But by the last decades before the war the movement had come to be composed not only of students and writers who had joined forces in exile and who carried on their activities from there, but also of Turkish officers of Arab origin who during the war became the military leaders of the Arab movement. Except for the central Arab sphere of influence of the independent Wahabi ruler, Abd-al-Aziz-Ibn-Saud, the national ambitions of the Arabs had never been directed towards the goal of complete independence from the Ottoman Empire and from the religious and secular rule of the Sultan and the Caliph. The break-up of Turkey was certainly not yet on the programme of this movement. It was not until the start of the war that secularised political thought made a breakthrough and permitted the destruction of the unity of the religious and political order which Islam had maintained inside the Turkish Empire.

After Turkey's entry into the war the desire for independence and the political ambitions of most of the Arab rulers proved stronger than the power of the Caliph. Even before the war Husein ibn Ali, the influential Grand Sherif of Mecca, had been in touch through his elder son, Abd Allah, with the British commander-in-chief in Cairo, Lord Kitchener, but they had failed to reach complete agreement. Several months after Turkey's entry into the war Husein's second son, Feisal, established the vital link with the Syrian nationalists in Damascus where the young Arab national movement set up by emigré Arab circles in Paris had established its illegal headquarters. After prolonged discussion of the future Arab attitude towards the Turks and the British the so-called Protocol of Damascus was finally drawn up in the spring of 1915. The Arabs decided to pursue their cause in a tactical alliance with the British because for the moment this seemed the most advantageous course. The ruthlessness of Turkish rule was too well known for the Arabs to put any faith in the promises made by Constantinople. The British on the other hand, after the failure of the

Gallipoli adventure about which there was by then little doubt, were more than ever dependent on the assistance of the tribes of the Arab peninsula. But there was no deep-rooted Arab desire to form an alliance with the British and to support their cause. The Arabs decided to exploit the circumstances created by the war of the Great Powers. Arab policy was based primarily on the consideration of first and always serving its own cause. On the other hand, much the same is true of British policy which only appears in a different light because of the romantic figure of T. E. Lawrence, who fought body and soul for Arab independence and made many friends among the Arabs.

In an exchange of letters, in which he used the Protocol of Damascus as a credential, Husein established direct contact with the British High Commissioner in Egypt and the Sudan, Sir Henry MacMahon, who was in charge of British policy in the Near East. The Protocol enabled Husein to appear as the spokesman of the Arab nationalist movement. He asked for recognition of the future political independence of the tribes living south of the 37th parallel. This line – although with some noteworthy deviations – runs along the southern edge of Anatolia. It cuts through the territories of the Kurds and also through Adana – inhabited by Turks, Greeks and Armenians – the old Armenian kingdom of Cilicia which lies between the passes of the Taurus Mountains and the coastal plain of Iskenderun, and which was a transit region where trade and transport flourished as long as there was no threat of war; it was also the threshold to Syria and the most important link between Ottoman Anatolia and the Arab peninsula. With the construction of the Baghdad railway the area was brought into contact not only with the economic life and communications system of the twentieth century but also with modern military strategy and organisation.

Sir Henry MacMahon's first reply was a typical piece of cautious British diplomacy: he was glad to welcome the new, promising ally but not prepared to commit himself. Anxious not to offend Britain's great European allies, Grey kept various irons in the fire and was not prepared to recognise Arab national unity.

Indeed Arab nationalism was and is full of religious, social and also personal problems. Within a social framework in which there were few differentiations a small number of tribal princes from the old ruling families had their way; and the religious conflicts within Islam were of political significance. The Wahabi reform movement of the eighteenth century had for long presented a permanent threat to temporal and spiritual Ottoman overlordship in central and southern Arabia. In the end the new sect was suppressed until Ibn Saud as the great tribal ruler took up the struggle against the Caliphate and even before the war caused the Sublime Porte serious difficulties with his conquests in the Persian area. The war of the Great Powers now offered him a unique opportunity to strengthen his position with the help of Britain at the expense of the Turks. He was Britain's born ally in these regions to which the influence of the Great Sherif and his family and that of the Arab brotherhood did not extend or where it was at any rate less than firmly established. British diplomacy made the most of this situation. As regards the final result, it mattered little that in its dealings with Ibn Saud the British relied primarily on the services of the India Office while Husein's contact was the High Commissioner in Cairo.

Ibn Saud was treated like the sovereign that he felt himself to be and that he basically was, although by European concepts the territorial limits of his rule were difficult to define – not least because they were constantly being enlarged. It was in the interest of British policy in the Middle East to keep this Arab ruler away from Aden, Hadramut and the British protectorates of Oman and Muscat and to direct his expansionist efforts towards the areas controlled by the Turks. A formal agreement concluded with Ibn Saud on 26 December 1915 and ratified on 18 July 1916 confirmed his independence and his conquests. Like a medieval Arab conqueror Ibn Saud went to war to unify the central Arab tribes and principalities in order to establish a state; in the process the leadership of the tribal chief, the *riasa*, became the *daula*, the state, which was one with a dynasty and was personified by it. Here to rule meant to conquer and continued to mean this; and conquest meant the establishment of a state. The process was still incomplete by the time the war ended. But it was never endangered by English reservations or objections. In their relationship with Ibn Saud the British were much less reserved than they found it desirable to be in their dealings with Husein.

If Ibn Saud was a potentate the Grand Sherif was more like a modern political leader and ideologist who preached Arab unity by emancipation from Turkish overlordship, an objective which he pursued with considerable diplomatic skill by making the most of the moment. Ibn Saud was the incarnation of ancient Arabia in search of new power. Husein represented the modern element in Arab nationalism which could rely neither on religious ties nor tribal links and which had as much need of the urban tradesmen and the urban intelligentsia as of the idea of national Arab unity which was fostered by the Arab Brotherhood. But even the family of the Grand Sherif concentrated in the last resort on the interests of the family community. It sought to establish dynasties at the head of new Arab states and in the end paid for its activities with bitter sacrifices and failures.

The first indication that the struggle for national emancipation had become a dynastic conflict came with Husein's decision to proclaim himself King of all the Arabs in Mecca. He did this in conscious response to the British agreement with Ibn Saud, the complete English text of which was communicated to Husein. On 4 November 1916 Husein crowned himself at the shrine of Islam. But by then he was fighting not only against Turkish soldiers and struggling with Ibn Saud for domination of the Arab peninsula. In secret the Allies had begun to pursue a colonial policy which in the long run was even more detrimental to Husein's ambitious plans than to the power of Ibn Saud.

Shortly after Turkey's entry into the war but still at the time when the Germans and the Russians were putting out peace feelers the Russian Foreign Minister, Sazonov, had obtained British approval for a plan by which under a future peace settlement Russia would receive Constantinople, the western shore of the Straits, the islands in the Sea of Marmara and off the Dardanelles as well as southern Thrace up to a line running from Enez to Midye and a stretch of the Turkish Black Sea coast east of the Bosphorus. This settlement was typical of the highhandedness of secret diplomacy in the style of nineteenth-century imperialism; the reservations made by Britain to safeguard its interests appeared tolerable to the Russians even though they had not yet achieved their historic objectives. Constantinople was to have a free port and Russia was to guarantee the freedom of merchant shipping through the Straits. In 1916 it was in return granted also the major part of Armenia and Kurdistan. This was seen as compensation and therefore tied to conditions: that the two parties pursued the war together to its victorious end but also that Russia agreed to the settlement of British and French claims to other parts of Turkey and to independent Mohammedan rule in Arabia. The eastern shore of the Sea of Marmara and of the Dardanelles did not form part of this deal. It seems that Russia was not to gain a foothold there.

In the London Treaty of 1915 Italy was given sovereignty over the

Dodecanese and – in the eventuality of the complete partition of European Turkey – large parts of the western coast of Asia Minor. At this period the Foreign Office still proposed to preserve the unity of Arabia. However, the French were granted the Lebanon region and western Syria as well as Cilicia to the north. Early in 1916 this area was extended to the future Russian frontier and to the Persian frontier. Southern Mesopotamia, with Baghdad and the Palestinian ports of Haifa and Akko, were reserved for Britain.

A little later the question of the future political shape of Arabia was to some extent decided in an agreement concluded by two diplomats, Sir Mark Sykes for Britain and Georges Picot for France, and confirmed by an exchange of letters between the two Foreign Ministers, Sir Edward Grey and Paul Cambon, in May 1916. The agreement noted that the Arab population of the peninsula rejected the Turks and that it was therefore possible to set up an Arab state or federation of states with close links with the Entente. This idea was to be realised not by setting up an Arab government or by some other form of self-administration for the regions concerned. The agreement envisaged that the area was to be divided into five separate zones. In the first some suitable form of political control was to be exercised by Britain, in the second by France. These zones were, by the way, largely identical with the territories already allocated to Britain and France in northern Arabia, or Anatolia in the agreements with Russia. In two further zones, situated between the territories referred to, an Arab state or federation of states was to be set up, one under British and the other under French protection and influence. The area of present-day Palestine constituted a fifth zone; it was exempt from these provisions and was later in agreement with Russia to be placed under international administration. Arabia was thus divided into an annexation zone to be shared out between Britain and France, a protectorate zone to be dealt with in the same way, and an internationally administered region.

In addition the agreement tried to settle various questions of communication and economic links between the zones, and in important spheres provided for partly British, partly joint British and French control. In an additional agreement demanded by Italy when it heard of the Anglo-French arrangements and drawn up at Saint Jean de Maurienne in April 1917, Italy too was given an area to be annexed and a neighbouring sphere of influence in south-west Anatolia including the important port of Smyrna. It was also in principle agreed that

Italy would be allowed a voice in the shaping of the international administration in Palestine.

With this almost complete partition of the Turkish Empire by secret diplomacy on paper a compromise appeared to have been found which safeguarded the interests of the great Entente powers entirely at the expense of Turkey and went some way towards disposing of the historic eastern question. In addition Britain had gained a future direct land route from Egypt to India. But the peoples directly affected had no share in these arrangements. For the time being they were not even informed of the existence of any secret agreements.

Britain did, however, to some extent prepare for the future political shape of the Arab peninsula by concluding with several powerful sheiks treaties in which Turkish overlordship was replaced by a British protectorate. In the interior of the Arab peninsula Ibn Saud was confirmed as a completely independent ruler. In addition he received big monthly payments from Britain but did not explicitly decide on action against the Turks. Several tribal leaders in southern Arabia remained benevolently neutral towards the Turks while others supported the Turkish regime or even attacked British troops on their own initiative. In the Yemen and the vicinity of the British crown colony of Aden the military position of the British remained insecure until the end of the war.

In these circumstances the attitude of Sherif Husein of Mecca, who was actually in control of most of the Hedjaz, was of the greatest importance. In the course of his exchange of letters with Husein the British High Commissioner decided – even before the Sykes–Picot agreement – to meet Husein's demands and to make some concessions to the Arabs. Through him Britain now announced that there would in future be an independent Arabia south of the 37th parallel. Western Syria and the Lebanon region, which were described as not being purely Arab, were to be excepted; under the Sykes–Picot agreement this region formed part of the French annexation zone which otherwise stretched northwards from the 37th parallel. The need to consider France's interest was clearly stressed in MacMahon's important letter of 24 October 1915. With regard to the remaining areas among which were the zones finally agreed upon shortly afterwards – including internationalised Palestine and the French protectorate areas in central and eastern Syria – MacMahon stated that Great Britain was in principle prepared to recognise and promote Arab independence and also to protect the holy places of Islam, Mecca and Medina from all outside attack. The Arabs were promised British assistance in the establishment of suitable governments as soon as the situation permitted. In return it was taken as agreed that in future the Arabs would ask for advice and assistance from Great Britain alone and that the European advisers and officials who would be called upon to help with the formation of administrations would all be British. In addition Britain reserved for itself special administrative and supervisory rights and also the control of military security in the Basra and Baghdad region, that is in the area which under the subsequent Sykes–Picot agreement it proposed to annex.

It would be wrong to say that the Sykes–Picot agreement was irreconcilable with this letter. However the important fact that Palestine was to have an international administration and that there was to be an additional French protectorate zone was kept from the Arabs. But in view of the proposed British protectorate the British High Commissioner's declaration can be regarded as a preparatory step towards an amicable settlement with Sherif Husein who had not yet decided on open opposition to the Turks.

But Husein was not prepared to recognise a special British zone of control or special French claims. In their exchange of letters MacMahon and Husein failed to agree on this point; each side insisted on its own point of view. Nevertheless Husein openly joined Britain in June 1916. But undoubtedly he did not expect and had no reason to expect that without even informing him Britain would give France a zone of influence in northern Arabia with the economically and culturally important urban centres of Aleppo, Damascus, Homs and Harma and also the important oil region of Mosul. The Foreign Office's secret negotiations did in fact result in far greater concessions to France than the resident representative of the British government in Cairo admitted to his influential and important Arab negotiating partner. But, because of its negotiations with the Arabs, Britain found itself from the start at an advantage *vis-à-vis* the subsequent French claims that were based merely on the secret agreement with Britain and not on any understanding with the representatives of Arabia. The vital decisions were thus made at two completely different levels: in the first place secret diplomacy was used to agree upon imperialist spheres of interest in all areas inhabited by dependent peoples who were seeking political emancipation; in the second place revolution was systematically promised among these peoples with the objective of producing an internal upheaval in the Turkish Empire.

The Allied war aim of liberating the peoples of the Near East from Turkish rule must be seen with these facts in mind. There was no mention anywhere that the peoples concerned had the right to determine their own fate, neither the Arab tribes, nor the national Turks of Anatolia, nor the Armenians, nor the Kurdish population, nor the Greek minority on the coast of Asia Minor and the off-shore islands. Both the Sykes–Picot agreement and the exchange of letters between MacMahon and Husein referred to the formation of Arab states. The few details that were laid down justify the use of the term 'protectorates'. But under these secret schemes worst fate awaited the Turkish peoples, who were left with nothing but a small exclusively agrarian state capable only of limited productivity in north Anatolia and around the city of Ankara. Several million Turks would have been subjected to Russian, French or Italian rule.

On the other side the Young Turk masters of the Ottoman Empire also promoted revolution among peoples under the rule of their enemies. Talât Pasha, the last wartime Grand Vizier, and the Minister of War, Enver Pasha, who had been responsible for the Turko–German alliance and for Turkey's entry into the war, attempted to stimulate in the Turks east of the Caspian feelings that would lead them to revolt even after the war. Their idea of a Turanian movement exploited the national idea by linking it with vague ethnic concepts on the common ground of Islam – under the authority of the Caliph – and by playing it off against the Russian rulers. But these activities, which were at times supported by Afghanistan, did not become a serious threat to Russian unity until the overthrow of Nicholas II, when separatism quickly became the dominating feature of political developments on the periphery of the Tsarist empire.

On the other hand, the Turks made no serious attempts to undermine British rule in parts of India. Whereas the Germans had expected Turkey's entry into the war on the side of the Central Powers to have considerable repercussions on Britain's position in the Middle East.

In the German Foreign Ministry there were two schools of thought. There were those who wanted to concentrate on Russia as Germany's most dangerous East European neighbour and then there were those who wanted to stake everything on the struggle against Britain. The relative influence of these two schools of thought depended on the general military situation. In conjunction with the plans to promote revolution among the peoples of the Tsarist empire an anti-British programme was prepared with the idea of inciting the Islamic world from Morocco to India to rebel against European rule and of carrying the war against Britain to the East. Persia and Afghanistan were involved in the plans to promote revolution in India; rebellion was also to be fermented in Egypt, the Sudan and – in the French colonial empire – in Morocco, Tunisia and Algeria. The only successful venture, however, was the attempt to persuade the north African Senussi to invade Italian Tripoli.

The promotion of pan-Islamic revolt against the rule of the old colonial powers, Britain and France, was the ultimate objective of Germany's Near Eastern policy which the Kaiser had outlined in a famous speech at Damascus in 1898 in which he assumed the role of protector of three hundred million Mohammedans. But the wartime efforts to bring the area from Morocco to India into the German sphere of interests fell far short of German expectations. It was after a considerable delay that the impact of these activities made itself felt, even though in a fashion which was by no means in line with the German intentions.

The German wartime attempts to promote revolution among the Russian people were of much greater importance than their efforts to ferment unrest, let alone revolt, among the Mohammedan populations of the British and French colonies. Although to some extent their purpose was to support their military operations on the Eastern front, they were concerned as much with political considerations as with strategic objectives.

Plans had existed at the start of the war to assist a revolt in Finland by the promise of future autonomy and to bring about a separation of the Poles and the Ukranians from the Russian Empire. For this purpose the German Foreign Ministry employed German and non-German socialists and through these men tried to win over Russian emigrés to the idea of revolution in Russia. The Russian-born revolutionary, Alexander Parvus-Helphand, publisher of the socialist journal *Glocke*, who was in close touch with the German ambassador in Copenhagen, Count Brockdorff-Rantzau, said in his journal as early as 1915 that the interests of the German government were identical with those of the Russian revolution. On the basis of this view the Germans had thought up the idea of dividing Russia into a number of states which in the discussions on Europe's post-war political order were allocated a position dependent on Germany.

Of the diplomatists of the German Empire Count Brockdorff-Rantzau was the most fervent advocate of the idea of importing revolution into Russia and of using it to break up the Entente. From that time onwards the idea of making a separate peace with a revolutionary Russia never disappeared. It gained in importance with the failure of the attempts to come to terms with the actual rulers of Russia.

After the collapse of these efforts all German sights in the East were set higher. Demands which had originated from a wish to protect Germany's future eastern frontier now assumed the character of extensive annexations. It was suggested that Poland should be made into a buffer state and claims were made on Lithuania and Courland. The aim of a 'decomposition' of Russia was not confined to promoting revolution among its peoples in quest of independence. This was seen merely as a condition necessary for a future occupation of the country and as part of the conduct of the war. But there were considerable differences in the way these peoples were to be treated. The intention was to give Poland limited autonomy dependent on the designs of German policy. (Thanks to the activities of emigré committees similar arrangements were envisaged for Lithuania and Estonia.) Effective assistance, on the other hand, was given to the national autonomist and separatist activities of the Georgians and the Ukranians among whom there were two movements seeking to break away from Russia, a conservative one, directed from Austrian Lemberg (Lvov), and a social and agrarian reform movement.

German policy towards Poland was in the last resort governed by Germany's insistence on strong safeguards which were considered necessary but which completely precluded the promotion of a broadly based national Polish movement capable of freeing the country from Russian rule. When the United States entered the war and the Poles in America were able to make their influence felt the national Polish movement worked against Germany's interests and became a serious problem at the eastern frontiers. But it was not only in view of this development that the proclamation of a Polish state, made on 5 November 1916 in deference to Austria and entirely without Polish participation, totally failed to strengthen the position of the Central Powers. The Lithuanians suffered no better fate, in contrast to the

Finns who from the early days of the war worked with determination for a rising against Russian rule. Given German policy it was logical that in Germany's immediate sphere of interest all autonomous or revolutionary trends were suppressed. This was so in Courland and Livonia, where the idea was to maintain and even to strengthen the influence of the Baltic Germans, and also in White Russia which was regarded as German occupation territory and considered for the settlement of Germans. Primarily, however, it was Courland that was envisaged as an area for large-scale German settlement after the Baltic nobility had announced its willingness to sell part of its possessions 'at market prices' to the German Reich for settlement purposes. The German authorities also considered the idea of resettling on Polish territory Poles and Jews living in the eastern regions of Prussia.

These ideas were never finalised or carried out. The guiding principles of German policy underwent kaleidoscopic changes and therefore do not always seem to fit into the context of logical considerations. The absence of definitive decisions in this as in other spheres permitted frequent reappraisals of ideas and objectives and allowed the development of certain concepts. These were gradually revealed where their realisation appeared possible during and after the negotiations for a peace in the East.

4. European socialism and the revolution in Russia

The most important domestic problem which confronted the governments of all the belligerent countries at the start of the war was created by the existence of the socialist parties. As the struggle continued this problem increased both for the Russians and finally also for the German government. The socialist attitude towards a war between the Great Powers could not be predicted. It was no more possible to foretell whether national unity could be preserved during the war in spite of continued social problems in industrialised society than to predict the course of the war. It is clear, however, that the assumption of a short war made the future appear in a much rosier light and more predictable than if people had known at the outset how long the struggle would be.

However, the problem of socialism had lost some of its urgency during the last pre-war years and the assumptions that press propaganda would help to assure the reliability and constancy of patriotic reactions was in fact not justified. In most European countries the great workers' parties had achieved overwhelming election successes just before the war; yet they were in a state of turmoil which made them susceptible to the manifold influences of the imperialist age. For decades the revisionists and the orthodox socialists had fought for supporters and clashed over programmes and forecasts about future political and social developments. Even in the great pre-war debates of the Second International – which, compared with the First, was a more loosely organised affair – the increasing strength of national in relation to international loyalties had become apparent. But in all the great national parties there were pockets of determined followers of the Marxist doctrine and their ranks grew as the bitter controversies continued. However, even these groups appreciated that much had changed since the days of Hegel and Marx, and the need for fundamental principles which could be flexibly applied and were plausible led them progressively to adapt the original ideas and teachings.

The workers' parties such as they had emerged from the nineteenth century treated imperialism as an economic, sociological and political fact and reacted to the intensified nationalism which it had brought in its wake by continual internal adaptation, the full extent of which was at that time difficult to foresee. Dominant among the doctrinaire supporters of the original theory was a type of intellectual who though in the minority left his mark in all countries and who fought against experienced politicians and old veterans as much as against the advocates of a liberal revision of party policy. The principles of a democratic organisation, in which all decisions were in the last resort based on the majority view, imposed laws of their own on this struggle, fought partly by theorists and ideologists among themselves and partly by the officialdom of the traditional party leadership.

In Italy the phases of this conflict followed each other more rapidly than elsewhere and the issues were already settled by the time the war started. This was due partly to the fact that in the Italian workers' movement the Marxists had never ruled supreme, as for example in Germany, that they were always in conflict with strong revolutionary and anarchist trends and had to defend themselves against attacks from the left. Another reason was that the Liberal governments of the early twentieth century, of Zanardelli and Giolitti, were in some respects sympathetic to the workers' movement and allowed it considerable freedom of activity; this was of benefit to the revisionists who for the price of certain social reforms were prepared to bring the party policy more in line with that of the government. In these circumstances the split in the Italian workers' party which became apparent almost at the same time as that in the German party, namely at the Party Congress at Bologna in 1904, was much worse than elsewhere. While the revolutionary syndicalists under Arturo Labriola shrank to a minority the national revisionism of Turati and Bissolati made further gains and completely won over the trade union organisation, the *Confederazione del Lavoro*. In fact from 1906 onwards the Italian workers' movement was largely behind the government; and in 1912 Giolitti made a gesture towards the workers by reforming the electoral law so as considerably to enlarge the franchise and to exclude from voting only illiterates.

This was the position when Italy embarked on the Tripoli war against Turkey. The step resulted in violent controversy in the revisionist camp and led to another split and to the breakaway of the group around Bissolati which reconstituted itself as a new socialist reformist party. It adopted a programme which was completely reconciled to imperialist policy and based on the principle of being interested in every opportunity for Italian economic expansion. The flood of Italian emigrants who came from the socially dissatisfied sections of the population must be seen as the logical consequence of the infiltration of nationalism into socialism.

But other groups were also attempting a synthesis of nationalism and socialism. The doctrines of Maurizio Maraviglia took the bourgeois, extreme right-wing *Associazione Nazionalista* and its journal, *L'Idea Nazionale*, a long way towards the extreme right of socialism. The post-war confrontation between the Communists and the Fascists under the leadership of Benito Mussolini – who at the start of the war, as editor of *Avanti*, was one of the journalist spokesmen of the socialist Left but later joined the Nationalist Right – really began during the war. But the final shaping of the Fascist Party as an alliance of right-wing socialist leaders with the military, agrarians, nationalist bourgeois, unemployed soldiers and down-at-heel aristocrats belongs to the typical and striking features of the post-war period. The development of socialist nationalism in Italy before and after the war was lastingly influenced by the *età Giolittiana*. After the war the distinguished Liberal, Giovanni Giolitti, during his fifth period as head of the government, tried once to form a national bloc in parliament and at first refused to take Mussolini's Fascisms as anything but a short-lived right-wing off-shoot of socialism produced in the course of its chequered history. This misjudgment of the true character of Fascism was based on certain features of the pre-war situation in Italy. In other respects Giolitti showed surer judgment. As early as 1914 he realised that the outcome of the war would in the end depend on the intervention of the United States; and from the beginning he had no doubt that the war would bring the collapse of Tsarist Russia.

Russia had remained a predominantly agrarian country, with almost eighty per cent of the population belonging to the peasantry. When the war started neither the agrarian Socialist Revolutionaries nor the Marxist Mensheviks and Bolsheviks had really recovered from the persecutions to which they had been exposed since the abortive revolution of 1905. During the long-drawn-out process of regeneration the composition of the leadership of the socialist parties underwent a fundamental change. Part of the intelligentsia joined the camp of the bourgeois constitutional democrats, the Kadet Party, and espoused the ideals of Pan-Slavism, often described as Neo-Slavism. With their support the war against Germany gained in popularity as being a Russian venture. At the same time the social democratic groups – whose numbers remained very small – acquired a new leadership which came from the ranks of the workers' trade unions and co-operative organisations. This leadership included a number of spies of the Tsarist secret police who kept their employers closely informed on what went on inside the party leadership and who did their best to encourage existing differences of opinion. The start of the war led to further splits and differences between the Bolsheviks and the Mensheviks. Although their joint group in the Duma unanimously voted against the war credits Plechanov, and with him the majority of the Menshevik leaders, made their peace with the government for the duration of the war. This step they justified with the argument that by far the greatest threat to the revolutionary Russian proletariat came from the possibility of a German victory; because German imperialism would exploit Russia without giving it an opportunity to develop its productive forces, to ensure the growth of its industry, of its working class and also of socialism.

Even among the Bolsheviks the influence of the anti-war group was at first limited. Its line was increasingly laid down from outside Russia by their leader, Lenin, who had been joined by another exile, the Menshevik Trotsky. Determinism had influenced the International as early as the beginning of the century. The theory was that all capitalist states were equally responsible for the outbreak of the war. Among the victors the reactionary, anti-revolutionary elements would become stronger whereas defeat would enable the revolution to triumph. The only conceivable conclusion to be drawn from this which was developed to a fine point was that revolutionary socialists must want the defeat of all belligerent powers. The defeat of the Tsarist state was 'the lesser evil for nine-tenths of the population'. Lenin was of the opinion that only a military defeat of Russia would create the conditions necessary for a victory of the revolution; therefore the revolutionary struggle must go on during the war and be consciously directed against the interests of national defence. Lenin did not restrict his interests to Russia but was always aware of the international development of communism; he tried to popularise the idea that with defeat and weariness the war must turn into a struggle of the proletariat against its capitalist rulers. 'The greater the sacrifices imposed by the war the clearer it will become to the mass of the workers that the opportunists have betrayed the workers' cause and that the weapons must be turned against the government and the bourgeoisie of each country,' Lenin said on 1 November 1914 in an appeal of the central committee of the Bolshevik Social Democratic Workers' Party of Russia. This was a restatement and a practical application of the idea that world war would become a vehicle for world revolution. The revolutionary party must devote itself entirely to this idea.

The tenacity of intellect which produced these theories was certainly totally irreconcilable with the emotions aroused by wartime patriotism. And yet patriotic motives and national feelings were by no means alien to Lenin. But once he had set his sights it was in his nature to pursue his objectives with monomanic ruthlessness, to subordinate everything to them and constantly to impress his purpose on his followers with tactical skill and logical penetration. He saw the revolution in Russia as only a Russian could see it, as an occasion for self-negation as well as for proud self-awareness, as a great task in the history of his country and also as the fulfilment of a mission and as an exhortatory example to the oppressed masses of the world:

We are full of national pride and for that very reason we hate our slavish past (in which aristocratic landowners led their mushiks into war so as to strangle freedom in Hungary, Persia and China) and our slavish present in which the same landowners supported by the capitalists lead us into war so as to strangle Poland and the Ukraine, so as to suppress the democratic movement in Persia and China. . . . We, the Russian workers who are full of national pride want at any price a free and independent, a democratic, republican and proud Russia whose relationship with its neighbours is based on the human principle of equality, not on the principle of subjection and privilege which degrades every great nation. Because we want this we say: in twentieth-century Europe (even in far Eastern Europe) one can only defend one's country by fighting with all revolutionary means against the monarchy, landowners and capitalists of one's country, i.e. against its worst enemies. . . . The interest of the national pride (interpreted not in a slavish sense) of Russia coincides with the socialist interests of the Russian (and of all other) proletarians.

The idea of freedom had originally come from Western Europe. A spark of it now set alight a store of strange but undoubtedly highly inflammable material and before long the flames of this fire lit up the whole world.

It was on these assumptions that Lenin's theory of imperialism was based. As on other occasions he was impressed and stimulated by earlier west European authors. In this instance it was the book which the radical liberal British anti-imperialist J. A. Hobson had written at the beginning of the century against the background of the Boer War. From this Lenin went on during the war to develop the thesis – which he published in the autumn of 1917 – of imperialism as the 'highest stage of capitalism' but also as the 'eve of the socialist revolution'. The world war would be the decisive turning point of the great historical drama; it was in this light that the significance of its manifestations must be judged.

At first, however, Lenin had little opportunity to direct any revolutionary developments inside Russia. At the outbreak of the war he was arrested by Austrian police in his Cracow exile; released again a few days later he went to neutral Switzerland and took up residence in Berne. From there it was almost impossible to exert any influence on his Bolshevik followers in Russia. As it had become known that secret preparations for revolution were afoot the Bolshevik leaders in the Duma were arrested, accused of high treason and early in 1915 sent to various places in Siberia. This meant the end of the Bolshevik organisation; all that remained were the emigrés in Switzerland. In consequence the Russian regime was spared serious internal unrest during the first two years of the war in spite of the military crises of the summers of 1915 and 1916 and in spite of a number of offensives into which great resources were thrown but which in the end produced no results. Lenin and the Russian socialists in Switzerland, however, began to operate in the international sphere and became a factor to be reckoned with.

The special position of the emigrés and the significance of Lenin and also of Trotsky are characteristic of a feature of the workers' movement in Russia not found in that form anywhere in the major belligerent countries in Europe. The situation was totally different in Britain where pacifism was strongest among the workers and where in the critical days immediately before the start of the war representatives of all workers' movements voiced their opposition to Britain's entry into the war. Even after the violation – unanimously condemned – of Belgian neutrality by Germany the Independent Labour Party under Keir Hardie and Ramsay MacDonald tried to uphold the pacifist line. But by then the majority of the Labour Party no longer shared this attitude and MacDonald was compelled to leave its leadership in the Commons to others. Yet even his group never went so far as publicly to oppose the policy pursued by the government during the war. It was content to maintain an independent attitude and to reiterate its desire for a negotiated peace, although there were no prospects whatsoever of this for the time being.

Of far greater consequence was the trade unions' change from dedicated pacifism to national patriotism; almost without any reservation they supported the government's basic policy. A large section of organised labour volunteered for military service. In the end Mac-Donald also lent himself to the recruitment campaign which was of vital importance while there was no conscription. Now and again there were strikes but they were not directly connected with the conduct of the war or with war policy. Henderson, MacDonald's successor as leader of the Labour Party in the Commons, joined Asquith's coalition cabinet. Lloyd George made him a member of the inner war cabinet and it was not until August 1917 that Henderson left the government because of his support for the international socialist congress at Stockholm. In addition to Henderson the trade union leaders John Hodge and George Barnes were also, at the end of 1916, invited to join Lloyd George's cabinet.

The situation in France seemed at first similar to that in Britain. Having played an active part in the pre-war inter-parliamentary conferences at Berne and Basle the French Socialists felt committed to a pacifist line, which was in fact energetically advocated by their leaders during the July crisis. Jean Jaurès, the outstanding figure of the international labour movement, said in speeches at the end of July 1914 that he felt convinced that it was imperial Germany which had encouraged Austria-Hungary in its moves against Serbia. But in the last resort he regarded it as his moral duty to preserve the peace and to this he subordinated everything during the crisis. Jaurès' standing was such that he had the ear of members of the French government. His representations led to the last conciliatory exchange of notes and telegrams between Poincaré, King George V and Nicholas II. After his assassination the Socialist Deputies continued to negotiate with the government from whom they obtained the promise that France would not declare war on Germany. But the hopes of peace collapsed when Germany incurred universal odium by becoming the aggressor. On 2 August Marcel Sembat, after Jaurès the most respected of the French Socialist leaders, outlined at a meeting what the Socialists' attitude would henceforth be: they must fight because war had been forced on France by the aggression of the German Reich; but they were fighting only to defend French civilisation and the freedom of the nations. In these circumstances and with the help of this formula it was obvious that the French Chamber would vote unanimously in favour of the war credits. At the end of August 1914 Jules Guesde, the main exponent of the Marxist doctrine in France and Sembat joined the war cabinet of the *Union Sacrée* without demanding special guarantees from the government. The overwhelming majority of French Socialists served their country loyally, just as the British, Russian and German socialists did what they regarded as their duties to their country. It was generally accepted that there could be no thought of peace while German troops occupied parts of Belgium and France. It was only after this point that opinions differed and as the war went on a small but determined anti-war group emerged. It left its imprint on the literature of the war and helped to create a modern realistic pacifism.

Before long, on the other hand, a small but by no means insignificant group of Socialists joined the nationalist camp. Among them was Gustave Hervé, the most radical representative of French pre-war pacifism, Marcel Cachin, who was later to lead the Communist Party, and Charles Andler who had always shown social–liberal inclinations, being as much an opponent of Marxism as of Jaurès and who now attacked the *Marxisme prussien* by seeking to establish a close relationship between Marxism and the historic spirit of Prussia.

Barely ten years before the war Jaurès had united the French Socialists. His death had fateful consequences. This is evident from the progressive internal split which occurred during the war. Several new problems were added after the start of the war to the old differences over which Jaurès and Guesde had fought at the turn of the century. The first criticism – of local significance only – of the party leadership and its support for an intensified war effort came from Haute-Vienne, a Guesdists stronghold. At first these voices remained content only to warn against the premature condemnation of the German Social Democrats which had by now become commonplace, and to reject all French war aims other than the restoration of Alsace-Lorraine. This criticism was significant because it provided the first visible sign that by no means the entire French Socialist Party was behind the war. Other groups followed suit and the idea of restoring international relations remained alive among socialists in Europe. It was in the course of 1916, the year that brought so many great sacrifices and military failures on both sides, that the majority of French Socialists began to change its viewpoint.

The socialist parties of the Central Powers were more or less in the same position at this moment in time. The Austrian socialists had less chance than any except the Russian socialists to express their views. The Austrian Prime Minister, Stürgkh, ceased to call the Reichstrat and suppressed all dissenting voices. Nevertheless pacifism gained a foothold among the Austrian Social Democrats as among others during the war. But from the outset there were marked differences within the leadership. Although the Austrian Social Democratic Party was spared a major internal conflict it had to accept the break with the Czech and Polish socialists. Its continued efforts to strengthen the links with the German Social Democrats, with whom it was in close touch even during the war, formed a historic prelude to Austria's attempts after the collapse to join forces with Germany. But Austria's intellectually independent socialists never became dependent on the German Social Democrats. The idea of a peace 'without annexations or indemnities' was formulated in unambiguous terms by Austria's labour movement before it was adopted by the German Social Democrats.

The story of the Social Democratic Party takes pride of place in the history of Germany's political parties, if only because of its quick and, in the pre-war period, seemingly irresistible rise. The Social Democratic Party, the biggest political mass organisation in Germany from the turn of the century until the rise of the National Socialists in 1932, played a decisive part in making the broad mass of the people politically conscious. Its growth caused its opponents to take counter measures. With a membership of three-quarters of a million it was the strongest party from 1903 onwards. At the Reichstag election in 1912 it had won four and a half million votes and had more deputies in the Reichstag than any other party. It was a force to be reckoned with in Germany, of a different order of magnitude to the Socialists in France who had 90,000 members and who gained 1·4 million votes in the 1914 elections to the Chamber. Social Democracy was a factor in Germany's constantly growing labour force well before the Social Democrats joined the government because they were the only party to have drawn fundamental social and political consequences from the fact of industrialisation. It was their strength but also their weakness that their theories were based on the teachings of Marx and Engels, substantial parts of which formed the foundations of the party's political programmes. But historically Marxism itself did not determine the attitude and development of Social Democracy and could not do so with any degree of permanence given the fluctuations of historical, social and political circumstances.

During the war Social Democracy did not remain altogether immune from nationalist and imperialist ideas and war aims. This was not surprising given the tendency of the party as a whole increasingly to accept the ideologies and illusions of the age. German Social Democracy was no exception in this respect.

Towards the end of the July crisis of 1914 the government was afraid that the Social Democrats would oppose the official policy and considered arrests and other police measures. The man largely responsible for the decision not to take any such step was Vice-Chancellor Delbrück who predicted correctly that the Social Democrats would behave as patriotically as all other Germans. To begin with the party leadership was at a loss how to behave and sent one of its members to Paris to find out how the French Socialists were reacting. But before long it was those who believed that it was in the future interest of Social Democracy to give proof of its patriotism who won the day. To varying degrees – while for the most part quietly assuming a German victory – they expected the workers to gain a growing share in the wealth of the nation and to benefit from new democratic institutions, above all the introduction of a democratic system of suffrage in Prussia for which they had fought for years. The most determined advocate of this viewpoint was the Mannheim lawyer Ludwig Frank who had come into the public eye before the war as a Reichstag deputy and also as leader of the Social Democratic group in the Baden Chamber of Deputies, where he had helped to found the 'great liberal coalition'. An able speaker and an active and energetic man with the temperament of a Lassalle, he was considered one of the rising stars of German Social Democracy. As an example to his party friends Frank volunteered for the army on the day of mobilisation and was killed on 3 December 1914. With him the Social Democratic Party lost one of its most active parliamentarians who was certainly not a nationalist but who in the historic hour carefully made due allowance for the triumph of national feeling.

The general acceptance of this attitude was in some measures due to the way in which the Marxist theory was handled. For years one of the most respected theorists of the party leadership, Karl Kautsky, had devoted much effort to a definition of the position and policy of social democracy in the imperialist age. Like the first leaders of the Social Democratic Party, August Bebel and Wilhelm Liebknecht, who before the turn of the century had referred to a future world war as a 'world catastrophe', Kautsky assumed a world war to be an inevitable feature of capitalist development. The question which followed and which had been raised before the war and to some extent answered for the majority of the party concerned the role of Social Democracy in a future world war. Kautsky argued that it could do nothing but wait. In practice it could behave passively or patriotically; its attitude would not influence the outcome of the war in any way. It had no responsibility and could not prevent political decisions. Kautsky proposed to ignore the victory of the German cause and to wait for the collapse for which, according to the Marxist theory, the entire capitalist system was heading. Only then could Social Democracy really gain political power and responsibility.

From the beginning therefore there were a variety of reasons which motivated the party to agree to the *Burgfriede*, the party truce, and which led the Social Democratic group in the Reichstag to vote for the war credits. At first, however, this fact was not fully appreciated. It is highly probable that none of those involved understood that the granting of government credit in this way started an inflationary trend the final point of which – according to a British historian – marked Germany's true social revolution in the twentieth century and the start of the collapse of the middle class.

The *Burgfriede* meant that the parties in the Reichstag unanimously supported the policy of the government and voted it the necessary funds. The contributions which the Länder made to the imperial treasury under the financial system of the Bismarckian empire were

totally inadequate to pay for the war. The political leadership was
continually in need of new large-scale credits to raise the necessary
funds. But for this the government needed to be sure of a majority in
the Reichstag; this was based on the *Burgfriede* and survived until the
last stages of the war. In addition the leadership needed unanimity
among all politically active persons so that the nationalist slogans
about willingness for sacrifice, readiness to fight and determination to
win would not be questioned.

In these circumstances the importance of the Reichstag could well
have increased as it was repeatedly convened to vote war credits in
addition to dealing with the regular budgets, approval of which had in
the preceding decades been its prerogative. It was, however, primarily
the leaders of the parliamentary parties who acquired a political standing *vis-à-vis* the Reich government unknown before the war. It is
true that in the Bismarckian empire the parties had acquired a broad
popular basis and that the government was compelled to pay some
attention to them; but the parliamentary component of the German
constitutional system had not developed on anything like the scale of
the rest of Western Europe. To start with the alliance between the
government and the parties – the *Burgfriede* – in fact immobilised the
Reichstag as an institution because its leaders were respected by the
government precisely because they had made it known that they were
not offering any opposition. It was not until 1917 that the situation
began to change fundamentally, although without the principle of the
Burgfriede being abandoned.

Early on in the war a small but growing opposition emerged within
the Social Democratic Party. After 1915 this pacifist minority made
itself felt also outside the Reichstag; it spread its gospel among the
armament workers of Berlin and finally branched out into organisational activities. It was influenced by the inexhaustible energy and
oratorical skill of Karl Liebknecht, who though not actually its leader
protested from the start at the parliamentary group level against the
granting of war credits and against the official Social Democratic
policy. The party leadership was thus faced with competition from an
opposition which grew from year to year, influenced the politically
organised workers in the big industrial cities and gained in importance
as the war dragged on and as it became apparent that the hopes of early
victory would not be fulfilled. From the start this opposition disapproved of the party leadership for failing to make at least the pro-

Belgian declaration which Viktor Adler, the leader of the Austrian Social Democrats, had demanded from the Germans. At meetings of the parliamentary party at the end of November and beginning of December 1914 Liebknecht submitted resolutions condemning the Reich leadership; but these were overwhelmingly rejected. Thereupon the minority with Liebknecht at its head demanded to be allowed to voice its views at a plenary session of the Reichstag. Again the majority insisted that there must be no deviation from the official party line. The conflict became apparent when Liebknecht refused to obey party orders and handed to the President of the Reichstag a special declaration; this was not, however, incorporated in the stenographic record of the proceedings. The opposition smouldered on, spread and developed on lines almost parallel with the situation in the French socialist party, except that there the opposition originally came from a few regional groups. In Germany it began earlier but for some time fought its battles entirely behind the closed doors of the parliamentary group and therefore news of it took longer to reach the public.

In March 1915, when the controversy between the Chancellor and the *Alldeutsche* over the public proclamation of war aims came to a head and when a move to the right threatened to break up the *Burgfriede*, the first visible signs appeared of a conflict among the Left. At a meeting of the parliamentary group twenty-three of the hundred deputies present expressed themselves against the granting of further war credits; and in the Reichstag two deputies for the first time voted openly against the majority after almost a third of the Social Democratic group had previously left the chamber.

In the twenty-five years since the Anti-Socialist Laws German Social Democracy had passed through numerous internal crises, always patching up the differences between the revisionists, the orthodox party leadership and the neo-Marxists but never resolving them. With the war several of the old issues were revived and received a new lease of life. But as in France after the quarrel between the Guesdists and the followers of Jaurès the old dividing line in Germany broke down over the questions raised by the war. New groupings emerged which would have been unthinkable in the pre-war era. As early as June 1915 the opposition group among the Social Democrats in the Reichstag attacked the annexation plans announced by the leading industrial associations in connection with pan-German war aim pronouncements. The Social Democratic opposition offered the clear alternative of peace based on voluntary settlements. When it came to the next vote on new war credits twenty Social Democrats voted against and the unity of the parliamentary group collapsed. As a result the minority disassociated itself from the majority and in March 1916 set up an independent group under the name of *Sozialdemokratische Arbeitsgemeinsschaft* (Social Democratic Association), the members of which were formally expelled from the Social Democratic Party soon afterwards.

While these things were happening in Germany the fruits of the ideas developed by Lenin in exile appeared to be maturing. A restoration of the international links between the great socialist parties broken off at the start of the war seemed possible. However, the old International with its permanent Bureau was not suitable for this task; and when the British section of the International Bureau convened a socialist conference in London in February 1915, the British, the French and the Belgians were the only ones to attend because of the military situation. The resolutions drawn up on this occasion were framed at the expense of the countries not represented. Those present held Germany responsible for the war, committed themselves to the principle of self-determination for the nationalities of the Danube monarchy and called for the liberation of the territories annexed by the Central Powers. The widely voiced demand for the reunification of Alsace-Lorraine with France was also reconfirmed. The socialist parties of the Entente countries represented in London would no more disassociate themselves from their governments' policies than the German Reichstag majority.

As we have seen the conflicts within the socialist camp became increasingly significant and were by no means restricted to Germany. But their significance showed itself in different ways and the trend was much more marked in Central Europe, particularly in Russia. As early as September 1915 a first international meeting of opposition socialist groups was held in the village of Zimmerwald near Berne. Most of the German Social Democrats kept away from the meeting; but the minority that was represented came to play an increasingly active part in Germany. After Zimmerwald the opposition socialists, in accordance with the decisions taken there, organised anti-government street demonstrations and advocated international solidarity across the trenches. They proposed to back up these campaigns with a succession of strikes and when conditions were favourable to transform them into political mass action. The rejection of war credits was naturally part of this programme.

A further meeting which took place at the end of April 1916 in Kienthal near Berne and which was dominated by the Russian socialists, Axelrod, Lenin and Trotsky, took the Zimmerwald decisions one important step further. Those present at Kienthal decided – while renouncing the previous insistence on simultaneous action – to fight for a peace without annexations in all belligerent countries, to the extent that the opportunities in each country allowed. There were now no obstacles to the aim of promoting revolution by exploiting the situation created by the war. Everywhere the international community of revolutionaries began to break away from the parties determined to preserve the national party truce. After the birth of the new Left in the middle of the war the impact of Lenin's slogans was strongest at first outside Russia. From this period onwards the trend in the German Social Democratic Party was irresistibly towards a split. The strikes organised by the radical Left were highly successful. The number of participants was proof of continued growth of the movement and indicated the revolutionary determination of many of the workers. Karl Liebknecht's fame as the most determined pacifist agitator threatened to eclipse that of the leaders of the Majority Social Democrats. The intellectuals of the so-called 'International Group' headed the German supporters of revolution. And in the Berlin armaments factories a new organisation grew up which took the form of trade union opposition. These 'revolutionary shop stewards' formed the core of the revolutionary cadres of 1918–19. But by then revolution had broken out in Russia.

The serious military setbacks which Russia – still inadequately equipped for some time to come – suffered after the great exertions of the autumn of 1916 led to a tremendous loss of confidence in the monarchy. The great mass of the Russian people worshipped the Tsar as the incarnation of religious orthodoxy and as the protector and saviour of Russia. They could certainly not be expected to revolt, but neither could they be expected to protect the monarchy. Opposition to the Court, where in the eyes of many the figure of Rasputin played a particularly evil role, spread first and most effectively among the middle classes and the aristocracy. It was led by the bourgeois, nationally inclined liberals of the Kadet party under the pan-Slav

Professor Milyukov, in whom the Allies, in particular the ambassadors of Britain and France in Petrograd, put their faith when it became evident that in spite of a worsening of the internal crisis at the turn of 1916–17 the Tsar was not prepared to make concessions in the form of constitutional reforms.

Meanwhile the Germans in the winter of 1916–17 intensified their efforts to make Russia weak both militarily and internally, with the increasing objective of an upheaval and a socialist revolution. The most important contact between the Chancellor, the Foreign Ministry and the Social Democrats was Parvus, who, from Copenhagen under the special protection of the Ambassador, Count Brockdorff-Rantzau, built up an extensive organization which stretched as far as Switzerland and as a sideline also pursued some economic objectives. An Estonian socialist contact of Parvus was the first to suggest the use of the socialists to foment revolution in Tsarist Russia. The assumption that the Mensheviks were receiving Entente money and that in case of a revolt and the establishment of a Menshevik government Russia was unlikely to leave the Entente camp led the Germans to concentrate increasingly on the Bolsheviks. Lenin's peace programme which promised full autonomy to the nationalities of the Tsarist empire seemed to fit in with the German wish to split up the country. But while Lenin's programme demanded peace without annexations or indemnities, there was no mention whatsoever of this by the Germans.

Having decided to support the Bolshevik efforts the Germans devoted substantial sums to this activity. If slightly exaggerated, there is a basic truth in the claim of the future Foreign Minister, von Kühlmann, that the growth of the Bolshevik party organisation in Russia in the decisive phase was made possible by German financial assistance.

But even before these efforts could bear fruit the signs of change in the Russian capital multiplied. In February 1917 there were mass demonstrations in a number of cities caused by food shortages. They were followed by strikes by munition workers which quickly assumed major dimensions. The troops sent in to deal with the unrest proved unreliable and mutinied. The Duma protested and openly opposed the regime. When the Tsar wanted to dissolve parliament on 11 March (26 February according to the Russian calendar) the majority of deputies resisted. The following night they formed themselves into an executive committee which assumed power, while in the streets and squares of

Petrograd the revolt took the historic, classical form: soldiers turned against officers and refused to obey orders, people gathered and marched, opened prisons and in various ways took revenge for past wrongs. The government was arrested and after receiving a Duma delegation at his headquarters Tsar Nicholas II on 14 March signed a declaration of abdication. A week later he too was arrested and taken with his family to Tsarskoye Selo. Their subsequent murder sealed the fate of the Russian monarchy.

On the model of the revolution of 1905 an executive committee of workers and soldiers councils under Menshevik leadership was formed to work in conjunction with the executive committee of the Duma. If there was not immediate open conflict between the two bodies it was because several politicians belonged to both bodies and were therefore able to exert a conciliatory influence. Outstanding among them was the lawyer Alexander Kerensky, a social revolutionary member of the Duma, who in addition to his talent for conciliation had become popular because of the oratorical skills which he displayed at large rallies. To start with, the political decisions lay in the hands of the Duma committee which appointed a provisional government under Prince Lvov of which Milyukov and Kerensky were members and which announced that elections to a constituent assembly would be held in the autumn.

At first the genesis of the French revolution seemed to be repeating itself. To begin with, the government was composed of members of the upper middle classes and of a few liberal aristocrats. It amnestied political prisoners and proclaimed the civil liberties. But when it offered no programme of social reform voices were raised asking for more than had been achieved and the second phase of the revolution began. This movement which was led by the councils, the *soviets*, was given its big chance when after the overthrow of the Tsar the provincial administrations collapsed and in many localities the soviets became the undisputed local authorities. But the soviets did not recognise the central authority of the Petrograd government. In so far as there was any central direction from the top it came from the executive committee of the workers and soldiers' councils in Petrograd which was responsible for the gradual shift of power to the left. To start with it was the Mensheviks who set the tone in the executive committee, whereas in the soviets it was primarily the social revolutionaries, a non-Marxist, democratic, revolutionary party whose objective was a radical land reform and whose chief support therefore came from the rural population which made up the greater part of the Russian people. But the future course of events was decided in the cities.

While the soviets in the country and in the army consisted of peasants and supported the social revolutionaries, it was the Mensheviks who gained ground in the elections to the workers' soviets in the factories. And in their wake came the Bolsheviks. The soviets had the advantage over the Petrograd government in that they were in close touch with the people and controlled local events in which the government had no say whatsoever. The relentless process of continual undermining of the power of the central government was bound one day to lead to his collapse.

The successes of the Lvov government remained confined to the sphere of foreign policy. As a result of its decision to continue the war on the side of the Allies it was immediately recognised as the lawful government of Russia by the Entente powers, the United States having shown the way only one day after the arrest of the Tsar.

But while the diplomatic representatives of the Allied powers, supported by delegations of British and French socialists, helped to extend and to strengthen the foundations of the Lvov government, the central executive committee of the soviets entered the arena of foreign policy by issuing a proclamation to all peoples at war calling for the end of the imperialist struggle. Thereupon the government took over the demand for 'peace without annexations or indemnities', and after serious internal clashes which led to a reshuffling of the cabinet and the inclusion in it of a number of socialists, presented this demand to the world and at the same time published the secret treaties of 1914 and 1915 between Russia and the Entente powers.

But no practical consequences flowed from this formula now that it was officially recognised by Russia. Kerensky used his position, strengthened by the cabinet reshuffle, as Minister of War and the Navy and as master of the armed forces to reorganise the army along the lines suggested by the Allied diplomats. By promoting revolutionaries and appointing commissars to the units as well as by an extensive process of democratisation he sought to restore discipline in order to use the army once more for an offensive against the Central Powers. It was the Mensheviks and the Bolsheviks who advocated immediate peace and who, responding to a suggestion made by the Dutch and the Scandinavian Social Democrats, together with the German Social

Democrats in early June 1917 attended a peace conference in Stockholm. But no agreement was reached as the Germans – under the eyes of their Foreign Ministry – insisted on the *status quo ante bellum* in Central Europe, in Alsace-Lorraine and in the German colonies while giving a curious interpretation to the formula of 'peace without annexations or indemnities' which they recognised in principle but applied in a most one-sided manner to insist on the right of self-determination for Poland, Finland, Ireland, Egypt, India, Tibet, Korea, Tripoli and Morocco.

Shortly before the Germans and the Austrians had invited senior Russian commanders to discuss an armistice. This gave both parties in the east a breathing space which Kerensky used to prepare a new Russian offensive. The attack began in July under Brusilov's command but – after a few initial successes on the Austrian sectors of the front – came to a halt without having achieved anything.

Meanwhile events inside Russia took another turn which was strongly influenced by the Germans. After the fall of the Tsar at the beginning of April 1917 the German Foreign Ministry had taken the decision, supported by the Army High Command, to send Lenin from his Swiss exile to Russia and to use him to promote revolution there. No direct contact was made with Lenin or apparently asked for. This is explained by the limited objectives of the Germans who were concerned only with the next goal, the elimination of Russia as a military force on the side of the Entente.

Lenin's return to Russia must be regarded as the decisive event which shaped the course of the revolution and the development of the new Russian state. Up to that time the Bolshevik party, divided into a left wing and a right wing, and led by a triumvirate without a clear political line of its own, had followed gropingly behind the Mensheviks. The left wing in the party organ, *Pravda*, represented the opposition to the Lvov–Kerensky government. In particular it opposed the continuation of the war and demanded all power to the soviets. The right wing was prepared to support the government and to negotiate an understanding with the Mensheviks. It was in this situation that Lenin, who was renowned as an agitator, arrived in Petrograd on 16 April to a triumphal welcome. He did not disappoint the expectations placed in him. His hastily prepared theses which he announced to the world the day after his arrival at a joint session of Mensheviks and Bolsheviks went well beyond the stand taken by the left wing. They represented a programme in which negation played a vital role and which permitted no stopping once the chosen road had been taken. Its most important points were: termination of the war, abolition of the army, the police and the bureaucracy, socialisation of the banks, control of production by the workers and distribution of the estates among the peasants. Lenin was unable to gain immediate approval for these extreme radical demands which he intended to be translated at once into action. But henceforth he was unceasingly active as the eloquent and insistent advocate of his ideas. Advancing step by step he set the small Bolshevik party on his course and made it into the most determined revolutionary force. He was assisted in his activities by Trotsky, who returned from America to Russia in May and who encouraged the Mensheviks to collaborate with Lenin.

In mid-July, during the Kerensky offensive, the Petrograd Bolsheviks tried to turn big organised mass demonstrations into a *putsch*. The attempt collapsed. It resulted in another re-shaping of the government in which Kerensky took over the office of Prime Minister in addition to his other posts but in which he relied more than before on the right, on the Kadets, whereas on the other side the Trotskyites now joined forces with the Bolsheviks. With Lenin's flight to Finland, Trotsky became the leader of the revolution in Petrograd. After an unsuccessful *counter-putsch* by the military commander-in-chief, General Kornilov, who regarded military dictatorship as the only way out, Trotsky was elected President of the Petrograd Soviet which discussed and finally decided upon armed rebellion and the overthrow of the provisional government. The conspiracy organised with military precision by Trotsky was a resounding success because of the complete penetration of the Petrograd soviets and troop commissariats by Bolsheviks reinforced with Trotskyites. On the first day of the meeting of the pre-parliament convened by Kerensky for 7 November (25 October) 1917 the call for action went out and it became evident that there were no troops prepared to resist. Almost all important points in the city fell to the rebels without a fight. Only for the Winter Palace, the residence of the government, was there a short struggle.

When the news of the successful revolution became known Lenin re-emerged. He demanded the establishment of a proletarian, socialist government with the total exclusion of the bourgeoisie. On the following day such a government was appointed by the all-Russian Soviet and given the name of 'Council of Peoples' Commissars'. It was led by Lenin; Trotsky was in charge of foreign policy for which Lenin had prepared the basic guidelines. The aim of the government was to achieve peace and to wait for the start of the socialist revolution in Germany and in western Europe.

The Council of Peoples' Commissars began its activity by issuing a decree abolishing the possession of landed property and legalising its distribution by the village soviets; these had been set up in the meantime and had assumed arbitrary forms. Next followed the decision to offer without delay a 'democratic peace' to all belligerent peoples.

After the failure of Kerensky's last attempt with Cossack troops to push from Pskov to Petrograd the power of the Soviets spread, although not everywhere without opposition, through the whole of Russia except for the Cossack territories in the south. But the agrarian population of the country as a whole was only gradually affected by the political events in Petrograd and Moscow. Given the position of the Soviet Government at the end of 1917 there was no doubt that its only chance was to end the war at once and thus to have a free hand for the task of internal consolidation.

At home the rulers established a radical, terrorist dictatorship and immediately restricted the freedom of the press which had existed for a few months only. Some weeks later all non-Bolshevik papers were banned. At the end of 1917 a secret police (Cheka) was set up which under Dzerzhinsky's direction proceeded ruthlessly against the opponents of the Bolsheviks and in some respects out-did even the Tsarist secret police (Okhrana). Under Lenin's leadership Bolshevism never aimed to develop humanitarian principles. Everything was subjected to the question of ensuring that the revolutionary forces in Russia and beyond would acquire power and strengthen their position. Lenin probably never doubted that this dictatorship could not be established without the use of force and terror. Ruthless persecutions and executions became the order of the day. But fear also had its effect. In spite of the catastrophic state of the economy and the breakdown of food supplies there was a split in the social revolutionary movement whose left wing joined the Bolsheviks. Meanwhile elections to the Constituent Assembly had been held. Although orderly elections had not been possible and only 36 million votes were cast the social revolutionaries remained the strongest group, gaining well over half of all seats and more than twice as many as the Bolsheviks, for whom the result was a bitter blow. In fact it did not correspond to the real situation. For Lenin this was the occasion to turn his back completely on democratic parliamentarianism. With the help of hastily summoned military units he put pressure on the Constituent Assembly which met on 18 January 1918 without the bourgeois groups even putting in an appearance. When the Bolshevik proposals were nevertheless rejected the extreme Left marched out; and on the next day troops prevented the assembly from meeting. Lenin thereby provided irrefutable proof of the fact that machine guns are stronger than parliaments when pointed at the latter. He simply declared the Constituent Assembly dissolved.

On 26 October 1917, in the midst of the second revolutionary phase, the second all-Russian Congress of Soviets adopted a peace resolution. Thereupon Russia's allies and also her enemies were telegraphically informed of the readiness of the new rulers to make peace. The Entente replied with a protest to which the Russians responded with an 'appeal to all workers, soldiers and peasants', sharply refuting the allied remonstrances and calling upon the fighting nations to oppose the continuation of the war. This propaganda which equated peace and revolution brought home to the Entente powers the new threat facing them from the direction of Bolshevik Russia. At the same time the secret Entente treaties were published.

The ties with the Entente were finally cut on 15 December when an armistice agreement was signed for the entire Russian front. A last Russian appeal to the Entente to follow this example remained unanswered and peace negotiations started at Brest-Litovsk a week later. In a situation almost as unpromising politically as it was militarily the Bolshevik government had not without skill, and certainly not without success, been seen by its own people and by the world to be doing its utmost to achieve the best possible result. It conveyed the impression that it had finally abandoned conventional diplomacy, for ever renounced secret treaties and regarded it as its task to explain to the people the situation and what action it proposed to take, the first and noblest being the early restoration of universal peace. As it claimed to speak not only for Russia but for all opponents of capitalist imperialism, success or failure in the negotiations could not change its attitude nor alter its predictable verdict on its superior negotiating partners. The new diplomats of revolutionary Russia started to discuss the

Central Powers' peace conditions without the ballast of a strict
objective, as a partner of the representatives of very different forces
which now set out to obtain the most substantial share possible of a
peace that was based on victory.

5. Twists and turns
in the year of the Russian revolution

From the start Berlin saw the situation in Russia only in the short-term perspective and through rose-coloured spectacles. The position in Vienna was somewhat different: Count Czernin was worried about a revolt of the nationalities of the Danube monarchy; indeed in July 1919 the Emperor Charles tried to make a conciliatory gesture towards them by pardoning the Czech leader, Kramář, found guilty of treason. But it was in Germany that things first began to happen.

After the great strike of ammunition workers in the spring of 1917 and under the impression of the February revolution in Russia the oppositionist *Sozialdemokratische Arbeitsgemeinschaft* set up the Independent Social Democratic Party of Germany (USPD); it held its first public party rally at Würzburg in October. The formation of this party presented a new threat to the *Burgfriede*, this time from the Left. The USPD was not inclined towards extremism; of this there can today no longer be any doubt in view also of the mass revolt of Kiel sailors at the end of July 1917. Like the Majority Social Democrats the USPD had a large following in the navy. Soon afterwards there were indications that the position of the USPD was being undermined by extremist activities of the decidedly revolutionary *Spartakus* group. Most socialist party members, however, remained loyal to the Majority Social Democrats and their leaders, Ebert, Scheidemann, Müller–Franken, David and Landsberg.

But gradually the parliamentary parties abandoned their passivity. Here again the year 1917 marks a turning point with the Kaiser in his Easter message adopting a new line on the Prussian electoral law. The most important event in the parliamentary sphere was the peace resolution moved by the *Zentrum* Deputy, Matthias Erzberger. This he put to the Reichstag under the impact of Count Czernin's peace moves and also of those which the Vatican was making at the suggestion of Austria, the fruits of which became visible to the world a month later when Pope Benedict XV offered his services as a mediator. Erzberger now made a courageous about-turn on the question of U-boat warfare and achieved a striking parliamentary success when on 19 July 1917 his resolution was approved by a majority in the Reichstag. For the first time the Social Democrats, the Progressive Peoples' Party and the *Zentrum* had made an alliance with the objective of persuading the Reich government to make a peace move. Although this Reichstag majority failed in its proclaimed intention, the July events which began with the fall of the Chancellor, Bethmann Hollweg, led to closer collaboration between the SPD, The Progressive Peoples' Party and the *Zentrum*. Henceforth their spokesmen met regularly at an inter-party committee which in the following year devoted itself with increasing energy to the problems of internal political reform, at times with the participation of the National Liberals. A permanent link was thus created between the parties, paving the way for the parliamentary coalition which later became the cornerstone of the Weimar constitution.

The moving force in this alliance was Matthias Erzberger, who from July 1917 onwards occupied an increasingly important position in the *Zentrum* and gradually broke completely with the right wing of his group. Erzberger sensed the needs of a given situation even if he lacked consideration and sometimes tact. His July moves were based on justified assumptions about possible developments in the Ruhr, where he rightly saw the mass of Catholic workers as a numerically significant part of the future *Zentrum* voters. In the summer of 1917 Erzberger regarded a reshuffle of the Reich leadership as the overriding consideration. But the idea of changing 'the system' arose because Erzberger had become convinced that without a basic reorganisation Germany could not 'come through' the war. He saw a confidence-inspiring leadership and a form of government which had the support of the people as the main requirement for future negotiations of any kind.

Not all the spokesmen of the parliamentary parties showed equal determination in their demand for a change. The *Zentrum* was led not only by Erzberger but also by cautious and fundamentally conservative tacticians. Among the Majority Social Democrats, Scheidemann was advocating determined inactivity as late as July 1917: nothing would be lost in a few weeks; they could be used for thorough preparation. The greater the misery the more power the Reichstag would acquire at the expense of the government. However basically correct this observation was, it remained uncertain how and for what end the passing time should be 'used'. On this point Scheidemann was silent.

The next fourteen months showed, however, who was really in charge. It was not the Reichstag but the Army High Command under Hindenburg and Ludendorff which after Bethmann Hollweg's fall finally pushed the civilian authorities into the background and took almost complete charge also in the political sphere. The Army High Command was anyway well placed to exercise considerable authority in internal matters because of the powers vested in its military district headquarters and fortress commandments under Article 68 of the Constitution of 1871 and the Prussian Law of 1851 (which was still in force) on states of emergency, and to an increasing extent the Army leadership adapted itself to the demands of total warfare by creating new spheres of regimentation in political and social life. Towards the end of the war the supreme commanders wielded more power than any military authority in the history of Prussia or of Germany. The press department was in charge of censorship and controlled and directed much of the political propaganda that was put out. The Prussian war department within the Ministry of War, the war economy department and the food department made the entire economy fit in with the requirements of the armed forces. A side effect of all this was the continuous growth of almost every branch of the administration, including the local authorities which were given important duties in connection with economic and military objectives. After the fall of Bethmann Hollweg, which was primarily the work of the Reichstag, it was the Army High Command and not the Reichstag that found a candidate to replace him. In fact during his brief period in office, Michaelis, a senior Prussian civil servant from the war economy department, depended totally on the military leadership.

The immediate effects of Erzberger's July moves pointed to a compromise rather than a strengthening of the parliamentary elements. On 20 July 1917 the Kaiser for the first time ever gave an audience to members of the Reichstag. Furthermore, with Michaelis's government, men now came to the fore who had made names for themselves in the bourgeois parties of the coalition of July 1917, although none of them had actually been among the leaders of the Reichstag parties. But this did not in any way affect the position and power of the military leaders of the German Reich, nor did it harm their public image.

Some of the senior commanders had gone into this long war with archaic ideas. They were unable to cope with surprise situations or depended completely on the judgment of their young staff officers. In the circumstances any exception to this rule, which applied to most of the old commanders, was all the more noticeable. Among the younger men it was Ludendorff, the chief of general staff, who stood out as a successful leader; while among the older men Hindenburg, the commander-in-chief, was regarded as Germany's most respected military leader, a reputation which was never questioned during the war. He was the saviour of East Prussia from the Russians, the conqueror of Poland, the victorious commander of the Central Powers in the east. His generalship, which was glorified by patriotic propaganda, was seen as a guarantee of victory, so that in the end he was looked upon as the real head of Germany's war machine. Strictly speaking Ludendorff assisted him. But the honours due to the 'commander-in-chief' were accorded to both generals, the older of whom was typical of the Prussian junker although he owned no land, while the younger was the incarnation of the military type produced by the *deutsche-nationale* middle class.

In France too the happenings in Russia had repercussions in the early spring of 1917. These were, however, confined to the military sphere and resulted from the disappointing development of Nivelle's great offensive. The bitter fighting of 1916 in which France suffered heavy losses produced among the troops a form of mental breakdown which led to a series of mutinies; for several weeks large parts of the French army were more or less paralysed and became temporarily unsuitable for the exhausting service at the front. But these potentially dangerous manifestations had no immediate repercussions in the political sphere. The French cabinets changed even more rapidly than before the war, although they now had a broader parliamentary basis. Between the start of the war and the time when Georges Clemenceau became Prime Minister in November 1917 and began an unparalleled process of stabilisation, France had six variously composed governments whose average period in office was just over six months. In the twelve months from December 1916 to November 1917 that were so depressing for France from a military point of view and that caused the great military crisis, there were four governments. The situation in the political sphere was therefore like that in the army leadership. First the Chief of the General Staff, Joffre, was dismissed after the fruitless sacrifices of

Verdun and replaced by Nivelle; when he too suffered setbacks Pétain took over and became the saviour in the hour of need; Pétain in turn was succeeded as supreme commander by Foch, the great strategist and organiser who as generalissimo of the allied forces successfully terminated the last phase of the war with the powerful support of American troops.

In Georges Clemenceau France found a ruler who combined a sure political instinct with brutal ruthlessness. By nature he was a left-winger, a radical and a life-long bitter opponent of the bourgeois nationalist Raymond Poincaré. The latter hesitated for a long time before entrusting the most important political office to Clemenceau who had been Prime Minister only twice, Minister of the Interior once and in August 1914 for a short time Minister of War, but who had brought down many cabinets of the Third Republic with his merciless criticism. Clemenceau, a native of the Vendée, was a passionate orator, highly cultivated, a doctor by profession, who had translated John Stuart Mill and written novels, plays and a book on the oratory of Demosthenes. Until the 'nineties' when by ill fortune he became in-volved in the Panama scandal and was defeated in the 1893 election to the Chamber of Deputies, Clemenceau was regarded as the outstanding parliamentary representative of humanitarian republicanism who in *La Justice*, the journal which he edited, fought with impassioned words for political and social justice. As one of the great advocates of pro-letarian interests and democratic rights he spoke up in 1876 for an amnesty for the members of the Paris Commune, espoused the cause of the revolutionary Blanqui and defended the right to strike. Clemen-ceau was steeped in the ideals of the French Revolution, of freedom, equality and fraternity, and firmly believed in man's moral perfection without the help of the Churches. His philosophy was deprived from the revolutionary elements which had determined the flow of French history from 1789 to 1848 and for which freedom, democracy and social justice were indivisible. Basically Clemenceau belonged to the past, not the present or the future. But he was as convinced of his ideas as of the greatness of France's political and cultural achievements. He knew how to communicate his convictions with passion and to make them generally acceptable in clear but extreme language. But above all as France's last war-time Prime Minister he displayed the qualities of a dictator pursuing his objectives with unswerving conviction in the justice of his cause. He revealed himself to be a man of relentless energy and passion whose great qualities had become tempered by much bitterness. This fact was brought home to those who stood in the way of his political objectives, like the pre-war Prime Minister, Joseph Caillaux, who was suspected of secret contacts with Germany and who barely escaped being shot.

For the rest the happenings in Russia affected the West European Allies mainly in the sphere of foreign policy and also had serious consequences on the military situation. This is true above all of Britain, where the revolution had no repercussions on the domestic issues. The British system of government more than any other proved equal during the war to the burdens placed upon it and showed itself capable of regeneration. The wartime changes had resulted in much of the political decision-making being transferred from parliament to the Cabinet, which in 1915 was joined by the leaders of the Conservative opposition. It became clear, however, that this body with its traditional duties was inadequate to cope with the many new tasks arising out of the war. It was enlarged and new portfolios were created. By the end of the war Lloyd George's Cabinet was composed, apart from ministers without portfolio, of thirty-three ministers in charge of specific departments, consisting both of traditional offices and of newly created departments which owed their existence to the demands of the war, such as the Ministry of Munitions, the Ministry of the Blockade, the Ministry of Shipping, the Ministry of Food, the Air Board and the Local Government Board. It was impossible for such a large body to take joint decisions. But although the position and pre-eminence of the Prime Minister was important in British history, the complicated problems created by new administrative tasks were such that it was impossible for him to settle them alone. The activities of the armed forces and the resulting problem of munitions and rationing, foreign policy, supply and allocation of food, and the provision of raw materials for the war industries were certainly closely connected, but depended on so many different factors that permanent and successful government in coalition conditions was possible only if the Cabinet acted as a committee under the chairmanship of the Prime Minister. With the enlargement of the Cabinet came the formation of a second and in some ways superior inner group which co-ordinated and decided the work of the Cabinet. As early as 1914 Asquith had set up a War Council of the Cabinet, but this body soon assumed dimensions which made it unsuitable for its original purpose. In November 1915 the place of the War Council was taken by a

Cabinet Committee, the membership of which quickly rose to seven but which in Maurice Hankey was given a permanent secretary whose abilities of co-ordination and whose services to the war leadership were such that Balfour could later say: 'Without Hankey we should not have won the war.'

Lloyd George then gave this body its final successful form and in the last two years of the war, with the increased demand on material and intellectual resources, the five-man War Cabinet, in which Hankey could display to the full his unparalleled organisational skills and general ability remained without change the instrument of British political leadership until victory. Hankey's rapid rise is one of the peculiar features of the war for which there is no parallel outside Britain, the United States excepted. Hankey had begun life as an officer and had made a name for himself in staff positions of political importance as a master of administration and organisation. His military training stood him in good stead; even in political matters Hankey later kept his direct, military-style approach. With him the type of the tireless, calculating organiser joined the Liberal and Conservative élite from which the British leadership had hitherto been drawn. He could be described as the technocrat of the political administration. It was fortunate that this outstanding expert became the valued aide of the tactically clever, brilliant, active, decisive and generally popular Prime Minister, David Lloyd George.

Lloyd George who took over the reins of British policy with firm grip from Asquith – having displayed his restless energy as Minister of Munitions and, after Lord Kitchener's death, as Minister of War – towered above his Cabinet colleagues. He combined a sense of power with personal charm and a tremendous eloquence which won him public support. He had some of the charismatic qualities of the great democratic leader needed by the nations in this war. It was fortunate though certainly not accidental that in both the first and the second world wars Britain at the decisive moment was led by great men who responded to unusual circumstances with unusual qualities. Both Lloyd George and Churchill had the fascinating ability to use the spoken word not as oratory in the classical sense but as a tool of political persuasion, to grip men and to win them over.

Before and during the war Lloyd George perfected the art of influencing and controlling men by means of the spoken word, harnessing language to the service of modern democracy. Other men before him had been masters of parliamentary debate. But none equalled Lloyd George in spellbinding the masses when necessary. He offered them clear, plausible ideas in simple, popular form; he was a man of passion and of passionate speech who knew how to give his opinions compelling appeal and who almost always succeeded in making his audience identify itself with views of the speaker. His ability to be both simple, restrained, clear and threatening, forceful and violent was often misunderstood and coldly received by his opponents of other tongues. He was even accused of hypocrisy. In his oratory he used telling nuances, always giving his opinions the cloak of moral justification, and by using elements of daily speech created the impression that he was familiar with the feelings and anxieties of the great public. Later Lloyd George tried to use this exceptional gift at international conferences, which played an important part in his diplomacy but failed to do full justice to the difference in surroundings. Yet in all his speeches something of his tremendous energy emerged.

The influence of the British Prime Minister on the men around him was considerable. He knew how to win them over, to stimulate them, to urge them on and to use their services to obtain his goal which was always crystal clear. As leader of the British government during the war he devoted himself totally to his tasks and displayed a dynamic initiative which he communicated in full to those around him. With the help of his Round Table collaborators Lloyd George also succeeded at the decisive hour in strengthening the links between the Empire and Britain. The first carefully prepared Imperial War Conference which met from 1 March to 2 May 1917 in practice began the transformation of the Empire into the Commonwealth. Even more important than the meetings of the Imperial War Cabinet during this session, attended for the first time by the Dominions as Britain's partners in decision making on the direction of the war, was the permanent participation of the South African Prime Minister, Jan Christian Smuts, in the inner circle of political co-ordination, the War Cabinet. For over two years Lloyd George enabled the most outstanding of the political leaders of the Empire to exert an influence on British war policy that cannot be overestimated.

Having become almost a national hero in the last years of the war, after the war Lloyd George's reputation declined and he was viewed with increasing suspicion even in Britain. Fundamentally this was the result of a number of changes in political relationships which occurred when abnormal efforts were no longer required. Once the great goal, victory in this terrible struggle, had been achieved and the pressure of emergency was relaxed, wartime habits, emotions and opinions gave way to other, more critical standards which allowed Lloyd George to be viewed in a less favourable light than had been conceivable before.

That Lloyd George was also a master of adaptation and of tactical finesse showed itself with surprising clarity as early as 1917 in connection with Britain's foreign policy and its Near Eastern policy. With the collapse of the Tsarist Empire in March 1917 Russia ceased to be one of the powers which claimed a stake in Asia Minor. The provisional Russian government was already committed to a programme of a peace without annexations. In November 1917 its Bolshevik successor declared null and void the agreements on Turkey and by publishing the secret treaties acquainted the peoples of the Near East with the nature and the results of the policy actively pursued by Britain during the war.

This was particularly embarrassing to the makers of British foreign policy who had drawn their own conclusions about the effects of Russia's collapse in the Near East. With Russia the strongest advocate of an international administration for Palestine had gone. This arrangement had represented a compromise thought up by the Foreign Office to meet the historic claims of the Tsars as protectors of the holy places of Christianity and of the Christians in the Ottoman Empire. When the fortunes of war turned in favour of Britain in Mesopotamia and their troops began to advance into Palestine the Foreign Secretary, Arthur Balfour, promised in the House of Commons that the Jewish settlers in Palestine, who had suffered much in the fighting, should have their national home. The great and lasting importance of the Balfour Declaration lay in the indirect official recognition of the Zionist movement which was almost as old as the beginnings of Arab nationalism. Balfour declared that Britain welcomed 'the establishment in Palestine of a national home for the Jewish people and [would] use the best endeavours to facilitate the achievement of this object'. The motives of the Foreign Office in giving way to the pressure of the British Zionist leader, Chaim Weizmann, were of a complex nature. Events in Russia and the attitude of the Russian Jews were as important as the wish of the Foreign Office to retain its influence in Palestine. But other considerations also entered.

This declaration of 2 November 1917 did not fit in with the Sykes–

Picot agreement unless the creation of a national Jewish home was seen as compatible with an international administration. But neither then nor later was it ever interpreted in that way. Nor did it aid the cause of Husein of Mecca. The growing feeling of uncertainty created by the devious ways of secret British diplomacy led a number of influential Arabs to make urgent representations to the British High Commissioner in Cairo, a step which the British government could not ignore.

But the situation had also been affected by the United States' entry into the war. While President Wilson's Peace Inquiry was preparing the basis of the peace message of the so-called Fourteen Points, Lloyd George on 5 January 1918 in a great speech in Parliament used all his persuasive powers to eradicate the unfavourable impression created by the Russian publication of the secret treaties. He said that as Russia had dropped out of the ranks of the Entente powers Britain wished in consultation with its Allies to revise the secret treaties, that Britain no longer intended to interfere with Turkish rule in Constantinople and in the Turkish regions of the Ottoman Empire and that Arabia, Armeni Mesopotamia, Syria and Palestine were entitled to recognition of their existence as nations. For the moment therefore the British Prime Minister seemed to disclaim the secret treaties made by his predecessor's government. His statement was in line with Point 12 of the Fourteen Points which Wilson announced three days later to Congress and which promised sovereignty to the Turkish part of the Ottoman Empire, the possibility of undisturbed autonomous development to the other nationalities and internationally guaranteed free passage through the Dardanelles. Compared with the content of the secret agreements these promises made the future prospects of the Turkish and also of the Arab populations seem much brighter if the Entente powers were to win.

But from the outset the British counted on discord and differences among the Arab tribes; indeed in international law there was some ambiguity about the credentials of Husein and of his sons who had negotiated in his name with the British and also with the Arab leaders in Syria. They were the representatives of rebellion, the spokesmen of revolutionary forces which conspired with the external enemy of the Turkish rulers, even though they did so for the sake of national self-determination for the Arabs. If it is accepted that under international law only sovereign states can make binding agreements the rebellious Arabs could not be said to be acting legally. That at any rate was how the diplomats who adopted the traditional point of view saw the situation. But the public statements of Balfour, Lloyd George and Wilson had a different effect. They contained politically highly significant promises which raised the hopes of both Arabs and Jews.

6. From the declaration
of Wilson's Fourteen Points to
the Treaty of Brest-Litovsk

No other historical event has had such far-reaching impact as the amazing rise of the United States. The effects of the creation in 1871 of the German Reich and its growth as the strongest military power of the pre-war era were put in the shade by the United States' advance to the position of the world's greatest economic and financial power.

Towards the end of the First World War the United States also proved itself as an impressive military power; its strength had never before been tested to the same extent and was for a long time underestimated by the Germans. The vast military and economic reserves at the disposal of the United States were misjudged by Germany's military commanders and also by its political leaders, and the political characteristics of the new great power remained largely misunderstood. A few men like Max Weber tried in vain to spread some knowledge about conditions in America. As early as 1905, after a visit to America the Leipzig historian Karl Lamprecht had published his impressions which had attracted the attention of the bourgeois public and had provided some insight into the life of the new great nation on the other side of the Atlantic. He was greatly impressed by the militant spirit of the volunteers of the American–Spanish war and even then saw this as one of the 'most striking phenomena' in the American people, although he recognised that it depended less on exaggerated national pride than on a sense of being physically equal to their job, a feeling which he found in many of the people of the plains. For Lamprecht it was the ever-present memory of the frontier experience that explained why the American was a born warrior who could at short notice develop soldierly virtues. The growth of the United States' military strength during the war was not all that surprising. But if it was foreseen or suspected by only a few people, the military experts on the other side never even considered such a possibility.

The United States' political position in the world was not based primarily on the military potential of which it gave such impressive evidence; and the fact that it was in the process of becoming the greatest maritime power beside Britain was a by-product and must not be regarded as a cause. North America's undisputed position in the world was due exclusively to economic factors. It was based on its wealth and on the financial dependence of other great powers on the United States. The war fundamentally altered the relationship between creditor and debtor nations, transforming the greatest, most fertile and most productive debtor country of the world into the greatest creditor nation and the greatest financial power of the world. There were few countries which did not in the course of the war become indebted to the United States. States which before the war had been financially in a strong position now became debtors of the United States. This situation caused problems later when most of the countries indebted to America found it difficult to repay their debts by exports as the United States' industrial capacity continued to expand at a fast rate. The trade balances with America therefore remained passive so that no settlement could be achieved that way. This vitally important factor was one of the main causes for the rise of the reparations problem which grew beyond the war indemnity question and for half a generation became an international issue of the first magnitude.

The United States' assumption of the role of a world power is thus of epoch-making importance and fraught with consequences for several reasons. The Americans' behaviour in the theatre of war was very different from that of the European belligerents. This was partly the result of President Wilson's prophetic gestures and missionary determination; he found suitable words for the mood and political ideas of the American citizen and expressed them with authority and effect in his great messages to Congress and to the general public. He spoke of the 'hope of the whole world' being focused on America. It was Wilson's intention to keep this hope constantly before the eyes of his people. As the American people were growing into a nation this incessant appeal to their better nature gave them the historic role which was suited to their political self-consciousness.

'The new things in the world are the things that are divorced from force. They are the moral compulsions of the human conscience.' This impressive statement which Wilson made before the war had actually begun throws light on the lines which the President followed when it came to making political decisions for America during the war. In his view the United States should and could intervene in the war with a new watchword. Convinced of America's unique role Wilson coined the formula 'peace without victory'. He identified America's policy with future world policy: 'The United States have not the distinction of being the masters of the world but the distinction of carrying certain lights for the world that the world has never so distinctly seen before, certain guiding lights of liberty and principle and justice.' The expression 'ethical imperialism' may justly be applied to the role which Wilson had in mind for the United States. His ideas, which owed much to the Quakers, centred on the belief that if they were to be realised the political principles of the United States must be identified with the principles of humanity. This was a revolutionary idea which if accepted would change the world and create a 'new system of law and justice' among the nations; this system the American President at first referred to in general terms and then gradually outlined in great detail.

It is in this light that we must see the Fourteen Points proclaimed by Wilson on 8 January 1918 in a message to Congress. They had been prepared by an expert group which became known as 'the Inquiry', convened by Colonel House at Wilson's behest. At first the Fourteen Points found little understanding among European politicians. The British Foreign Secretary Arthur Balfour, called them 'certain admirable but very abstract principles', thereby clearly disassociating himself from the view of the American President who described his principles with great finality not only as a programme of world peace but as 'the only possible programme'.

The Fourteen Points asked for open covenants of peace openly arrived at and rejected all secret agreements. This demand was based on the view that there would only be reliable safeguards for peace if the nations knew as much about international politics as about domestic policy and that they must be in a position to control international affairs so as not to be pushed into commitments, conflicts and wars by the obscure and uncontrollable machinations of secret diplomacy. This approach reflected the Anglo-Saxon view of democracy as being based on a strong public opinion closely and indissolubly linked with the power of the law.

The general principles expressed in the Fourteen Points included complete freedom of navigation in peace and in war, the removal as far

as possible of all economic barriers, the exchange of adequate guarantees for the lowering of national armaments and a frank, open-minded
and completely impartial settlement of colonial claims.

This far no distinction was made between the parties to this war.
Only the subsequent points contained conditions for the Central
Powers. It was in line with the principle of peace without victory to
demand the evacuation of all Russian territory and complete freedom
for Russia's development, the evacuation and restoration of Belgium
and of the occupied territories of France. How the American President
and his advisers imagined the future Europe becomes evident from the
clearly defined outlines of a generous territorial settlement and of the
proposed political transformation. Germany must return Alsace-
Lorraine to France; Austria's future frontier with Italy must be settled
on nationality lines. The peoples of Austria-Hungary must be given
the freest opportunity of autonomous development.

Analogous with the conditions imposed in the Russian and French
theatres of war the Fourteen Points insisted that the military conquests
in south-eastern Europe must be abandoned and that the occupied
states of Rumania, Serbia and Montenegro must be evacuated and
restored. Serbia should in future have access to the Adriatic. This could
be done only by taking Hercegovina and Dalmatia, territories that
formed part of Croatia and Bosnia, from the Danube monarchy. The
movements to break away from the Danube monarchy that existed
in all these areas were now openly assisted by Wilson's message and
the question indirectly arose of what their political future should be.
Serbia's demand for access to the sea had wider implications. With it
reappeared the idea of the great south Slav state that had long been one
of the aims of Serb nationalism and had loomed large in the pre-war
crisis in Austria-Hungary.

A similar fate was to be Turkey's. The guarantee of assured sovereignty was restricted to the Turkish portions of the Ottoman Empire
whose future territorial limits were not defined. The Straits, however,
were to remain completely free. The autonomous development of the
subject nationalities was to proceed absolutely unmolested.

The penultimate of Wilson's Fourteen Points referred to the
establishment of an independent Poland which was to cover all areas
indisputably occupied by Polish people and to have free and secure
access to the sea. The last point referred to the setting up of a League of
Nations 'for the purpose of affording mutual guarantees of political

and territorial integrity to great and small States alike'. This 'Covenant of the League of Nations' was Wilson's greatest and most important idea with which he hoped to safeguard peace and to end the age of imperialist power politics. The principles of power politics were to be replaced by the principles of a universally recognised law, and disputes and conflicts were to be solved in an orderly way jointly by all states. This idea presupposed permanent United States participation not only in happenings in Europe but in international affairs, indeed it presupposed America's permanent presence as the guardian of this idea and as the superior power in the system of great powers.

This was certainly an ambitious goal. For Wilson the United States' entry into the war on the basis of his political programme as set out in the Fourteen Points provided the historical opportunity for the achievement of the greatest conceivable objective of American foreign policy. In the light of this great idea the circumstances and individual events that preceded America's entry into the war become unimportant particles of a tremendous process of change that was to affect the whole world. But the Central Powers were bound to regard the points directly related to their future fate as the immediately relevant and most important parts of the American President's demands which at first failed to find full support anywhere.

The sum total of the American President's proposals amounted to: (1) the termination of the occupation conditions created by Germany's military successes and the restoration of France's former frontiers, including Alsace-Lorraine, the complete restoration of Belgium and of the other occupied states. (2) The general revision of the political map of the age of imperialism, primarily of the political map of Europe and the Near East with the objective of doing away with antiquated systems of government which for several peoples had clearly meant a state of oppression, and of giving the peoples of these territories full rights of national self-determination. (3) The application of the right of national self-determination to the world as a whole and the creation of a permanent safeguard of the nations' right to life and self-determination in the shape of the League of Nations.

Later, when the war was approaching its end, the American President completed his message of 8 January 1918 with 'Five Particulars' which he announced on 27 September 1918 and in which he reinforced and enlarged the Fourteen Points with reference to the setting up of a League of Nations. The first particular insisted on justice to friend and foe alike; the second denounced all national and diplomatic separate interest; the third provided that there should be no alliances within the future League of Nations; the fourth forbade all economic alliances within the League of Nations and the fifth reaffirmed the prohibition of secret treaties. These further refinements of the President's ideas understandably met with undisguised criticism from his Allies as they were of benefit to the Central Powers whose defeat was predictable if it had not already occurred. It was doubtful therefore whether these Particulars would ever have the approval of America's Allies.

On official Germany the proclamation of Wilson's Fourteen Points made no impression at first. Any government responding at that moment to this new American pronouncement would certainly have been thrown out by the *Alldeutsche*, the *Vaterlandspartei* and above all by the Army High Command.

The German hopes of victory revealed themselves in the bold designs translated into reality with great ruthlessness at Brest-Litovsk. They were also behind the military and political arrangements of 1918 when not only the army thought that victory was within reach. An easier winter and better food supplies compared with the horrors of the winter of 1916–17 and the spring of 1917 encouraged confident predictions, although signs of internal upheaval – such as the sailors' mutiny at Kiel and a series of strikes, above all the great strike of munition workers in January 1918 – were multiplying. The position was worse still as regards Germany's ally Austria-Hungary; even before the sailors' mutiny at Cattaro there were alarming signs of disintegration in the dual monarchy. But the German military leadership and with it the civilian authorities were not impressed and remained confident.

It seems explicable only in terms of the curious psychological climate of the time that at the beginning of 1918 the Germans had reached a peak of confidence and expectation of victory that was equal almost to the hopes of August 1914; this was no longer true, however, of all sections of the population. Germany's rapid disintegration between January and October 1918 revealed the fragility of this will to win and of the assumptions on which it was based.

After almost two and a half months of intermittent negotiations the peace treaty of Brest-Litovsk was finally signed. In the history of this peace several phases can be distinguished.

The negotiations opened on 22 December 1917 with a surprising Russian initiative; the leader of the delegation, Joffe, presented a six-point programme which left no doubt that the revolutionary government proposed to present the peace in the east to the world as a model for the settlement of the war. This programme, formulated in general terms and applicable not only to Russia, showed that the demand for 'peace without annexations or indemnities' was in fact very close to Wilson's 'peace without victory'. It called for the liberation of the territories annexed by force, the rapid withdrawal of troops from the occupied territories, the complete restoration of the independence of those peoples who had lost it in the course of the war and for plebiscites on the political future of national groups who wished to break away from one of the existing states of which they formed part; it further demanded protection for the rights of national minorities, the analogous application of all these principles to the peoples of the great colonial empires and finally the complete abandonment of war indemnities.

The principles advanced by the Russian negotiators were well thought out, morally sound and announced for propaganda purposes; the leading representatives of the Central Powers, Prince Leopold of Bavaria, Major-General Hoffmann, Secretary of State von Kühlmann and Count Czernin, were therefore compelled at first to move cautiously. Their reply, which had been drafted by Czernin, was evasive and confined to reservations without directly rejecting the principles set out by the Russians. Both Czernin and Kühlmann were anxious not to make it appear to their own peoples that their policy clashed directly with the impressive declarations made by the Russians whose object it was to let the whole world participate in the events at Brest-Litovsk and to negotiate in public with the press in attendance.

But this beginning set off a storm of nationalist indignation in Germany and met with opposition from the Army High Command, although only a day later the diplomats followed up their first public reply to the Russians with a second confidential communication in which they demanded that certain areas between the Baltic and the Black Sea should voluntarily be separate from Russia. The Russian delegation was totally unprepared to accept this demand. It remained consistent, broke off negotiations and departed, leaving behind an atmosphere of uncertainty, of fluctuating and conflicting opinions. During the days that followed a crisis developed between Austria which wanted to proceed with moderation and Germany which proposed to show no consideration, and also between the Army High Command and the Foreign Minister not so much over the treatment of Russia as over that of Germany's obstinate ally. Ludendorff made it known that Germany no longer needed Austria's military assistance, that Bulgaria was without significance and Turkey a burden. Indirectly and probably subconsciously this was a devastating criticism of the whole of Germany's previous war policy. However, the general failed to convince the diplomats and politicians. The army leaders thought in the simple categories of crude power politics which saw no worthwhile objectives other than large-scale annexations. But for the moment Kühlmann successfully countered this with the view that Germany should aim at a political protectorate over large regions in the east and at secure economic relations with the rest of Russia.

Meanwhile, Trotsky, in charge of the foreign policy of the revolutionary Russian government, made an attempt to establish contact with the United States which he knew from the last phase of his exile. Although this interlude remained unsuccessful it cannot be completely ignored in view of Wilson's Fourteen Points which one might say competed in theory and reality with Lenin's peace terms.

The second phase of the Brest-Litovsk negotiations lasted only ten days and was dominated by Trotsky's determination to exploit every opportunity for propaganda purposes and whenever possible to appeal to the German public. The Bolsheviks now addressed their propaganda also directly to the German soldiers in the east. With the rejection of the German demand for a plebiscite in the areas which the Germans thought should be separated from Russia the negotiations quickly reached an impasse. The negotiations broke down again and the Russian delegation departed.

In the ensuing interval there were violent arguments in the Central Committee of the Bolshevik Party. The group led by Trotsky was afraid that a peace on German terms would have depressing consequences which might lead to the collapse of the revolution. Lenin on the other hand saw no alternative but to make peace regardless of the conditions. He saw the negotiations only in terms of the transition to a new situation in which the revolution would before long spread through *Mitteleuropa* and overthrow the existing systems. In contrast to Trotsky he regarded the victory of the revolution as certain and the need for peace as imperative; the people wanted peace and Russia could not go on fighting. Lenin's estimate of the situation was certainly more accurate than that of Trotsky, Bukharin and others and his was also the more practical programme for the immediate future.

The third phase of the negotiations started from the compromise of 'neither war nor peace' decided upon by the Central Committee; in pursuit of this Trotsky now resumed his previous tactics. He was helped by signs of disintegration, by unrest and strikes among the Central Powers and by renewed tension between Germany and Austria. In order to safeguard food supplies for the future, peace was concluded on 9 February at Brest-Litovsk with a Ukranian government dependent on the Central Powers; presented with a *fait accompli* the Russian delegation left Brest-Litovsk shortly afterwards for the third time.

As the armistice concluded in December expired on 17 February the Army High Command's plans to resume the fighting and to gain Germany's objectives by force of arms came into their own again. The decision was taken at the Crown Council on 13 February. As at many previous Crown Council meetings there was tension between the civilians and the military who wanted to attack at once; one of their aims now was to bring about the overthrow of the Bolsheviks – whom they had helped to power – by sparking off a counter-revolution through renewed German military action in Livonia and Courland. In the end a weak compromise was reached. The Foreign Ministry hastily arranged, before the end of the armistice, for cries for help from the territories not yet occupied by German troops. Thereupon the Russians were presented on 21 February with an ultimatum to which an answer was required within forty-eight hours and which contained the harshest German conditions yet, including Russian renunciation of the northern Baltic provinces, the conclusion of peace with the Ukranian government (recognition of which was achieved by this method), the transfer of the trans-Caucasian frontier districts and an explicit abjuration of Bolshevik agitation in all German-occupied territories.

On the Russian side Lenin had just had his way completely, and by a small majority it had been decided to accept the original German conditions. Although the Russian decision was communicated telegraphically to the Germans on 19 February it could not stop the rapid advance of German troops. In a state of feverish excitement the Russians now discussed the latest German terms and with ruthless

arguments Lenin ensured their acceptance, a decision which was telegraphically communicated to the German government on 24 February.
On the following day the Russians returned to Brest-Litovsk.

The peace treaty was signed on 3 March. Under it Russia lost over a
quarter of its European territory, of its arable territory and of its rail
network, a third of its textile industry and almost three-quarters of its
heavy industry and of its mines. With good reason the peace treaty of
Brest-Litovsk has been described (by Georg von Rauch) as one of 'the
most unfortunate peace treaties in history'. In Russia's history it
represents a stage the importance of which is as great as that of the
second revolutionary change which followed the events of October
1917. Lenin frankly admitted the harshness of the peace but sought to
throw out a ray of hope at this low point of Russian history by repeated
references to Prussia's position in 1807. One of the direct consequences
of Brest-Litovsk was the collapse of the last Russian coalition government. The left-wing social revolutionaries who had voted against
ratification of the treaty left the government of Peoples' Commissars
and the Bolsheviks who had been responsible for all important decisions
in the recent past remained in sole charge. On 6 March at the Seventh
Bolshevik Party Congress it was decided at Lenin's proposal to name
the party the Russian Communist Party (Bolshevik), a conscious
reference to Marx and Engels' concept of communism. A new era in
the history of socialism had thus begun. The Bolshevik government
moved to Moscow and installed itself in the Kremlin, which for the next
fifty years became its permanent domicile and the symbol of its rule.

But inside Russia the peace produced the effects which Trotsky in
the first phase of the Brest-Litovsk negotiations had warned Lenin and
his followers to expect, and the collapse of the state seemed imminent.
Strong White Russian counter-revolutionary units gathered in distant
Siberia, where they were later led by Admiral Kolchak and began an
offensive which with Allied assistance temporarily took them back into
European Russia. They also had the support of the well-supplied and
well-armed Czech legion which had been recruited from Russian
prisoner of war camps. Even before the start of the thrust from the east
there was a rising by the Danube Cossacks; this was the beginning of
many years of civil war activities by counter-revolutionary elements
which in southern Russia were commanded by Generals Alexeyev,
Kornilov, Denikin, Krasnov and Wrangell, and in the north by
Generals Yudenich and Miller. The position of the Bolshevik rulers

became precarious as early as July 1918 when during the Fifth All-Russian Soviet Congress there were risings of social revolutionaries in twenty-three cities; before that they had repeatedly expressed their bitterness about the peace treaty and had been encouraged by the French to do so. By assassinating the German plenipotentiary, Count Mirbach, they tried to disrupt diplomatic relations between the Bolshevik government and Germany.

The Allies regarded the German operations as a threat and from March 1918 onwards there were extensive landings of British and French troops. Their activities soon went beyond the immediate objective of protecting the Allied supply depots at Murmansk, Vladivostok and Archangel; they tried to influence the military situation in Russia and also to protect the important oil fields in the Baku region against attacks from both the Central Powers and the Bolshevik forces. The intervention of the Allies and their support of the White Russians whom they supplied with materials and military advisers fanned the flames of the civil war in Russia. In that way Brest-Litovsk had not brought a solution for Russia either. The Allies now embarked on a phase of ruthless opposition to the Soviet government which was seen as the enemy. On another page of the history of the war is written the story of the intervention of Japanese and finally also of American troops behind the back of the Kolchak army in eastern Siberia. These activities began a new phase of the struggle in eastern Asia but were no longer directly connected with the European theatre of war.

But among the immediate effects of Brest-Litovsk another factor deserves attention. During the two and a half months of negotiations that preceded the signing of the treaty the revolutionary Russian government both at home and abroad used every means of propaganda to proclaim its determination to end the imperialist war and to make peace. But in spite of this world-wide propaganda it was realistic considerations which in the last resort persuaded the Russians to accept the German conditions. Apart from the realisation that the military situation was hopeless it was the alarming signs of the evident disintegration of the old Russia that finally persuaded the Russian rulers, urged on by Lenin, to accept the enemy's harsh terms. The Russian plenipotentiaries signed the treaty under conditions of duress which made it appear a *paix de violence* not only to Russia but also to the Entente countries and to the neutrals. This fact subsequently, after the defeat of the Central Powers, did not help the victors of the dictated peace of Brest-Litovsk. The socialists in the Entente states noted with pained surprise that not even the German Social Democratic Party press found much to criticise in this peace treaty and that only the independents were wholly opposed to it. But there was also widespread severe condemnation of Russia's decision to stop fighting, for which Lenin was primarily responsible, and it was not long before suspicions were voiced of a plot involving German socialists, particularly the shabbily treated Parvus. The international links between the majority of European socialists who since the Kienthal Conference refused to establish closer relations with the Russian party under Lenin and Trotsky suffered permanently as a result. In the end this was of help to the Bolshevik initiative during the restoration of the Communist International. But during the war Wilson's Fourteen Points were bound to seem highly attractive to the moderates and liberals among the majority of socialists.

7. The military collapse of the Central Powers

With Brest-Litovsk and the peace treaty with Rumania, which was signed at Bucharest and which set the seal on Germany's military triumph in the east, many of the German war aims seemed to have been achieved. The designs of the Army High Command which were viewed sceptically by the Foreign Ministry went beyond the achievements of Brest-Litovsk. There were also economic pressure groups advocating a federation of states under German control on the territory of the former Russian empire. This federation was to include Livonia, Estonia, the Crimea, the territories of the Kuban Cossacks and of the Don Cossacks, the Caucasus region, the territories of the Volga Tartars and of the Astrakhan Cossacks, Turkmenia and Turkestan. This calculation was of course based on the assumption of a 'revolutionised' Russia. There was no thought of strengthening Bolshevik or any other Russian rule. The Foreign Ministry on the other hand appreciated that the extent of the territorial losses already suffered by Russia, and above all the loss of all access to the European seas, would lead a consolidated regime to fight for the lost territories. Russia would either re-emerge as an imperialist power or disintegrate completely.

But the Army High Command was not impressed by the critical analyses of a few officials in the Foreign Ministry. The military advance in southern and northern Russia did not come to an end with the peace treaty. In March the Germans reached the Rostov–Belgorod–Polozk–Narva line. A supplementary peace treaty with the Ukraine established the basis for the economic exploitation of southern Russia; this was reinforced politically by the military dictatorship of General Skoropadski set up with German help. These activities were difficult to reconcile with the peace treaty of Brest-Litovsk. Secretary of State von Kühlmann's protests against this policy made him so unpopular with the Army High Command that his position became increasingly precarious.

With the victory in the east, victory in the west seemed within Germany's grasp. After Brest-Litovsk Ludendorff spoke of the 'blow in

the west' which would now follow; the peace in the east had created
the conditions necessary for its success. How close the links between
the happenings in the east and in the west were thought to be, and how
in the absence of an adequate understanding of the basic differences
they were misjudged, is shown clearly by a jotting of the Kaiser dating
from early 1918:

> The victory of the Germans over Russia was necessary for the
> revolution, the revolution was necessary for Lenin and Lenin for
> Brest. The same is true of the west. First there must be a victory in
> the west with the collapse of the Entente, then we shall make our
> conditions which they must accept. These will be made to suit our
> interests alone.

These illusions were based entirely on the assumption that the
enemy was weary of the war. Germany was in no position to continue
the struggle. Its military position was untenable in the long run. A few
politically influential civilians began to appreciate this fact under the
impact of the great strike at the end of January. Liberals like Friedrich
Naumann, Ernst Jäckh and the industrialist Robert Bosch said in a note
to Ludendorff that the mood of the population would not tolerate a
delay in ending the war.

Even the General Staff began to have some doubts after the failure
of the five great offensives in the west which began on 21 March and
were designed to lead to a breakthrough in the second half of July.
But for the time these doubts were expressed in veiled form only. In
June Ludendorff gave his blessing to a propaganda campaign designed
to stimulate a peace offensive which would aid the army's activities and
take into account the growing criticism at home. But it became clear
that the High Command was still not prepared to abandon its military
objectives when three weeks later Freiherr von Kühlmann responded
in the Reichstag to comments made by General Smuts and ex-Premier
Asquith and said openly for the first time that 'given the vast size of
this coalition war and the many powers involved – also from overseas
– no definite end [can be] reached by military action alone without
diplomatic negotiations with the enemy'. This statement was unambiguous and realistic. A sensation was produced when the conservative
party leader, Count Westarp, made a sharp reply and amid loud applause
from the entire right described a military victory as the only road to
peace. Thereupon the Army High Command seized its opportunity

and insisted on the dismissal of the Secretary of State at the Foreign Ministry whom it had long viewed with distaste; Kühlmann went in spite of opposition from the groups supporting the Erzberger resolution.

But at the latest by the 'black day' which at the western front was 8 August, it was clear that victory had finally eluded the Germans. The great plans for the promotion of national and social revolution in the east boomeranged on to the Central Powers. For the Army High Command this was a sudden fall from the clouds; because the optimism which it had carefully cultivated had affected even the coolest brains. There was surprise at the Great Headquarters when it was realised to what extent Ludendorff's judgment of the situation had been influenced by considerations of military prestige.

For a long time it was not appreciated, and Ludendorff did his best to hide the fact, that the real turning point in the west was 18 July. Ludendorff was motivated partly by a wish to cover up his own mistake, which had been not to listen to the urgent representations of the capable chief of the general staff of the fourth army, General von Lossberg, who wanted several armies to be pulled back and to be kept in readiness along a shortened front for defence purposes. In not following this advice Ludendorff was swayed by political considerations and by fears of the impression which such a move would have made on the enemy, the army and the people at home. After a further deterioration of the position at the front Ludendorff was forced with great sacrifices and under strong pressure from the enemy to agree, too late, to the demand for a withdrawal.

But even at a time when the collapse in the west was already predictable the Army High Command continued to pursue its aggressive policy in the east. As late as the beginning of August Ludendorff advocated a new offensive in the east when after British landings the Deputy Peoples' Commissioner for Foreign Affairs, Chichernin, asked the Army High Command to help the Bolshevik government. On 28 August the supplementary treaties of Brest-Litovsk were ratified without the Reichstag being consulted because it was not expected to approve them. Under these treaties the border states were separated from Russia and Russia agreed to make extensive deliveries of war materials to the Central Powers in addition to an indemnity payment of six milliard gold mark. Russia benefited by the evacuation of the territories east of the Beresina, for which it paid dearly of course, and by the German promise not to intervene in the Russian civil war. The then Foreign Minister, Paul von Hintze, who as an Admiral and as former naval attaché at St Petersburg was in close contact with the military, regarded the Bolsheviks as 'awful people'. But this did not prevent Germany from getting as much out of them for as long as possible. While the fears of the Bolsheviks being ousted proved unjustified the hopes associated with the survival of their regime were also shown to be completely misplaced.

Only after the collapse of Bulgaria at the end of September 1918 was Ludendorff prepared to agree that the army was finished and that the western front could give way any day. He said so for the first time at the meeting of the Great General Staff on 1 October. On 29 September it had been decided at Spa to ask for an armistice. On the same day plans were for the first time discussed and set afoot for parliament to be given political responsibility. This innovation went back to an idea of Paul von Hintze who wanted a 'modernisation' of the Reich so that the nation could close its ranks for its 'defence in the final struggle'. The fact that at the last moment Ludendorff agreed to and even supported the idea of parliamentary responsibility is explained entirely by the situation in which the Central Powers found themselves after the failure of the High Command's military plans. Now the American President's peace formula was urgently taken up. Both the Army High Command and the Reich government recognised the Fourteen Points as a basis for future peace negotiations and Ludendorff demanded that the American President should immediately be approached with a request for an armistice; this proposal was accepted after the hopelessness of the military situation had been emphasised. The collapse of 1918 therefore started as a military crisis resulting from the strategic errors of the Army High Command. In the subsequent phase the parliamentary majority in the Reichstag gradually took over the country's political leadership.

Recent research has shown that earlier interpretations which stressed the dependence of the political scene on the decisions of the military leadership need to be examined afresh. More important is the fact that towards the end of the war there ceased to be effective collaboration between the military and the civil authorities. The military failure produced a crisis in the course of which this collaboration became increasingly intermittent while at the same time the paths of the political parties began to diverge. In August 1914 the unity of all political groups had seemed a reality, although before the war nothing was more unimaginable than co-operation between the socialists, the bourgeois parties and the conservatives and agreement between them and both the civil and the military leaders of the Reich. In fact this unity survived for a relatively long time. The subsequent collapse of the 'national unity front' has therefore in retrospect often been attributed by nationalist historians to irrational decisions and has not been recognised as the important political event that it was. In fact the political upheaval of the so-called November Revolution is nothing but the final manifestation of the breakdown of this collaboration. Undoubtedly it occurred under the impact of devastating military decisions in the theatre of war, but there were also domestic causes. Behind the façade of the 'national unity front' there had been a shift in political strength which in the end led to the emergence of democratic ideas and programmes and to the rise of the parliamentary groups behind them.

The central question in the autumn of 1918 was how, in view of the previously proclaimed annexationalist goals, Germany could now make its peaceful intentions creditable both at home and to the enemy. Hintze's information from Washington was that for any peace campaign to be effectively supported by the American President Germany needed to produce a new, broadly based government and a constitutional reform. But from the point of view of the military leadership it was also essential to have a 'Ministry of National Defence' which would demonstrate once more the unity of the whole nation and include the Social Democrats.

The programme formulated by the SPD on 23 September 1918 contained some proposals that formed part of Wilson's Fourteen Points or were at least in line with them: Germany was to join Wilson's proposed League of Nations; Belgium, Serbia and Montenegro would be restored as part of a general peace treaty and the Brest-Litovsk conditions set aside – a proposal that came close to Wilson's peace without victory for the Central Powers; occupied territories should be given civil administrations; Alsace-Lorraine would be granted autonomy; at home universal secret suffrage would be introduced everywhere and the state of emergency brought to an end. The programme was not without influence on future developments. On 28 September the inter-party committee agreed on a formal programme under which parliament would play a greater role. The programme was based on both the SPD demands and on the guidelines drawn up the day before by the national liberal group. These had been the result of a draft submitted by Deputy von Richthofen and also demanded autonomy for Alsace-Lorraine and a more parliamentary form of government. Up to that point the *Zentrum* representatives in the inter-parliamentary committee had supported the Hertling government. But as Hertling opposed the new programme which had the approval of the Reichstag majority the *Zentrum* changed its line.

At this point the Army High Command took the initiative and on that very same 28 September a telegraphic order went out from Spa calling Hertling, Count Roedern, the Prussian Minister of Finance and Secretary of State of the Reich Treasury, and Secretary of State von Hintze to Spa where the Kaiser, the Crown Prince, Hindenburg and Ludendorff invited them to discuss the reshaping of the Reich government. The surprising change at the Great Headquarters was due largely to the position of Germany's allies: the political aspect of the situation had hitherto been disregarded but its dramatic military consequences could now no longer be ignored. The precarious situation in the west was aggravated by the collapse of the Macedonian front which led to Bulgaria's withdrawal from the war and, on 29 September, to its capitulation. As a result of the turbulent happenings in the Balkan peninsula the surviving Austrian and German units were forced to beat a hasty retreat. Having been militarily stable since the peace of Bucharest the situation in the south-east was thus suddenly upset. Politically Germany could no longer turn a deaf ear to the representations of the Austrian Emperor and Burián, who had once again taken over from Czernin and who both appreciated that in quick peace moves lay the last hope of saving the Habsburg Empire.

The wear and tear of the long war had greatly damaged the ties which had held the Danube monarchy together for centuries. The civil service and the officer corps were the basis of Habsburg rule over the multination system of the dual monarchy. But the heavy losses of the war, more in prisoners than in dead and wounded, which it was necessary to make good by new recruits had brought about fundamental changes. The empty places in the old officer corps were filled with reserve officers whose loyal ties to their own nationality were stronger than their devotion to the Habsburg state and who contributed substantially to the progressive disintegration of the army.

No less fraught with consequences were the administrative defects of the Danube monarchy which was not prepared for and proved unequal to the demands of the war and above all to its long-term effects. The lack of centralisation and particularly the trade barrier between the Hungarian and the Austrian half of the Empire made it very difficult to ensure that the country was supplied with food. The parts of the monarchy with agrarian surpluses, above all Hungary and Bohemia, obstinately resisted any form of planning, so that in practice this was successful only locally. As a result there was large-scale distress which after 1917 led to endless hunger revolts in the big cities of the Austrian half of the Empire, although the monarchy as a whole produced more food than it required and could even have come to the assistance of the German population.

These revolts, some of which produced military counter measures, quickly spread to the army. There were more incidents of this nature with the return from Russian prisoner of war camps of roughly one and a half million soldiers after the peace of Brest-Litovsk in the spring and summer of 1918. These men came back with revolutionary ideas, although in the individual territories of the monarchy they took a nationalist rather than a communist form.

New forces from outside also made their influence felt on the national groups. After the United States' entry into the war, groups of peoples of the Danube monarchy played an increasingly political role in the United States. Like the Poles, the Czechs had first-rate advocates of their cause in America. They were headed by Thomas Masaryk, a highly respected scholar, religious philosopher and outstanding exponent of Slav history of thought who had been a professor at Prague University. Masaryk was the son of a Czech mother and a Slovak father who had been a serf in his youth. He had married an American who belonged to an influential family and he had made a great impression on President Wilson during his American exile. Masaryk had once been one of the spokesmen of the Czech national movement in the Austrian Reichsrat but had in the end parted company with all the Czech parties. When the war broke out he had gathered around himself, at first in Prague, a secret national Czech opposition group tellingly called the 'Mafia' – which to start with was only a political general staff without an army – and had worked tirelessly to convince the enemies of the Central Powers of the need to break up the Habsburg monarchy and to establish an independent Czech state. He was the incarnation of the unity of the Czechs and the Slovaks which was put into words in the Pittsburg Treaty of 30 July 1918. This agreement, which was subsequently disputed, had the support of Wilson and also the approval of the Slovaks resident in America. On the same day the Czech national committee under Beneš and Stefánik was officially recognised by the Allied powers and given supreme control of the rapidly growing Czech contingents at the Entente fronts. It was the political aim of all Slav national groups in the dual monarchy to emulate this development.

The Slav exile groups in the Entente camp could certainly not have become so influential if in the last weeks of the war their ideas and programmes had not been visibly confirmed by events inside Austria-Hungary. Up to that time the Vienna monarchy had not been unpopular among the conservative Czech middle classes. But the last phase of the war proved too much of a test and national trends were now helped by events. There had been desertions from non-German-speaking units of the Austrian army since the second and third year of the war. In 1918 these assumed such dimensions that complete units were formed on the Italian side and used at the front. Francis Ferdinand hoped to preserve his empire from disintegration by playing the peace-maker. The Germans could no longer ignore his activities, although they remained ignorant of the form and extent of the talks that went on in Switzerland mostly at unofficial level.

On 30 September William II dismissed Count Hertling and broadened the basis of the government by bringing in a number of parliamentarians. But the most important part of these changes which showed which way the wind was blowing was the then unpublished decision to authorise the future Chancellor to send a peace offer to Wilson and to accept his Fourteen Points. After some hesitation and disagreement among the Berlin parliamentarians the liaison man between the Army High Command and the Chancellory proposed as candidate for the Chancellorship Prince Max von Baden, a man whose liberal views recommended him for this office. In the end the progressive deputies Haussmann and von Payer persuaded the inter-parliamentary committee unanimously to agree to this choice and then the Army High Command gave its approval. The official proposal which followed came from the head of the Kaiser's civil cabinet.

Thereupon Max von Baden was summoned to Berlin and informed of the Army High Command's call for an armistice; he did not, however, immediately agree to accept the post which the Kaiser proposed to give him. Prince Max said plainly that in his view a peace offer of the kind that he had in mind could not come after a request for an armistice; priority must be given to the preparation by the government of a viable programme of reform. But the military was not prepared to give up the ultimate decision. The Foreign Ministry shared their view and Hintze informed Vienna and Constantinople of the proposed course of action as though it was a *fait accompli*.

The decisive word was spoken by Hindenburg at a conference on 2 October attended by the Chancellor candidate, Payer, Hintze, Roedern and the head of the Kaiser's civil cabinet: he said that within eight days he expected the Allies to launch a new major attack and that he could not guarantee that this would not lead to a catastrophe. Eight days was a very brief period in which to develop political ideas and plans and the civilian participants at the meeting were therefore bound to regard the situation as catastrophic.

On 3 October Max von Baden made a last attempt to dissuade Hindenburg from his demand for an immediate armistice on the ground that it was an admission to the world that Germany was defeated; he expected it to strengthen the enemy's chauvinism without benefiting the cause of peace. When he failed to move Hindenburg he demanded for his personal protection a written declaration from the Army High Command to the effect that the military position at the western front no longer allowed any delay. The letter which Hindenburg wrote in reply did not contain this unambiguous declaration but reiterated the army leadership's view that it was essential to break off the struggle so as to spare the German people further sacrifice; every day's delay would cost the lives of thousands of brave soldiers. But Max von Baden continued to have reservations and tried, unsuccessfully, to gain a clearer picture of the situation by addressing detailed questions to the Army High Command. In response Ludendorff said that at present the situation was not threatening but that a new major offensive might be launched shortly. Then it would be of vital importance whether the German army had obtained the urgently needed armistice twenty-four hours earlier or later. Behind the Army High Command's insistence on an armistice there was evidently the idea of extricating themselves as best they could from the victorious offensive war waged by the Allies.

When this became clear Max von Baden gave way to the Army leaders. He signed the request for peace and an armistice and agreed to accept the Chancellorship. The pacifist in him won the day, maybe also the officer who obeys orders, or perhaps he saw himself called to save the situation. He made a great political and personal sacrifice by falling in completely with the demand of the Army High Command whose aim it was to preserve Germany's military strength in the immediate future so as to avoid an internal collapse following on a military defeat.

The problems of forming a government were solved when the new Chancellor decided to accept office. Among the Social Democrats in the Reichstag, Ebert had favoured the idea of joining a government, whereas Scheidemann was opposed to participating in what he regarded as a 'bankrupt enterprise'. But events now moved fast. On 2 October parliament learned with horror what the situation was really like when a military spokesman of the High Command painted the situation in the blackest colours to the party leaders. A few days he said would be enough to decide the fate of the army and the future of Germany. Given this situation the new Reich government was formed in the most unusual fashion from the top men of the inter-parliamentary committee and the acting secretaries of state of the Reich Ministries. The Chancellor candidate was presented with a *fait accompli*. Here again decisions were taken regardless of Prince Max's own ideas and intentions and he was relegated to the position of a supreme representative.

In the night from 3 to 4 October the German request for an armistice was sent to the American President via Switzerland; without entering into detail and without reservation Germany accepted the Fourteen Points of January 1918 'as the basis for peace negotiations'. The German note reached Wilson on 7 October, at the same time as an almost identically worded Austro-Hungarian request for an armistice.

8. October reform
and November revolution in Germany

The unexpected turn of events on top of the Chancellorship crisis had a disturbing effect on the German public which had so far been fed nothing but optimistic reports. Even before the publication of the American President's first reply voices were raised demanding that Germany should go further, that the Kaiser should resign, that there should be a complete break with the past. Characteristic of the mood that was gradually spreading is a phrase used in a letter of 11 October 1918 by Max Weber who described himself as a 'sincere supporter of monarchical institutions, although with parliamentary restraints': 'If he [the Kaiser] goes now without external pressure, he goes honourably and has the chivalrous sympathy of the nation. But above all the position of the dynasty is assured. If he remains he too will inevitably be accused of serious errors of policy; this is unavoidable.' But the standing of the monarchy survived in spite of William II's loss of popularity. As for the myth connected with Hindenburg and Ludendorff, this survived even the end of the hopes of military victory in July 1918.

The Chancellorship crisis had been settled relatively quickly. The heir apparent of Baden, a man whose political qualifications were unknown, was to build the bridge to peace and to a new Germany. But the change of leadership did not make the political decisions any easier. The men around the American President knew and liked the Prince's personal friend and political adviser, Kurt Hahn, who had played a part in the events leading up to Max von Baden's name being put forward for the chancellorship. But by and large the new man was regarded as the tool of the Kaiser and of Germany's military leaders and was widely regarded with suspicion. This was certainly not a fair view of Max von Baden who had for some time been influenced by Hahn's ethical ideas. But it is true that he was only slowly and without conviction won over to parliamentary government.

An unfortunate event which Washington heard of just at the time of the German peace move seemed to confirm the suspicions of those who distrusted the Prince. A French press bureau had got hold of a letter which Max von Baden had written nine months previously at the height of Germany's illusions to Prince Alexander von Hohenlohe; he had said that Germany must take full advantage of its military successes and had totally rejected the formation of a parliamentary government in Germany. A few days later the American President received information from the British Secret Service which threw doubt on the tactics pursued in the occupied eastern territories by the new Foreign Minister, Solf. The effect of this news on Wilson can hardly be overestimated. The report of a Foreign Office official in Washington, Sir William Wiseman, testifies vividly to the American President's fears of 'old Prussian trickery and cunning'. He voiced them at length in a conversation with Sir William and in the days to come behaved with suitable caution. The President's suspicions were if anything surpassed by those of Secretary of State Lansing, who was motivated also by the thought that stronger pressure on the Central Powers could only end the war sooner. But we must also bear in mind that the war fever in the United States had long reached a point where a reconciliation with the German Kaiser seemed unthinkable.

The decisions that were taken at the White House were undoubtedly determined by Wilson's desire to see the exchange of notes with the German government culminate in peace. Moreover both Wilson and his advisers wanted at any price to prevent Bolshevism from spreading to Germany.

Although the situation and the motives of the Americans were complex their aims were completely unambiguous. But complex also were the German reactions. The third American note of 23 October which went into the proposed constitutional reform of Max von Baden's government was very strongly worded. It claimed that in fact the German people were powerless to compel the military authorities to do what the nation wanted, that the King of Prussia had as much control over Reich policy as before, and that the old rulers of Germany continued to have the initiative. This note led – after preliminary, unjustifiably optimistic reports by an army press officer on the mood in the German capital – to a moment of madness at the Great Headquarters.

On 24 October Ludendorff issued an order to all army groups to continue the struggle with the utmost energy. The general's almost incredible autocratic decision to prevent the acceptance of 'dishonourable conditions', to make renewed use of military force and to fight on had been predictable a week previously when it became known that no immediate armistice could be had. On 17 October Ludendorff surprised the Chancellor and the Secretaries of State with a relatively favourable estimate of Germany's military reserves and hinted that if the worst came to the worst the struggle should be resumed. Prince Max von Baden probably ceased to have any confidence in Ludendorff as early as 17 October. But after the order of 24 October he made energetic representations to the Kaiser supporting the Foreign Minister's demand that Ludendorff must be dismissed, which he was.

Almost at the same time as the Chancellor achieved this first real victory over the military leadership the Reich government accomplished the parliamentary reform of the constitution which was approved between 24 and 28 October by the Reichstag, the Bundestag and the Kaiser. The most important of these October reforms were the introduction of universal suffrage in Prussia and a number of significant changes in the Reich constitution: declarations of war and peace treaties were to be subject to the approval of the Reichstag and the Bundestag; the Vice-Chancellor, his representatives and the Minister of War were made responsible to parliament; the Chancellor was given the right to approve the appointment of supreme commanders, and the Minister of War the appointment, promotion, and dismissal of officers and military officials. These reforms were in line with some of the proposals which had been made by the parliamentary parties before the war, and which seemed close to realisation as early as 1917. However the draft electoral law submitted by Count Hertling in November 1917, when he became both Reich Chancellor and by tradition Prussian Prime Minister, although it had provided for direct secret ballot had not adopted the principal of one man one vote. The overwhelming majority of conservatives, many national liberals but also a few *Zentrum* were opposed to one man one vote. It needed the urging of the Army High Command in the last month of the war to persuade these groups to accept universal and equal suffrage.

A second important complex of reforms relating to the central government was anticipated by the formation of Max von Baden's 'broadly based' cabinet. The constitutional reform merely legalised the political *status quo* by enabling members of the Reichstag to be at the same time members of the Bundestag, which was as much an instrument of legislation as the Reichstag, and by making the Chancellor responsible to the Reichstag and dependent on its confidence. There the reforms ended for the time being. But after the Kaiser had in practice lost all his rights as 'Supreme Commander' there existed in the eyes of many only a thin dividing line between the monarchy and a republic. It collapsed completely under simultaneous pressure from inside and outside.

But in this respect events happened faster in Austria-Hungary than in Germany. On 14 October 1918 clashes occurred in Prague where a socialist-influenced revolt movement was led by reserve officers with nationalist Czech leanings. Although for the moment the use of the army prevented a proper rebellion it was evident that the survival of the monarchy was at stake. The Austrian Emperor took the initiative and on 16 October addressed a generously formulated manifesto to the peoples of the Habsburg Empire. This, however, bore no fruits whatsoever. Two days later Lansing sent the American reply to the Austrian request for an armistice. It stated – a devastating piece of news for Vienna – that the American President no longer regarded mere autonomy for the Czechs and the southern Slavs as enough and that these peoples must be made the sole judges of their future relationship with the Austro-Hungarian government. In the days that followed there was total chaos in Agram (Zagreb), Lemberg (Lvov) and Budapest. On 26 October the Austrian Emperor informed William II by telegram of his decision to ask for a separate peace within twenty-four hours. But this haste could not improve the situation nor stem the relentlessly advancing tide of events. On 28 October there was a demonstration in Prague in favour of a Czech state, watched helplessly by the governor and the army. On the fo llowing day the fate of Bohemia was decided. The German Consul-General in Prague hastened to recognise the new authorities.

Before long similar developments took place in Budapest, Lemberg and Agram. The Reichsrat members of the German parts of the Austro-Hungarian Empire met in Vienna on 21 October and after much discussion invited the German Reich to protect the interests of the German-speaking regions. They thus prepared the way for the decision of the provisional national assembly on 12 November to declare the German regions of Austria part of the German republic. The national committee of the German Bohemians had come to a similar decision. The collapse of the Danube monarchy happened with surprising rapidity before the Emperor had time to issue his last manifesto renouncing any claim to intervention in the affairs of state. The separation of the crown lands took place almost automatically, at first without incidents but then there were clashes and finally fighting which in some regions assumed warlike proportions.

While in Austria–Hungary the situation deteriorated under the pressure of the nationalities question which determined the fate of the monarchy, in Germany the question of the future form of the state was linked up with the attitude of the Kaiser. The course of the war, even the pre-war crises caused by William II's personal rule, and above all the events of the summer and autumn of 1918 had led to a continued loss of confidence in the embittered and resigned Kaiser. Even a number of south German governments and princes interpreted the third American note in such a way as to consider it advisable to urge for the Kaiser's abdication. The Left, which supported the government, thought it important in view of the unrest that was spreading among large sections of the population not to lose touch with the revolutionary developments. But the Kaiser could not bring himself to move in any direction and on 29 October surprisingly returned to the Great Headquarters at Spa to await the further course of developments. On 4 November the Prussian Minister of the Interior, Drews, called on William II and impressed upon him what the situation was really like, something which nobody had dared to do until then. But as Drews received no support from the generals he returned to Berlin without having accomplished anything. At that moment it might still have been possible to save the monarchy, although not the throne for William II.

The political upheaval of the 'November revolution' temporarily interrupted both the close relations between the socialists and the bourgeoisie which had existed since Erzberger's peace resolution and had reached their climax in Prince Max von Baden's cabinet and the relations between the civil and military leadership. The contracts between the latter were restored with surprising rapidity, more quickly than between the former. But the monarchy was swept away for ever.

The influence of the Bolsheviks from Soviet Russia affected the workers and the Independent Social Democrats. This influence was of a propagandistic nature rather than material, although there is no doubt that at least one of the leaders of the Independents, Emil Barth, was given money by the Russians to purchase arms. It is against the background of the failure of the German plans of the spring of 1917 which did not lead to the permanent destruction of their opponent but in the end to a revival of radical opposition inside Germany that we must see the growing dread of Bolshevism and the fear that the Russian example would be emulated by Germany; a view incidentally shared by Lenin. In fact fear of the Bolsheviks and anti-Bolshevism spread as rapidly among the bourgeois parties as among the Majority Social Democrats and among the military leadership, which henceforth concentrated its efforts on determined opposition to the revolutionary elements at home.

What proved more important than the direct contacts with the Bolsheviks was Karl Liebknecht's agitation. When the social democratic members of the government obtained an amnesty for the political prisoner, Liebknecht, this revolutionary who was one of the Majority Social Democrats' most determined opponents found himself once more at large in mid-October. He set to work immediately and arranged for the revolutionary shop stewards to co-operate with the Spartacus League which had grown up as a revolutionary cadre within the Independent Social Democrats. With Liebknecht and Rosa Luxemburg, who intellectually was Liebknecht's superior and influenced him in several ways, a markedly activist spirit began to pervade these organisations and gradually prevailed in spite of differences and difficulties. The shop stewards who were trained in the trade union approach and accustomed to traditional strike tactics came to accept Karl Liebknecht and Rosa Luxemberg's idea that in the situation as it then was the object of all activity should be to keep the workers moving. The revolutionary ideology and its slogans were to be spread in an atmosphere of constantly growing tension created by demonstrations, campaigns and the provocation of counter-pressure and counter-measures. The situation would thus be brought to a state of revolutionary readiness which would eventually result in political change.

Although Liebknecht's influence in Berlin was great he could not stop the revolutionary shop stewards from hesitating until 9 November. As a consequence the decision remained with the Majority Social Democrats. The view taken by the revolutionary shop stewards at this moment of the attitude of the broad mass of the workers diffused substantially from that of Liebknecht and the intellectual Spartacists.

But the last hopes of a peaceful settlement of the situation were destroyed by the high-handed decision of the naval leaders to risk a last naval engagement. This was the spark that set off the revolutionary explosion. The attitude of the naval command is comparable with that of Ludendorff. The naval leaders objected to the cessation of un-restricted U-boat warfare demanded in Wilson's third note as another precondition for armistice negotiations and after 28 October prepared for one last naval sally against Britain. The move was unlikely to affect the outcome of the war but it gave the naval command the illusion of having found a final military gesture with which to refurbish the tarnished image of the German navy. To their way of thinking it was a point of honour not to haul down the flag without striking 'one last blow'. Military considerations no longer applied, from a political point of view their decision merely hastened an undesired development.

When on 30 October the fleet was given the signal to sail the stokers of the big vessels refused to obey orders. Although a mutiny was prevented by the arrest of the ringleaders the fleet could not sail; in the days that followed there were big demonstrations of sailors and dockers in Kiel and on 3 November, after a clash with a detachment of NCOs, open revolt broke out. The rebels' demands continued to be moderate but were no longer confined – and this was characteristic of the changed situation – to matters of food and complaints, to leave regulations, forms of address and the need to salute when off duty which had headed the list a year previously; instead they were given a decidedly political flavour with the insistence on the termination of the war, an amnesty for the sailors sentenced in the summer of 1917 and the abdication of the Kaiser. There was a general strike of dockers and on 4 November, for the first time on German soil, there were elections of workers' and soldiers' councils; officers were dismissed and finally the councils took over control of the city and also of the garrison. The infantry units hastily brought in from the interior of the country joined the rebels or allowed themselves to be disarmed.

The Social Democrat, Noske, and the Progressive member of the Reich government, Conrad Haussmann, rushed to Kiel on 4 November and were able to settle matters during the night, more or less to the satisfaction of all involved. But the situation remained tense; the authori-ties in Berlin feared a spread of the Kiel sailors' movement to other cities. These fears were confirmed on 6 November and there was unrest in Hamburg, Bremen and Lübeck. The following day the spark jumped to Munich and then to most cities in the Reich.

The revolutionary movement won its first victory in Munich where after the Austrian armistice there was fear that the Italians might march in. A great peace demonstration overthrew the monarchy and a 'provisional government of workers', soldiers' and peasants' councils' was proclaimed under the Independent, Kurt Eisner. Immediately after the proclamation of the Bavarian revolutionary government, on 8 November, the Duke of Brunswick signed his abdication. In Oldenburg and Stuttgart the transition was made soon afterwards, almost without incidents. The other states followed suit in the days that followed.

The Kiel events were like a signal upon which there was immediate and spontaneous revolutionary activity. On the Kiel model the revolutionary movement took the form of workers' and soldiers' councils. But behind this name there were widely divergent developments. Some of the soldiers' councils confined their activities to military matters. The workers' councils set up by factory workers usually joined forces with the local soldiers' councils. In some instances completely unrevolutionary elements gained the upper hand. Elsewhere, particularly in the industrial regions of central Germany and in the Ruhr, revolutionary tacticians assumed control and on occasions maintained their hold with dictatorial intransigence. During the later weeks of the transition period and also repeatedly in the months that followed there were clashes which yielded nothing in violence to the civil war battles in the capital, Berlin, in January and again in the spring of 1919, or to the fighting against the Upper Bavarian communist dictatorship. Among the centres of unrest during the first phase of the upheaval were the great industrial North Sea cities and ports, Hamburg, Bremen and Wilhelmshaven.

As the news of what was happening in Kiel spread the leaders of the Majority Social Democrats insisted on a break with the Kaiser. Their aim was to forestall the plans of the Left which had leaked out and had in part even been anticipated in uncontrolled or undirected actions. The date to be remembered is 6 November 1918. On that day the Quartermaster General, General Groener, who had taken over from Ludendorff met the leaders of the Majority Social Democrats on whom the further course of events appeared to depend. The SPD spokesmen then still favoured the preservation of the monarchy but at the price of the Kaiser's immediate abdication, a proposal which Groener felt it necessary to reject. Thereupon Ebert ended the meeting on behalf of himself and his party followers with the observation that in these circumstances no further discussion was possible. Events would have to take their course. According to an eye-witness he took leave of Groener with an expression of thanks for their frank discussion and said that henceforth their ways must part.

In view of what happened shortly afterwards these words appear melodramatic and out of place. They met again, sooner than at first seemed likely. The break lasted precisely four days; then the link between the Majority Social Democrats and the Army High Command was restored, although at first only with a telephonic but highly significant conversation between Ebert and General Groener. In the subsequent literature on the subject it has been said, and not without justification, that an alliance was made on this occasion. But in fact on 6 November there was still an unbridgeable difference of opinion on what attitude to take towards the Kaiser; this made agreement impossible and led to all discussions being broken off. In the course of the next four days the Social Democrats turned against the existing regime, in so far as this meant the monarchy. Regardless of their own involvement in the Reich government they now put pressure on the Chancellor, Prince Max von Baden, who found himself in a hopeless position between on the one side the Great Headquarters which continued to reject out of hand any idea of an abdication and the other the SPD leadership. All his plans seemed to have failed. He had brought about neither peace nor the armistice demanded by the Army High Command; and even after the October reforms it had proved impossible to preserve the existing system of government. The SPD was now strongly influenced by the movements on the left wing of the workers.

After a joint session on 7 November of the party executive and the SPD Reichstag deputies Scheidemann demanded the abdication of the Kaiser, thereby demonstrating that the Majority Social Democrats had joined the revolutionary camp. At the same time efforts were made to achieve a rapprochement with the Independents in order to restore Social Democratic unity at this historic hour. The rivalry between the different socialist organisations for leadership of the masses now developed into a race to be there when it came to the last decisions.

A few days previously the revolutionary shop stewards had prepared an organised action by Berlin's industrial workers designed to develop into a great uprising. The original plan was to strike on 4 November but then, as the SPD leadership learnt, it was decided to postpone the operation until 11 November, the idea being that Berlin must not attack too early but must be certain of help from the hinterland; because it was thought that the strongest resistance would be encountered there.

The idea which appears repeatedly in socialist tradition, that the social process must be allowed to reach culmination point and that then it becomes the task of the socialists to follow the trend and to benefit from it, found its most extreme manifestation during those days in the hesitations of the Independent Social Democrats. Their leaders, plagued by scruples of responsibility, longed for the uncertainty to end and to know what would happen after the collapse of the monarchy and the authority of the army and who their new opponents would be. For the revolutionary shop stewards the dilemma was less complex. They intended to oppose both the government of the October reforms and the antiquated monarchy, to put a stop to the 'rubbishy democratic state' and to set up a soviet republic on the Russian model. The Russian example was expected to provide all the answers to the difficulties of the situation, although nothing was known of the details and the circumstances of the Russian model.

The SPD on the other hand had taken measures to counter 'Bolshevik revolutionary phraseology' as early as the second half of October. Appeals by the party leadership and handbills warned its supporters against hasty steps likely to cause blood to be shed at home when it had ceased being shed at the front. A decisive factor was the arrest on 8 November of the leader of the revolutionary shop stewards. As a result the last meeting planned to be held by the leaders of the Independent Social Democrats and the shop stewards did not take place. Emil Barth, who was a member of both organisations, in the course of the night of 8–9 November penned a last appeal for an immediate mass strike; but this was not distributed on any scale.

On that day the commander in the border regions who had correctly interpreted the signs of unrest began to bring military units into the centre of Berlin, while Prince Max von Baden remained determined to save the monarchy. At the last hour when definite news had failed to arrive from Spa he took it upon himself to announce the Kaiser's abdication. This was followed by the proclamation of the republic. The social democrats, Ebert, Scheidemann and Bauer, left the Reich government. In an act of conscious formality Prince Max entrusted the office of Chancellor to Friedrich Ebert, the leader of the Majority Social Democrats, who now held in his hands the fate of the new state which could no longer be a monarchy.

Although it had been Ebert's intention to form a new government on the basis of the coalition which had supported Prince Max von Baden, events took a different course on 9 November. The unrest among the Berlin population, intensified by news of the revolt in Munich and of uprisings in other places, had the effect of preventing anything more from happening than a rapprochement between the two socialist parties, the SPD and the Independent Social Democrats, a move which had the determined support of the leader of the Independents, Hugo Haase. But it soon emerged that the Independents were no longer united and that the authority of their leaders was weak. It was in the discussions on the formation of the government of 'peoples' representatives' that Karl Liebknecht emerged as the most determined spokesman of the revolutionary movement. His demand taken over from Lenin for 'all power to the Soviets' was briefly agreed to and he thus sought to give the situation a new look and to recover missed opportunities. The revolutionary origins of the new Reich government whose composition had been arranged by the leaders of the SPD and the Independents was retrospectively proclaimed at a big, hastily summoned meeting of deputies of the Berlin workers' and soldiers' councils which claimed to be representing the councils of the whole Reich. The gathering appointed an executive council which in accordance with the prevailing fashion was to be the supreme consultative and executive authority. At the same time it approved the establishment of the council of peoples' representatives which had emerged from the discussions between the Independents and the SPD and confirmed the new Prussian government. Under the new system of administration two men of equal standing were appointed to the head of each Reich ministry, an Independent and a Majority Social Democrat, so as to ensure complete parity. Outwardly there appeared to be a similar distribution of power in the council of peoples' representatives. But in fact the leader of the Majority Social Democrats, Friedrich Ebert, continued to make full use of the pre-revolutionary title of Chancellor when he did not use that of Chairman of the Council of Peoples' representatives. In practice he took charge of the permanent direction of the Reich chancellory and Controlled the old Reich ministries, some of which remained in the charge of their former secretaries of state while others were taken over by new men.

The Army High Command at Spa was caught completely off guard by these events. At first there was talk of a soldier's death for the Kaiser. But soon the main preoccupation became the threat of revolution which would arise if the Social Democrats left the government. In view of this danger, the reality of which remained disputed, some of the military turned from the need for a dignified end for the Kaiser to the completely new thought of taking up arms against the rebellion at home and of using military means to counter the threat of Bolshevik revolution. It was General Groener who refused to withdraw the army from the front for use at home and who rejected such a venture as a complete mistake. But in view of this situation the person and position of the Kaiser became less important in the eyes of the more far-sighted members of the officer corps. Finally Groener dared after all to take the last step; he persuaded the Kaiser to abdicate and to leave Germany.

In Berlin the die had already been cast because Prince Max von Baden had not waited for the news from headquarters. But Groener's step was of the utmost importance because it left the officers of the German army the choice of severing their ties with the ruler in one of two ways – by resigning or by remaining in the army. Otherwise it would have been impossible to put the remaining but rapidly diminishing military forces at the disposal of Ebert and his government.

But no one in the Army High Command had any intention of placing the army and its officer corps unreservedly at the disposal of the Council of Peoples' Representatives. For these officers traditions and customs were at stake to which they had devoted themselves body and soul. However, the transition was made easier by the prestige of Hindenburg to whom the Kaiser had entrusted the supreme command. Once the ties of the oath of loyalty were severed the officer corps could transfer its allegiance by being conscious of its patriotic duties. This attitude was based on a traditional code of honour and caste and on a strong corps spirit which in principle stood completely aloof from the form of the state.

The reorientation of the officer corps began with its political use by the new government in the fight 'against radicalism and bolshevism'. That was the real basis of the alliance which General Groener made with Ebert in his famous telephone conversation on the evening of

10 November 1918. Groener emphasised subsequently that he had Hindenburg's approval for this move and that the officers at the Great Headquarters were behind him almost without exception. But the officer corps of the old army needed to be legitimised by the authority of the state if after the overthrow of the monarchy it was to preserve its role as a national élite and to retain the established military hierarchy. It therefore made a pact with the only group with which at this moment it could make a pact, with the Majority Social Democrats under the leadership of Ebert who was in charge at the Reich Chancellory. The Army High Command chose the least of the evils from its point of view so as to save the old officer corps; Ebert chose it so as to stabilise the domestic situation as rapidly as possible.

The objective of Ebert and his supporters in the Social Democratic Party was to silence their political rivals on the left in order to bring the ship of state safely into the calmer waters of stable conditions. Ebert wanted to speed up the process of consolidation, not least because he wanted to regain freedom of action in foreign policy of which at the moment, before the conclusion of the armistice at Compiègne, there could be no question; but it was certainly the domestic considerations that were decisive. Ebert was anxious to restore with maximum speed the authority of the state, to consolidate the confidence of large sections of the German population in the new order and to put a stop once and for all to revolutionary movements. In practice this meant the rapid convening after a general election of a constituent assembly and the ruthless suppression of any interference with this plan.

The three Independents among the six Peoples' Representatives tried at first to foil this plan and then to delay it because they feared with good reason that they would be distinctly worse off as the result of an early general election. On the other hand the Spartacus League and later the Communists pushed ahead with their revolutionary tactics and opposed Ebert's plans with determination, although they quickly gave up hope of being able to change the course of events. Their aim was to bring together and to reinforce with the help of demonstrations and campaigns the radical elements among the workers, the strength and significance of which they greatly overrated.

At first, however, the situation was far from clear and it took some weeks before relationships crystallised. The councils did not develop uniformly and declined in importance, even in Berlin. This was largely because the executive council and later, after a Reich conference of workers' and soldiers' councils in December 1918, the 'central council of the German socialist republic' was unable to play a truly decisive role. The activity of both was increasingly confined to declarations and occasional clumsy and not very successful attempts to interrupt the work of the Berlin administration.

In the meantime workers, soldiers' or peasants' councils had sprung up almost everywhere in Germany. The idea was that in their local sphere of activity they should imitate the Russian soviets which historically in fact played a very different role from that of the German councils. The soviets developed into the local offices of the revolutionary movement whose headquarters were at Petrograd; in the end the Bolsheviks gained the upper hand in the soviets and then used the 'Red Militia' as their executive organ. These characteristics of the Russian soviets were not shared by the German councils. Clear-cut revolutionary concepts were revealed in the theories of individual members of the revolutionary shop stewards and the Spartacus League only after the National Assembly had met. Most of the councils were unfitted to be instruments of a revolutionary movement if only because they became the stage and thus the victims of the split and the struggle for power in the socialist parties. What Lenin characterised as the 'dual government' of the Russian transition period under Kerensky's regime never existed in that form in Germany.

Of a 'dual government' it is possible to speak only in another sense: to the extent that developments began in the first days of the revolt in the *Länder* that were in no way directed or controlled by Berlin; governments were set up and took over whatever had remained intact of the administrative machinery of the *Länder* on lines similar to the government of peoples' representatives under Friederish Ebert taking charge of the Reich ministries in Berlin. Bavaria remained the only state in which under a provisional basic law of January 1919 the councils, at the sacrifice of parliamentary rights, became a legally recognised institution even though their importance was transitory. Under the influence of the methods and still more of the plans of the determined extreme Left the leaders of the Majority Social Democrats in most state capitals and also in Berlin had broken off their links with the bourgeois parties and formed coalitions with the Independents. The exceptions to this rule were the coalition governments in Stuttgart and Karlsruhe in which the bourgeois parties were represented. But all governments were in control of administration.

In view of this situation the tacticians of the extreme Left, the revolutionary shop stewards and the Spartacus League under the leadership of Karl Liebknecht, Rosa Luxemburg and a number of others, took immediate action. Before the year 1918 was out these groups joined forces, broke with the Independent Social Democrats under Haase and Dittmann and called themselves 'Communist Party of Germany' (KPD).

But the counter-revolution started already before the effects of Liebknecht's agitation began to be felt. The Reich government took determined and ruthless precautionary measures; firmer still was the stand of the military leadership which in November drew up the outline of an anti-revolutionary campaign and under the pretext of bringing back troops from the front began in December to assemble large units in and around Berlin. This entry into the capital was presented as an outwardly splendid occasion, although the facts of the situation were very different. In spite of the serious military defeat and the uncertainties that cast a shadow over the future the military were ceremoniously welcomed and the civilian representatives of the new order accorded them the highest honours.

The face of the real situation was revealed immediately afterwards when the newly formed *Generalkommando* Lequis which was responsible for the Berlin area proceeded at the orders of the leaders of the Majority Social Democrats to take military action against a 'peoples' naval division' composed of indefinable elements. Although this motley body which had gathered in the Berlin Marstall district was not a serious fighting force and although its resistance was characterised more by resignation and despair than planning, the military proved unequal to the situation in spite of superior equipment. After a few hours most of them gave up. In fact the old army had collapsed and none of the old units was really fit to be used.

For the moment this incident put a stop to the plans of both the Army High Command and the Berlin politicians and gave considerable encouragement to the other side. But throughout the crisis of Christmas 1918 Ebert never lost sight of his plan and even allowed a break to occur with the Independents in the Council of Peoples' Representatives. In the process his dependence on the military became even more apparent. However, he behaved as hoped for and expected by the bourgeois politicians, senior civil servants and diplomats who had remained loyal to the state, and also by large sections of the population.

Immediately in the New Year the lessons were drawn from the December experiences and a completely new army was built up. The link between the social Democratic Party leadership and the military organisers of the Army High Command, was Noske, who had made his name as a mediator during the Kiel rebellion and who was now given the traditional military command of *Oberbefehlshaber in den Marken*. Henceforth he controlled the military force which began to reorganise itself in the shape of *Freikorps* and which was used against Spartacist and Communist revolutionaries in Berlin. On the outskirts of the city Noske assembled volunteer units composed partly of the cores of existing units and NCOs and officers who were mostly drawn from the old army but which also accepted inexperienced volunteers who were introduced to the military trade in the course of the civil war. These new units immediately took over the protection of the capital and at the beginning of January 1919 clashed with the extreme Left during demonstrations. Bitter street battles kept on recurring in the spring and cost the lives of several thousand people. The revolutionary leaders, Karl Liebknecht and Rosa Luxemburg, were arrested and murdered in a ghastly manner.

Freikorps were formed also outside Berlin. By and large they had the support of the bourgeois and national sections of the population and were used primarily in the industrial trouble centres where revolutionary Independents and Communists had temporarily gained the upper hand: in the Ruhr, in central Germany and Saxony, in the big cities of the Baltic but finally also in Upper Bavaria, particularly in the Munich region.

In spite of all this Ebert was able to carry out his schemes as planned. The German National Assembly was elected in January and met at Weimar to begin discussions on a new German constitution. In the elections to the National Assembly the parties of the 1917 coalition obtained a large majority – the SPD, the German Democratic Party, which had grown out of the Progressive Peoples' Party and for a short time acted as a magnet for most middle-of-the-road bourgeois, and the *Zentrum*. In the course of a few weeks the opposition of the extreme Left was steamrollered into the ground with the help of the army. But the fate of the revolutionaries was by then already sealed. Liebknecht's tactics of creating unrest by using every opportunity to keep the masses on the move and by accustoming them to violence had failed signally.

For Karl Liebknecht, the only workers' leader who had proved a determined revolutionary agitator and tactician during the internal crises of pre-war social democracy, Lenin felt something akin to admiration and esteem. He even spoke of 'brotherly confidence in Karl Liebknecht and in him alone'. No other of Lenin's non-Russian contemporaries was singled out by him in this fashion. But this must not tempt us into discovering a close spiritual kinship between the two revolutionaries. Although there was a certain similarity of temperament, of rabble-rousing skill and also of untiring activity we cannot ignore Liebnecht's humanitarian, but unrestrainedly radical, militant pacifism which did not date from the war years and the war experiences but had been known throughout the world long before, from the armaments debates in the Reichstag and from his violent attacks on the 'gun international' of the armaments industry, from the military strike debate and the treason trial of 1907.

Liebknecht was an avowed anti-imperialist and anti-militarist throughout his life and continued in the radical democratic tradition of his father who had been an only half-hearted disciple of Marx and of the theorists of the class struggle. Lenin was first and foremost a Russian and looked consciously not towards Europe but to Asia, indeed he really built on Asia and the Asian part of Russia. In Marx he had discovered the idea and the programme with the help of which he would galvanise into action the infinitely static masses of the predominantly agrarian Near and Far East so that they might realise the social ideal which he himself on occasions described simply as 'collectivism'. 'Backward Europe and Progressive Asia' was the title of a *Pravda* article which Lenin wrote on 31 May 1913. He reversed the generally accepted view, turning it upside down – as Marx had done with Hegel: the bourgeoisie was European; Asia knew no bourgeoisie in the European sense. Hence for Lenin only the population of Asia which was as yet uncontaminated by bourgeois manifestations and developments was 'progressive' and could thus swell the million army of 'fighters for a better future'.

In 1905 the centre of world revolution had shifted to Russia where the beginnings of a strong capitalism had developed belatedly but rapidly and where social contrasts in the cities were particularly marked and uncompromising. The main emphasis in Lenin's programme was certainly not on the planning of a democratic Russian state. The question of overriding importance in the phase of struggle was how to gain power. How the power would be used was a question that could be decided later and on which no thought was wasted. Here Lenin and Liebknecht saw eye to eye. Lenin was not interested in the problems of the West European workers' movement, in franchise, parliamentarianism and practical social policy. He referred to the workers' leaders who concerned themselves with these issues variously as 'social Chauvinists', 'social pacifists' or simply as 'traitors to the working class'. He approved of and recognised only the small minority of the revolutionary wing which acted as he did or intended to do in Russia.

But however outstanding Lenin's tactical genius and however unmistakably he proved himself as a revolutionary strategist who could start a world movement in an advanced industrialist age, his judgment of political situations must not be overestimated. His political desires and ideas occasionally almost blinded him to the facts. His successes were always primarily of a tactical nature. He knew how to gain and to consolidate power and how in favourable circumstances to harass his enemy to the point of collapse. He was wrong in his estimate of what would happen in Germany, being convinced that civil war would break out, that the revolutionary movement would spread to Germany. In his final address to the workers of Switzerland in 1917 he called the German proletariat the 'most faithful and most hopeful ally of the proletarian revolution of Russia and the whole world'. After Ebert and Schiedemann joined the government of Prince Max von Baden he said confidently in a letter to the Russian central executive committee that the crisis which was beginning in Germany would inevitably end with the transfer of political power to the German proletariat. Lenin had kept his faith in revolution although long years in exile in Germany, Austria and Switzerland might have given him repeated opportunity to come to know not only the revolutionary groups among the workers movements but also their opponents. In some ways he reminds one of Marx and his prognosis of revolution in the eighteen fifties. But compared with Lenin, Marx had a much more intimate knowledge of Western Europe.

In fact 9 November 1918 was not Germany's great historic hour of socialism predicted in the literature of the theorists. It merely gave social democracy a chance to escape from its role as an intellectually fossilised opposition condemned to passivity. If the historian confines himself to the known facts and eschews unhistoric and unrealistic simplification made with hindsight he finds that after the collapse of the monarchy the prospects were by no means equal for the various alternative roads open to Germany. The political line that may be associated with the name of Friedrich Ebert appears in the last resort as the shortest road with the least obstacles. Ebert preserved in a remarkably direct way the contacts established at the end of the war with the internal forces that existed independently of the monarchy. He won the help of the civil service and of the army. And the alliances with the bourgeois parties, with the administration and the army demanded opposition to the revolutionary Left.

9. Armistice

The dates of the armistice agreements concluded one by one by the Central Powers reveal some significant differences concerning their attitudes during the last act of the war. Militarily the war came to an end for Germany shortly after the start of the revolution and the overthrow of the old regime, although the decision to ask for an armistice had already been taken by then. Between these two events lay more than seven weeks which were filled with the German–American exchange of notes and in which the internal situation in Germany underwent a fundamental change. This period saw a total reappraisal of the military and foreign policy assumptions on which the Germans had based their decisions and in the light of which they continued to withdraw their troops from the French front. With the total collapse of the alliance of the Central Powers the growing pressure of the advancing enemy was concentrated more and more on the German troops and the circle around struggling Germany narrowed from week to week.

The Bulgarian armistice agreement amounted to a capitulation and was followed by the political collapse of the country; the monarchy, however, was saved by the abdication of the Bulgarian Tsar Ferdinand. The advance of French, Serb and Italian units in the Balkans and the southern regions of the Danube monarchy in October interrupted the land link with Turkey. After the resignation of Talât Pasha and the fall of the Young Turk committee of 'Unity and Progress' in the middle of October the new Grand Vizir and supreme commander, Izzet Pasha, saw no alternative in a hopeless military situation but to lay down his arms and to throw himself upon the mercy of the enemy. By doing so he hoped to preserve Turkey's ancient institutions and to save the sultanship for Mehmed VI who had become sultan only in July and therefore felt no responsibility for Turkey's war policy.

The armistice was concluded on board a British vessel in the harbour of Mudros on 30 October 1918. Turkey fulfilled its remaining treaty obligations by demanding a respite of four weeks for the German troops to withdraw while British and French troops were moving in to the intended zones of occupation. *De facto* the Arabian peninsula was therefore now cut off from Europe. All of the Arabian territory liberated from Turkish rule including southern Kurdistan which had so far not been touched by the war, together with the oil region of Mosul, remained under allied military administration as occupied enemy territory pending a final settlement in the peace treaty with Turkey. A few days later, on 7 November, Britain and France in a joint proclamation to the Arabs promised the establishment of indigenous governments in Syria and Mesopotamia but also hinted – with some caution – at the role which they themselves proposed to play in this area: they would give effective support to and ensure the normal working of the governments and administrations concerned, promote economic development and further education. These noble objectives in themselves implied far-reaching control of all important events in these Arab countries. But the two powers maintained that in international law these regions were still part of the Ottoman Empire. They thereby avoided the awkward problem of recognition of the Arab independence movement, although it must be said that the political shape of this movement, other than its military activity during the war and its representation by the Sheriff of Mecca and his sons, had not yet become clear. However neither the British nor the French appeared especially interested in clearing up the problems created by the political development of the Arab movement. The British commander-in-chief in the Near East and supreme chief of the military administration, Field-Marshal Lord Allenby, acted as the protector of the provisional Arab administrations in accordance with the principles of the joint declaration of 7 November. For the rest the activities of the two powers after the cessation of fighting were such as to bring about a distinct change of mood in political Arabia. At the orders of the military authorities the blue flag of the Hedjaz, which during the war had become the symbol of the struggle for liberation from Turkish rule, was removed from public buildings in Damascus and Beirut. The days when the Allies and the Arabs had fought side by side as comrades-in-arms appeared to be over and a new era of colonial administration seemed to be starting. National Arab suspicions of British and French policy were given ample food by the Russian publication of the secret wartime partition treaties which the Turks also did their best to circulate.

The remaining conditions which the Allies imposed on Turkey resulted in the immediate demobilisation of most of the Turkish army,

the transfer of the navy to the Allies and the occupation of the fortifications on the Straits by troops of the Entente. Allied control was
imposed on all ports, railway lines and telegraphic communications.
The treaty of Mudros also gave the Allies the right to occupy more
territory in two instances: if their safety was threatened or if there was
unrest in Armenia which during the war had once again been the
victim of Turkish ruthlessness and brutality.

The immediate reaction in Turkey was bitterness against the Young
Turk movement whose leaders, above all Talât and Enver, had made
Turkish policy during the war and who had been responsible for its
obvious failure. This understandable reaction led to an attempt to
revive the ideals and institutions of old Turkey, to bring back dynastic
absolutism, to restore the Caliphate which during the war had lost
much of its old prestige and to dismiss the Young Turk period as an
interlude alien to the Turkish people and its sovereign. This was
certainly the attitude of the Sultan and his circle; but during the
weeks of uncertainty and transition it was universal in Constantinople and was adopted also by the Turkish press, which after the
strict censorship of the Young Turks was now in a state of newly
achieved freedom and able to take its revenge on the immediate
past.

Before the Mudros armistice the Austro-Hungarian Army High
Command, faced with the disintegration of the monarchy and a great
Italian offensive, preparations for which had gone on for a long time,
appointed an armistice commission under a general. Without waiting for
Wilson's latest reply preparatory talks began with the Italians. Emperor
Charles informed the Kaiser telegraphically of the step which he was
about to take, and after a few involuntary delays the Austro-Hungarian
delegation on 31 October at Padua accepted from the Italian chief
of general staff, Badoglio, the draft of an armistice prepared by the
Supreme War Council of the Allies. The conditions, which were to be
accepted or rejected *in toto*, surpassed the worst expectations. Disarmament and the immediate demobilisation of most of the army, the
surrender of half of the army's artillery equipment, the occupation of
Istria, Friuli and southern Tyrol up to the Brenner seemed to the
Vienna government just acceptable as interim arrangements provided
they did not prejudice the provisions of the forthcoming peace treaty.
More humiliating still was the demand for the immediate withdrawal of

all German troops and for complete freedom of movement on Austrian soil for the Allied troops.

But in Austria too it was the military who wanted decisions to be taken and in the end it was they who were responsible for them. Emperor Charles, who was himself in favour of the armistice, on 2 November laid down the supreme command so that the military decisions were now made exclusively by the Chief of General Staff, Arz von Straussberg. In view of the state of the imperial army he ordered all units to cease hostilities in the early hours of 3 November without even waiting for the enemy's last reply. The objections of the armistice commission in Padua did not arrive in Vienna until after the order for the immediate signing of the conditions had been sent off. The time difference between the Austrian cease fire, on the morning of 3 November, enabled the Italian troops to achieve a final unparalleled triumph: without encountering any opposition they took 350,000 prisoners of war and captured vast quantities of arms and material.

The crushing blow of these events – rounded off for later generations by the last-minute secret contacts with the French and British chiefs of mission which the new Foreign Minister, Andrassy, established via the Berne embassy – made the disintegration of army and state inevitable. In Wilson's last messages which reached Vienna and Budapest simultaneously on 8 November the *Staatsrat* of German Austria and the government of Hungary were recognised by the Americans in the same fashion as previously Czechoslovakia and southern Slavonia. This was consistent with the *de facto* situation. The days that followed were spent in complicated discussions on the wording of Emperor Charles' abdication statement, without the decision itself being seriously questioned. The last manifesto which Charles addressed on 12 November 1918 to the 'peoples of Austria' was a verbal work of art; a model of legal subtlety, it was difficult to interpret and left open the important question of whether the monarch's renunciation applied to the crown lands outside Austria. Charles did renounce in unambiguous terms any share in matters of state but refrained from releasing the officer corps from its oath of loyalty to him. His declaration differed basically on this point from that made by William II. The matter had been carefully thought out and its consequence was that many officers who felt themselves tied by their oath refused to serve in the armies of the newly formed states. Charles saw himself still as emperor and king but without political power and without ruling, a historic figure responsible as ever for his lands. The extent of this conviction is demonstrated by his restoration attempts in Hungary in 1921.

The day after Charles's abdication Count Károlyi's Hungarian government concluded a special armistice with the Allies, a military convention at Belgrade, which formed the basis for the demobilisation of part of the Hungarian troops. Hungary's eastern, southern and northern border regions were occupied by Allied troops. But free Hungary still stretched from the Carpathians and Neumarkt (Târgu–Mures) to Arad, Fünfkirchen (Pecs) and Pressburg (Bratislava).

In contrast to the situation in Austria the conclusion of the German armistice took place totally independently of events inside Germany. The German armistice delegation led by Erzberger met the Allied representatives under the leadership of Marshal Foch on 8 November 1918 in the Forest of Compiègne near Paris. From the start of the negotiations the Germans never really knew what was happening in Berlin, nor did they have any contact with the old government or the new government of the Council of Peoples' Representatives. News of the situation in the capital reached the German negotiators belatedly and exclusively via the French High Command. On the evening of 10 November the German delegation received a directive from the Army High Command ordering it on Hindenburg's authority to sign the armistice at all events. This agreed with the stand taken by the Field-Marshal when Erzberger had called on him at the Great Headquarters on his way from Berlin to the front. The military leadership's only concern was to finish the fighting as quickly as possible and to withdraw the army from contact with the enemy so that it could be brought back home quietly and preserved intact for the future.

A few hours after the telegram from Spa an uncoded telegram arrived at Compiègne signed 'Chancellor', explicitly authorising the leader of the German delegation to sign the armistice conditions which had been transmitted to Berlin. There was no room for serious negotiation. The German armistice delegation nevertheless strove for concessions on some points. In this it was not without success. It achieved some changes in timing without, however, being able to alter the main conditions laid down by the Allied Supreme War Council. These conditions were severe. The Allies wanted to be sure that the Germans could in no circumstances reopen the fighting. There was a strong suspicion that the German Army Command merely wanted to gain time and to assemble new forces after the failures and losses of the summer of 1918 so that it could renew the attack in more favourable circumstances. But during the preparation of the armistice conditions, at the end of October, the situation inside Germany and south of the German frontier was such as to make fears of this kind almost unnecessary.

These conditions were handed to the German negotiators in the form of an ultimatum and were accepted in the early morning of 11 November. They already contained some important preliminary decisions concerning the shape of the peace to come; they also put the seal on the absolute superiority of the Allies and on the total helplessness of their opponent. The armistice which initially had been timed to last thirty-six days was renewed three times, the last time on 16 February 1919 for an unlimited period with the proviso that it could at any time be terminated within three days. This was the background against which the peace negotiations were conducted, the conditions handed to the Germans and the treaty finally signed at Versailles.

The thirty-four articles of the armistice agreement provided for a number of important preliminary steps on the part of the Germans. These included the liberation of the prisoners of war captured by the Germans, without for the moment any reciprocal action on the part of the Allies, and the withdrawal of German troops from the east to the territory of the Reich. This condition was complied with during the next three months as was that demanding the complete evacuation of France, Belgium and Alsace-Lorraine within fifteen days after the start of the armistice.

The preliminary steps which the Germans were asked to take before the final settlement included the explicit cancellation of the treaty of Brest-Litovsk which the Bolshevik government on its part annulled two days after Compiègne, so that Russia was now once more at war with Germany. The peace treaty with Rumania was also annulled. Finally Germany was made to return the Belgium, Russian and Rumanian gold which it had seized during the war.

Behind the remaining provisions was the Allied desire for military security. They included the surrender of heavy arms and vehicles, the evacuation within twenty-five days of the entire territory on the left bank of the Rhine and the occupation by Allied troops of this zone as well as of the bridgeheads of Mainz, Coblenz and Cologne on the right bank of the Rhine, together with a surrounding stretch of thirty kilometres, the surrender of all submarines and the disarmament and internment of most of the German navy. But the harshest condition, at first which was criticised even in the Allied camp, was the temporary continuation of the blockade and the ban on German merchant navy activity. The magnitude of the defeat, admitted belatedly by the Army High Command, and the burden of the Allied conditions which made this defeat a definite fact corresponded to the length and the bitterness of the struggle, to the strength of Germany's thwarted will to win and to the size of its war aims.

PART TWO

The Restoration of Peace

10. The problems of peacemaking and the assumptions of the Paris Peace Conference

With the two world wars of the twentieth century in mind and the way in which they were brought to an end peacemaking has been described as a 'lost art'. The historian appreciates that it has become incredibly difficult to make peace successfully. If the problems that confront the peacemakers arise out of a historical explosion which involved many powers and if the state of these powers at the end of the military conflict makes it impossible to guess how they will develop and what their relations with one another will be, then only partial solutions can be offered. The transition from war to peace involves operating with unknown future quantities, just as starting a war means stepping into an uncertainty of which nothing is known but that there must be sacrifice of life, of spiritual and material values until some solution is found. This is true of the great historic catastrophes which led to complicated and sometimes incomplete settlements, such as the Thirty Years War in which the whole of Europe was involved, the series of wars that followed the French Revolution and Napoleon's wars of conquest at the turn of the eighteenth century, which also affected all of Europe and at times even parts of North Africa and indirectly America, and finally above all the two greatest wars of all, the 'world wars' of the twentieth century.

All these were really 'world wars' in the sense that all the great powers of the age were involved, even if the geographical zones in which the military action took place, in which campaigns were planned, armies recruited, battles fought and allies wooed, and which became the scene of destruction and chaos, were largely restricted to the regions of political and diplomatic interest to the powers concerned. Advances in technology and transport and, following in their wake, armed colonial and political expansion in the nineteenth century finally drew the whole globe somehow into the great wars which as a result became much more complex politically, economically and militarily. To cite only a few instances: there was the commercial war at sea and the novel possibilities and consequences in international law arising from the invention of the submarine and the underwater torpedo; there was the modern war in the air with airships and aeroplanes, the air raids which followed the development of modern air strategy, the use of large-scale aerial bombardment and of bombs with ever greater powers of destruction; finally in the wake of the atom and hydrogen bombs the development of ballistic and guided missiles, which is as far as we have got for the moment. With the global extension of war, with its new techniques and also with the number of large and small powers involved or affected the practical aspects of peacemaking have of necessity become more numerous and complex.

A further feature of these 'world wars' is the ideological and possibly religious elements bound up with differing political ideas. These play a large part in determining the frontiers of war and in dividing friend and foe; on their presence depends the intensity and duration of the conflict and also the magnitude of the sacrifices made. Only the lasting commitment of his intellectual faculties to a certain idea enables the individual – or better perhaps the citizen who by nature is not a combatant in the military sense – to be involved in the struggle. As far as possible *societas civilis* is transformed into *societas militans*. Without ideologists and ideologies outbursts of mass enthusiasm are unthinkable, the decision to fight cannot be legitimised and nations cannot be mobilised for war both spiritually and physically.

In its last stages the Thirty Years War was a perversion of warfare because the main protagonists could not find peace and therefore continued to fight to the point of exhaustion. But the preliminaries, start and early stages of the war were the result of the conflict which grew out of the religious schism of the sixteenth century. The great military achievements of the late eighteenth and early nineteenth centuries were based on the *levée en masse* and the creation of the enormous French revolutionary armies; in the end they served the idea of Napoleon's empire which was modelled on the classical ideal of the *Imperium Romanum*. Both became important elements in the history of the modern French nation.

A question of secondary importance is whether ideologies precede the conflict and affect it or whether they mature during the war as a result of nationalist ideas and emotions. In the twentieth century they were fostered artificially. We saw this happen in the First World War when nationalist and chauvinist extremism was promoted by continuous press activity and by specially created state-controlled departments whose task it was to offer subjective opinions in place of reliable information. A decisive role was played by the conveyors of the most successful, because most popular, forms of propaganda. Nobody would doubt today that television can be of considerable political importance. But this presupposes that most people have television sets. In the Second World War television played as yet no role although it had existed for several years and went on being developed. The importance of radio, however was greater than that of the press; and in the Second World War the cinema was incomparably more important as a propaganda medium than in the First World War when the written word which could easily be disseminated by the press and in leaflets remained the most important propaganda instrument. Where the written word was not enough – and also but not only in revolutionary circumstances – the spoken word of the agitator assumed its age-old political function.

A number of features of these wars invite comparison, particularly as regards the extent of the sacrifice and the destruction as well as the magnitude of the effort: large sections of the population became caught up in the military side of the war and the economy was geared to the struggle, either by producing directly for war purposes or by providing the financial means needed by the leadership to continue the war. Although strategies changed, the underlying principle never varied; its extreme formulation in German is found in Schiller's *Piccolomini* where Wallenstein says that war feeds on war.

Both world wars grew into total wars. But let us remember that the important word 'total' must always be understood within the limits of the technical possibilities and experiences of the age. What we describe as 'total' can never be defined for all times. Each totality in a given period can subsequently be intensified in some direction or other; that is it can become 'more total'.

Ideally real peace presupposes a full understanding of the true causes of a war; it demands the complete removal of these causes and the replacement of old political and economic structures by new ones which have none of the qualities known to cause wars. No doubt this is a Utopian principle, a truth that has not become reality anywhere. But it should be voiced if only to highlight the difficulty of judging peace treaties and to point out the magnitude of the task of peacemaking – if the establishment of peace is to mean something more than the end of war. The gap between these two conditions is indicative of the extent to which the war was a 'total' one.

Emphasis has rightly been put on the basic difference between past peace treaties which frequently contained some special clause explicitly providing for what Fritz Dickman has called the 'forgetting that helps to establish peace', and the discriminatory settlements of recent times. The origins of the latter go back beyond Bismarck's early and unrealised ideas about peacemaking after the Franco–German war and his wish to pass judgment on Napoleon III, and with him on journalists, parliamentarians and ministers, and to discredit them forever. The absolute enemy who is fought not only with armies and military equipment but above all with ideological weapons has been known since the days of the wars in which the French revolutionary armies took part. At the same time wars have tended to become longer, more nations are likely to be involved and not only have the efforts and sacrifices become greater but so has the implications of defeat. Profound political differences between adversaries who shared neither a common faith nor respect for each other's sovereigns demanded a polemical peace to put a seal on the military victory and, on the road to peace, a last, irreversible judgment to eliminate for ever the forces responsible for the war.

Determined to defeat Napoleon I his opponents continued the war – which was in fact the first 'peoples' war – until they had crushed the man who was ultimately and inescapably responsible and those of his followers who stayed with him to the end. It was of no avail to Napoleon when his power was broken to place himself 'like Themistocles' under the protection of the laws of the British people and, seeing what his fate would be, 'solemnly before heaven and men' to protest against the violation of his 'most sacred rights' and against the brutal decree concerning his person and liberty. Napoleon was aware of the hostility of the European powers, but he overestimated the effect of his gesture and his appeal to history because he failed to comprehend the extent of this universal and passionate enmity and the new emotions of the peoples whose rebellion and struggle for 'people and country' destroyed his power. In the last resort he was defeated by the strength of a new creed which allowed no compromise but only victory or destruction. The Vienna Congress which outlawed Napoleon is reminiscent of an international tribunal passing the final verdict. But even more significant is the fact that in the whole of Europe no doubts were voiced about the moral condemnation of 'General Bonaparte' whom the victors expressly stripped of his monarchical dignity and reduced to the status of a rebel.

The irreconcilable hostility of vital principles is reflected in the ideological struggle between political systems. Bismarck's remark quoted in the introduction illustrates the Prussian conservative's contempt for the parvenu among the monarchs and shows his attitude towards pressmen and parliamentarians who he regarded as enemies. Such contempt prevents any objective analysis of who was really responsible for a war.

In the First World War the differences between peoples and ideas rapidly became extreme. By 1917 the Allies were convinced that they were fighting for a democratic world against antiquated monarchical autocracies. But from the start it was assumed that German policy was to blame for the war and that the Kaiser must be held responsible. Clemenceau and Lloyd George and also Wilson thought so. But in the conclusions they drew from this they were agreed only in the need to overthrow the Kaiser. They differed profoundly in their approach to the practical and legal implications of Germany's assumed guilt and to the peace treaty.

The concrete problems that presented themselves to the peacemakers at the end of the First World War arose from the discrepancy between Wilson's material proposals and above all the spiritual content of his peace messages and the irreparable situation created by the war. The peace which Wilson wanted, his 'new order of things', was to be a peace of justice and of clear conscience; it would end the age of imperialism and create a new world under the auspices of the 'Covenant League of Nations'.

Most of the negotiators concerned with arranging the peace terms were incapable of rising to such spiritual heights. The expression *sacro egoismo* describes in lyrical form the attitude of the Italians whose claims were made at the expense not only of their erstwhile enemy but also of Serbia and Greece, until recently their allies. The term can equally be applied to the variety of national emotions and claims which were the complete antithesis of the American President's ideas; and it was to these ideas that the decisions of the peace makers were in the last resort to be geared. With his formula of autonomous development and national policies for the peoples who had once been ruled by the Russians, the Habsburgs and the Turks, Wilson himself made a timely gesture to the idea of the national state, a gesture which took account of actual developments. To Wilson peaceful collaboration in a permanent alliance of nations was the highest obtainable political state, one that left no room for autocratically ruled monarchies. But at the peace conference a different reality revealed itself. The 'Covenant' between the Allies assumed an unexpected shape and was responsible for an apparently insurmountable gulf between the former protagonists. Its immediate effect was not to produce peace but new enmities which took up wartime differences.

For this cardinal failure of the peace conference the Germans and others have blamed particular individuals and in the process have levelled a variety of accusations against the most important of the statesmen involved. But such behaviour only brings out the magnitude of the problems raised by seeking to make peace after a world war. The statesmen concerned could plead in mitigation that if the peace conference fell short of Wilson's League of Nations ideal – suspiciously criticised by some from the start – and became a battleground of national interests, it was because they were faced by a unique task. Because many of the negotiators were aware of this the principle of gaining as much as possible for one's own nation guided the course and outcome of the conference. Yet the ideas set out in the Fourteen Points which Wilson proclaimed on 8 January 1918 and which he confirmed, supplemented and explained in a speech to Congress on 11 February and in speeches at Mount Vernon on 4 July and at New York on 27 September, were recognised as the only basis, not just by the Germans but generally, for the negotiations that began at Paris on 18 January 1919. In his important speech of 27 September, that is to say a week before the Germans asked for peace and an armistice, the President had called for 'impartial justice' without preferential treatment or distinctions. It is obvious that this phrase was designed to discourage illusory speculation on the part of the Central Powers and also to dampen the exaggerated ideas that began to appear in the Entente camp. The full significance of the phrase is revealed only if we examine Wilson's concept of justice. For the President the slogan of fighting for the ideals of democracy with which the United States had entered the war remained fully valid after the war. It defined the main assumptions on which future peace settlements would be based and was certainly closely related to the principle of 'impartial justice'. Anyone who knew the roots of the President's principles and who was aware of the profound missionary intensity with which the American President sought to follow them would not ignore this.

A close examination of Wilson's Fourteen Points reveals that only some of them were suitable to be used as the basis for negotiations. Many of the specific demands, for the evacuation of Russia, Belgium and the French territories, for autonomy for the peoples of Austria-Hungary and also for the evacuation of Rumania, Serbia and Montenegro, had been complied with before the armistice or formed part of the armistice agreement with Germany and Austria-Hungary. Other points looked ahead and laid down principles or programmes for a future world order. They could not be regarded as binding in international law on the Allies or their vanquished enemy but needed to be confirmed by future agreements. A League of Nations seemed more suited for this purpose than a general peace conference. This was another reason why the League of Nations was from the beginning extremely important for a peaceful world settlement. A third group of points also contained principles and programmes but of a variety that required the general type of settlement that would form part of the peace treaties, such as the settlement of colonial claims without giving any offence. Finally there were the points which said that there should be no annexations, no contributions and no punitive provisions, that the nations' right to determine their own fate should be preserved and that peoples and territories should no longer be pushed about between states against their will. *self determination*

But quite apart from the issue of whether or not Wilson's principles would provide the basis for negotiations the Paris discussions were only partly concerned with these matters. In part they were devoted to problems not touched upon in Wilson's messages, which originated from other aspects of the history of the war and finally pushed into the background the American President's noble but in the context impractical principles. This caused more than one serious conflict, none of which the President himself ever evaded. It was his firm conviction that peace and the new order based on the League of Nations could only be the result of agreements voluntarily arrived at. Acting in accordance with his principles he went to Paris to participate in the negotiations directed by Clemenceau.

Wilson did not come to Europe with a definite agenda. He was deeply convinced of the decisive importance of his personal presence and the enthusiasm with which he was welcomed by Western Europe confirmed him in this view. The Wilson critics – who appeared in Europe with the wave of disappointed hopes, were found in the United States as early as 1919 and in Germany came to the fore somewhat later – presented the President alternately as a weakling, a dissembler or a credulous idealist of limited intelligence and saddled him with a large share of the responsibility for the failure of the peace of Versailles.

The evaluation of American policy towards Germany has become a highly controversial issue for Wilsonians and anti-Wilsonians. It must be remembered, however, that the reasons behind this policy were complex; they reflect more than party groupings and differences of a party political nature. During the weeks of internal upheaval in Germany there was considerable hopes among the liberal middle classes but also among the leadership that America would solve the problems of the world and give Germany's fate a turn for the better. Evidence of this came from men like Prince Max von Baden but also from the Army High Command, where Quartermaster General Groener thought that he could count with some measure of confidence on the supreme commander of the American troops in Europe to exert political pressure on American foreign policy. Although there were some indications of the existence of secret diplomacy on the part of the American military there was no way of judging its intentions or possibilities. But other nationally minded Germans who basically mistrusted Wilson's ideas stuck obstinately to the Fourteen Points in the hope that their failure would one day morally cause the President's downfall, compromise him for ever in the eyes of the world and thus justify in retrospect the policy pursued by Germany towards America during the war. Wilson's Fourteen Points, together with his elucidations made in connection with notes exchanged between Germany and America before the armistice, have frequently been regarded and also described as a binding preliminary contract (*pactum de comprahendo*) from which the result of the Paris Peace Conference is said substantially to have departed to the detriment of Germany. Responsibility for this breach of contract was attributed primarily to the American President. He was looked upon as the only legitimate representative of the Allied powers whose statements were binding for them all, even though during the German cabinet's discussion of the formulation of the first German note not everyone present attributed the same significance to the observation that Germany desired a peace 'on the basis' of the Fourteen Points.

The highly emotional criticism of Wilson did not remain confined to Germany. But nowhere else was the theory of the binding force of the Fourteen Points and of the exchange of notes between Wilson and Prince Max von Baden presented in such extreme form. Outside Germany even the most determined critics of the Versailles treaty mostly adopted a subtler approach to their discussion of the course and results of the peace conference. But there can be no doubt that of all the statesmen at Paris it was the American President whose reputation suffered most and that the true historical importance of this man and of his behaviour during the war and at the peace conference has been tragically misjudged.

It is generally agreed that during the Conference Wilson gave up some of his most important points and revised parts of his message to Congress of January 1918. But recent historical research which has had access to informative material on the course of the negotiations has revealed that Wilson's failure at Paris was not due to lack of character or energy. He was defeated by objective factors which he, like every other statesman of the age, was unable successfully to resist. But it was fateful for the course of the negotiations and for the position and reputation of the President that Wilson could no longer count on the support of the majority of Americans.

If the Paris Peace Conference or any of its outstanding personalities are considered from a purely national angle, the verdict must necessarily differ from that reached if full account is taken of the circumstances in which the conference opened. Because the war had been fought in many parts of the world and because many peoples and states had been involved the peace settlement required the participation of all these states. It is true that from the start there were a number of undisputed priorities which determined the order in which problems of global or regional importance were taken up. This list alone is sufficiently extensive and varied to bring home at a glance the many difficulties that from the beginning beset the negotiators who were supposed to give world peace. The great international problems of the imperialist age, which pre-war diplomacy had shelved until the big explosion, were waiting for a comprehensive solution; and several other no less important problems had joined the list during the war.

Political rivalry with Germany was the central theme of French and British policy. While France concentrated on redressing the balance of power and – with regard to Alsace-Lorraine – on territorial arrangements, Britain was interested in the destruction of the naval power which Germany had built up with such unfortunate results and, together with the Dominions, in the colonial settlements. But the traditional spheres of conflict and crisis in overseas policy were not at all confined to colonial questions. There were also the problems of the Near and the Far East where Germany's disappearance from the ranks of the Great Powers had by no means clarified the situation. In the Near East the differences between Greece and Turkey were shortly to play an important role. There was less than complete harmony between the British and the French in that part of the world; and the Arabs and the Zionists both advanced claims which were to have even more disturbing effects later. In the Far East Japan had gained a foothold by occupying the German leasehold of Kiachow on the Chinese mainland; and in connection with the Allied intervention during the civil war in Russia it temporarily extended its sphere of power and occupation as far as Lake Baikal in Eastern Siberia before the United States, which was worried by the expansion of this new great power in East Asia, induced it to give up the occupied territories.

The disintegration of the Danube monarchy and its transformation into nation states brought to light new claims and new problems and conflicts, as was the case when German policy during the war led to the break up of the border zones of the old Russian empire in eastern central Europe and north-east Europe. From the start these problems involved conceptual issues arising out of commitments entered into during the war, primarily by the French but also by the Americans. Almost at once these questions loomed as large as the tension between Austria and Italy created by Irrendentist agitation against Austrian rule in south Tyrol and Istria in the immediate pre-war period and the first months of the war, or as the conflict between Serbia and Austria which had led to the war in 1914, or as the Rumanians' attitude towards the dual monarchy which was coloured by the ruthless minorities policy in the Hungarian part of the empire. With the realisation of the plans for a 'greater Serbia' and the creation of a south Slav state which took possession of most of the west coast of the Adriatic and placed it under the energetic direction of the Belgrade government, a further element of tension was introduced during the first phases of the peace negotiations because of Italy's critical relations with the new Adriatic state.

What was at stake was Germany's future in Europe, the future shape of *Zwischeneuropa*, eastern central Europe and south-eastern Europe, and also the political future of the territories and peoples of the ruined Ottoman Empire. There were other factors that played a significant role. First of all was the attitude of the West European Great Powers and the United States towards the new Russia; then there was the view taken of future developments in east Asia which most concerned the United States; great regard was also paid by everyone to the peoples of the colonial empires who had participated in the war and sometimes made great sacrifices. But most important of all were the developments in Europe where people continued for years to be influenced by the nationalism unleashed during the war but where there were also strong pacifist trends, new hopes for the collapse through revolution of a world dominated by imperialism and capitalism, and dreams of a new society. Shaken by violent upheavals and rich in contrasts the social and political stage of Europe remained the setting for powerful movements even after the war. Nor were the victor states spared; their domestic crises heralded significant changes in the balance of power between the political parties in the immediate or at any rate not too distant future. A factor of decisive importance in the sphere of international politics was that after the events in Petrograd in November 1917 the revolutionary socialist movement looked with growing attention, if varying degrees of sympathy, to European Russia which was having an increasing ideological influence on the world around it and even indulged in purposeful intervention in the internal re-shaping of old states and the creation of new ones in central and eastern Europe.

The war had ended with the collapse of the strongest military powers in Europe; they could therefore not make any significant contribution to the discussion on the shape of the future peace. For the moment the Allies were therefore objectively free to decide their policies without limiting factors. While the nationalist exaltation continued and the war psychosis survived it was possible for the ephemeral but apparently irresistible view to prevail that the solution best suited to the circumstances was to assemble as many war aims as possible, somewhat as the Germans had done during the period of their great or apparently great military triumphs. But in those days, ideas of this kind had found expression only in programmes and memoranda, except for the short-lived eastern peace treaties.

The Allies coalition did not prove nearly as firm and reliable as during the war. Then one objective had motivated all action: to persevere with the struggle and to win. Opinions about the ways and means might have differed; but in the end the threat to the existence of the struggling nations was recognised in its full significance and was considered before all else. Yet the differences between the Allies could be ignored successfully only for a limited period of joint hardship. With the end of the war and the disappearance of direct pressure from the enemy very different questions which went back to pre-war controversies came once more to the fore. What we see here is a phenomenon characteristic of coalition wars – although it manifests itself in different ways. It is clearly more difficult for a great coalition to prove as effective in peace as in war when there exists a determination to win. This again made peacemaking more difficult.

The controversial presence in Paris of the American President during the later stages of the negotiations did less to influence the outside world than his actions in the last phase of the war and was not enough to achieve a compromise, the need for which Wilson had recognised clearly and in time. The full extent of the secret arrangements and long-term commitments of the West European Great Powers which seriously affected the decisions of the peace conference was revealed only in the course of the negotiations. Britain and France had concluded treaties with both Rumania and Greece, similar to the treaty of 1915 which had preceded Italy's entry into the war and had made concessions that could by no stretch of the imagination be reconciled with Wilson's principle of national self-determination. Later it emerged that the French were not prepared to abandon any of the basic points of the Sykes–Picot agreement of 1916 because in their view France's security in Arab North Africa depended on having an influence there and sharing in the rule of the Arab peninsula. This made Lloyd George think that he should exploit the situation and obtain concessions for Britain from Clemenceau. The Arabs on the other hand did not benefit from these compromises.

What had a wholly disastrous effect on all participants during the conference were mistakes in planning and organisation. War aims existed; but it was probably because there were so many of them and they were so ambitious that there was no carefully considered and generally acceptable plan on how to run the peace conference. Memoranda and proposals were circulated among groups of experts and occasionally given a controversial general airing. But there was no clear joint programme. Neither before nor after the armistice was the peace conference prepared for its tasks in a manner which befitted its importance.

The conference was less aware of the need to agree on programmes before the start of the negotiations – if it was aware of such a need at all – than of the great obstacles that stood in the way of any agreement. Moreover, Wilson's Fourteen Points, which all the world knew and knew also that the vanquished recognised them as a basis for a future peace, were regarded by many as a sufficient basis for peace negotiations, a view that ignored the many reservations and objections on the Allied side.

Almost from the start differences were revealed between the attitude of the United States' representatives, primarily Wilson, and that of the West European statesmen. By insisting on certain principles which it regarded as vital for lasting peace America had no need to surrender any of its own claims or interests but was asking for various not inconsiderable sacrifices from the European powers. The French principles as they emerged during the conference amounted to a demand for safeguard guarantees against the Germans, regarded as essential after the loss of the Russian ally, and – connected with this – for the establishment of lasting French influence on the left bank of the Rhine. The British already had certain ideas on the partition of Germany's colonial possessions. And in view of their economic position, which was a result of the war, and their big war debt both France and Britain were extremely anxious for a generous war indemnity settlement. Lloyd George had been committed to this since November, since the election campaign, while France tied its own hands in April by agreeing to pay compensation to all Frenchmen who had suffered from the war. Italy was not in the least prepared after the wartime hardships to forget either wholly or in part the big concessions of the London treaty and in the face of the complicated ethnic situation on the shores and islands of the eastern and north-eastern Adriatic to submit to the principle that its future frontiers should coincide with those of its own nationality. The great nations had known great deprivation and sacrifice and experienced every type of national upset and tension. For years the Allied statesmen had urged their peoples not to give up and therefore did not want to renounce and probably could not renounce without a fight the spoils of war which their peoples expected. Other powers meanwhile sought to exploit this situation in order to gain whatever they could for themselves.

The Fourteen Points had already been the subject of detailed Anglo-American discussions. In an interview on 16 October 1918 with Sir William Wiseman, the British government's representative in Washington and a close friend of Colonel House, President Wilson had enlarged on some of the practical consequences of the Fourteen Points, on the whole in a fairly conciliatory spirit. Just as the Supreme Council of the Allied Powers in Versailles was about to lay down detailed armistice conditions, Wilson's right-hand man, Colonel House, with the peace negotiations in mind produced commentaries on the Fourteen Points the aim of which as far as Wilson was concerned was to cushion the blow of the armistice conditions: 'The heads of the governments will probably have to modify the terms because the soldiers and sailors will make them too severe.'

For these commentaries House had on 29 October telegraphically requested his President's approval which Wilson gave with the instruction that 'details of application mentioned should be regarded as merely illustrative suggestions and reserved for peace conference'. With the help of these interpretations, prepared for him by his colleagues Walter Lipmann and Frank Cobb, House hoped to avoid lengthy discussions in the Supreme Council and to co-ordinate Wilson's principles and the intentions of the West European powers. He explained the Fourteen Points with logical consistency and in the light of the existing situation. Recognition of the principle of freedom of the seas therefore did not yet include the lifting of the blockade and the demand for disarmament was understood and accepted as a principle the practical aspects of which would be considered later by a special commission. In principle the German colonies were at the appropriate moment to be regarded as the property of the League of Nations but would be handed to suitable mandatory agents to administer. It was here that the Americans officially introduced the mandate idea as the answer to the colonial question. This solution which American experts had been examining during the preceding year was advocated also, in a slightly different form, by the South African Prime Minister, Smuts, but was given a somewhat critical reception by the spokesmen of the 'New Imperialism' in Britain. Until then Wilson himself had shown no particular interest in this form of administration and House had said to Sir William Wiseman that having produced the world's best colonial system, Great Britain would make a very suitable mandatory power.

Of far-reaching importance were several carefully reasoned modifications clearly concerning matters of principle of some of the Fourteen Points. Little Belgium, which without any fault of its own had been involved in the war and had suffered greatly, was granted full compensation for all costs arising out of the war; and France which faced the difficult task of rebuilding large devastated areas was to be compensated for all war damage suffered by its population. Italy was to have the Brenner frontier, a provision that fell far short of its wishes but nevertheless separated a large German-speaking area from Austria. However, the German part of the population was to be given full autonomy within Italy. In line with actual developments and past declarations the peoples of the Danube monarchy were expressly assured of complete independence, although on the condition that the anticipated minorities would be given protection. In the Near East the British presence was confirmed: Constantinople and the Dardanelles zone were to be placed under international control and the future administration of Palestine, Arabia and Iraq was to be entrusted to the British. Greece was to be given the mandate over Smyrna and the surrounding regions and Armenia was to become an independent state under the protection of a great power. Turkey would thus have been confined to the interior of Asia Minor as had in principle been envisaged in the secret treaties concluded by the Entente powers during the war. Finally there was a restatement of the demand made in the Fourteen Points that at the peace conference Poland should receive access to the Baltic, which as matters lay it could only be given at the expense of German territory. House's important interpretations also contained concessions to one of the Allies' wartime enemies. The United States granted Bulgaria the whole of the Dobrudja, Western Thrace and parts of Eastern Thrace.

Although of some Points nothing much remained by the end of the peace conference it is true to say that a substantial part of these interpretations found its way into the future peace treaties. They represented a compromise which gave concrete form to Wilson's demands while taking into account the situation as it now was. But remembering the commentaries' primary link with the Fourteen Points as we must do in view of their assumptions and their origins, it is impossible to underestimate the influence of Wilson's ideas on the peace treaties that were subsequently concluded. The differences arose from the West

European desiderata not considered at all by the commentaries. But these certainly not unrealistic and important concessions to the European powers and their positions at the time, with which House was familiar, were insufficient to provide the conference with a basis for lasting agreement. The gathering quickly assumed the character of a large congress whose discussions were based to only a limited extent on firm assumptions and in the course of which a variety of new points of view emerged.

No details of these important variations on the Fourteen Points were known to the Germans. But the last of the American notes of the US–German exchange before the armistice, Lansing's note of 5 November, referred to American talks with the Allied governments and in a phrase indicating their fundamental importance recalled the 'interests of the peoples involved' to whom the armistice must give 'unrestricted power' to 'safeguard and enforce the details of the peace accepted by the German government . . .'. From a memorandum by the British government the note quoted two explicit reservations subject to which Wilson's peace principles would be acceptable as a basis for negotiations with the German government. These reservations related to future interpretations of the 'so-called concept of freedom of the seas', on which Britain was not prepared to commit itself in any way, and to the war indemnity question. Britain states explicitly that Germany 'shall pay compensation for all damage caused by its attacks on water, land and in the air to the civilian population of the Allies and to their property'. A modification of Wilson's principles was visible therefore already at this stage of the US–German exchange of notes, even though only a few large areas of Allied reservations were clearly outlined in summary form.

The German government accepted the last pre-armistice note without comment. But it is clear from Hindenburg's written instruction to the armistice commission that the Army High Command at any rate had no illusions about the extent to which the formulations were binding: 'We have unreservedly accepted President Wilson's Fourteen Points without being clear about the interpretation of these Points, their effect on Germany's future shape, or possible further Entente demands.' This observation describes with complete accuracy the actual situation.

The reason why no further progress was made with preliminary agreements was that a seemingly unbridgeable difference between the

French and the American viewpoints emerged at an early stage and in an extreme form. Exactly one month after House had modified his President's peace principles the French took the initiative by proposing a new agreement in line with their own ideas. In Washington Ambassador Jusserand produced a peace programme which not only contained several sensible and fruitful proposals but also included a number of preliminary demands that give a foretaste of the problematical severity of the peace treaties of Versailles and Sèvres. But the most painful aspect of this move was the perhaps not totally unintended clumsiness with which it was made. Jusserand submitted no proposals for discussion but produced counter-theses to Wilson's Fourteen Points which the French explicitly rejected and which they described as being unsuitable to form the basis of future peace treaties. Perhaps the French may be credited with remarkable frankness but certainly not with superior insight or better intentions than the American President. At any rate the move was bound to offend Wilson and to a man of his character there was no alternative but to answer firmly in the negative. The most charitable assumption is that it was the intention of the French to shock the President into an awareness of their determined counterposition. The shock effect seems indeed to have been achieved; because as far as we know Wilson made no attempt to enter into a dialogue with France before the start of the peace conference or to seek an explanation of the French position, although he must by then have realised that it was more than doubtful whether his scheme for world peace would be adopted.

But an understanding which ignored the United States was reached a few days later by the political leaders of the European Great Powers. At a meeting between Lloyd George, Clemenceau and the Italian Prime Minister, Orlando, on 2 and 3 December 1918 in London there was partial agreement on several points at any rate between the two closest wartime allies. They decided to appoint two joint commissions, one to examine the German ability to pay war indemnities and the other to investigate the need for food aid. In addition it was decided to bring ex-Kaiser William II before an international court of justice. Finally it was agreed that the British Dominions should have the right to attend the peace conference on questions involving their interests. This was likely to lend support to the British claim to mandates over former German colonies and also to their call for extensive German indemnity payments which Lloyd George had made part of his election programme and which the Dominions also wanted. But no agreement was reached on the important question of whether Russia should be invited to the conference table.

All other points were left for the conference to clarify. The conference therefore did not assume the character of a congress at which there was open negotiation as envisaged by Wilson, but from the start became the stage for secret diplomatic activity among the Allies who tried, with the future shape of Europe in mind, to agree on what to demand from their opponents. It is hardly surprising that infinitely more attention, labour and effort were devoted to this problem than to the negotiations with their totally defeated enemies.

In these circumstances Wilson's disputed decision personally to participate in the conference discussions was of the greatest significance. The statesmen assembled at Paris operated cleverly and – given almost intimate knowledge of their partners' peculiarities – with diplomatic skill. And the authority which Clemenceau and Lloyd George commanded in their countries in fact entitled them, no less than the President of the United States on account of his constitutional position, to speak on behalf of their peoples. But this was true only of that short period in which the mood of triumphant victory prevailed and in which they could count on the support of vast majorities and were able to consolidate their positions with plebiscites. It was necessary for the statesmen of the Entente Powers to exploit the hour and the situation by word and deed so as to prevent discouragement and disappointment from spreading among their peoples. Clemenceau knew that he expressed the views and feelings of nationally minded Frenchmen as long as the memory of the war lived on. Because of his great tactical ability, flexibility and resourcefulness Lloyd George managed for a while to retain the unique powers enjoyed by British prime ministers in wartime. Wilson was the first to be exposed, with the most serious consequences, to a change of public opinion in America and to be attacked by the newly formed opposition in the Senate and the House of Representatives. But the situation would probably have been no different even if the President had decided not to go to Paris.

Whatever is thought about the disadvantages of Wilson's presence at the conference it is undoubtedly true that his cause would have suffered unless an equal American partner counter-balanced the great weight of the personalities of Clemenceau and Lloyd George. In the light of his convictions and of his political aims we should be less

critical of Wilson's unhesitating decision to attend the peace conference – in spite of his lack of success there – than of the tactics of the
obstreperous republican opposition among whom Wilson unfortunately
failed to find anyone whom he could trust or win over to his point of
view. Wilson's decision wholeheartedly to back the peace programme
which he had proclaimed and which was irrevocably associated with
his name speaks for his strong sense of responsibility and his determination to show the world that America was serious in its efforts and
to demonstrate to his own country the importance of the peace about to
be made. It is very much to his credit that he was the first President
of the United States to go to Europe, faithful to his conviction that
American isolationism was a thing of the past. The historic importance
of this decision must not be judged only in the light of his subsequent
failure.

Certain of the President's characteristics, his inclination to adhere
strictly to principles and ideas which without being formalistic were
always based on theories and abstractions, together with his stubborn
imperturbability which made it difficult for him to compromise, alien-
ated his European negotiating partners. His difficult task was not made
easier by being constantly confronted by the clever logic and quick,
eloquent argumentation of Clemenceau and the agility of Lloyd
George. Today there can no longer be any doubt that in his energy, his
sureness of aim and – a few exceptions apart – in his familiarity with
the subject matter he was in no way inferior to his opponents and in
some ways even understood the position better than they. His strict
morality, the sovereign self-awareness of the qualified legislator and a
confidence reminiscent of James Mill in the beneficial and irresistible
effects of democratic common sense made Wilson seem to them like
a being from another planet, if they did not prefer to regard him
as a great fool. More important was the fact that Wilson's physical
collapse at a decisive point necessitated his absence and that his place
was taken by House, who was anxious for quick agreement and who
could not stand up to pressure from the European statesmen with
nearly the same determination and steadfastness of principle as the
President. He did not want the United States to become isolated from
the great powers with which it was allied, a situation in which it had
found itself before and which House wanted to avoid in view of the
establishment and work of the future League of Nations. In the further
course of the negotiations Wilson himself also made several far-reaching

concessions to Clemenceau. This was apparently done for the sake of what was undoubtedly the most important of the American objectives and with a view to the opportunities for revision which the League of Nations was to have.

Meanwhile Wilson had seen the change of public opinion in his own country and had recognised the threat to his position and his policy. Unfortunately this coincided with a change of opinion in Britain, where there was a rapid spread both of the reservations about Wilson personally and of the criticism of American foreign policy which had been general for some time past among Conservative politicians and had occasionally found drastic expression. From then on Wilson took more account of definite trends and proceeded very cautiously as soon as he saw himself at odds with the statesmen of the three great European powers.

The United States relapsed visibly into its pre-war isolationism and as a result of the determined activities of the Republican opposition far greater emphasis than before was placed on the sacrifices made by America in Europe.

When the fighting ended the United States had a force of 4.8 million men. More than 2 million had been brought to Europe and 1,390,000 men had been sent into action in France. Even more impressive than its military accomplishments were the economic and in particular the financial achievements of the United States. Its varied types of assistance which had included not only deliveries of war materials but also an extensive food aid programme and other humanitarian measures, were very expensive. They necessitated restrictions, resulted in big tax increases and in numerous ways imposed tangible burdens on every American family. For the first time in its history America had an income tax of a steeply progressive nature. It was largely because of this that between 1 April 1917 and 30 April 1919 the United States found almost $22 milliard for its war and nearly $9 milliard for loans to the Allies, to which were added in the following months several hundred million by way of financial assistance to several of the new states. At first the American people carried this burden with great selflessness because it looked upon the war, through Wilson's eyes, as an inescapable crusade fought for eternal ideas of justice and for future world peace. Thanks to a well-organised and cleverly directed propaganda campaign America developed a patriotism the like of which it had not known since the War of Secession. Rigorous action was taken against the small minorities which did not fall into line, the farming community of the upper Mississippi area which had always been isolationist in outlook and the small but active group of socialists in the industrial regions of the north. The complete changeover of the economy from peace to war created tremendous prosperity with a rising cost of living and rising wages; and war profiteering assumed exorbitant dimensions. The number of millionaires increased by about a quarter between 1917 and 1920.

But now that the war was over and that there were signs of a decline in prosperity the United States was faced with the need to put into reverse gear the great machinery of war production which had just been started up with indisputable success. The demobilisation process created problems for all the great states involved in the war. Producers found it difficult to sell their goods, factories closed down and there was bankruptcy and rapidly growing unemployment. In common with other countries the United States suddenly saw in a new light the world war which had produced the quickest and greatest boom ever. In these circumstances the enthusiasm for remaining involved in Europe disappeared and a growing part of the American public, led by the Republican majority in the Senate Foreign Affairs Committee under the chairmanship of John Cabot Lodge, demanded a return to 'normal' pre-war conditions. The situation was made more difficult by the fact that Wilson's 'nationalities policy' never became generally popular although the principle of self-determination was, given the American political tradition, always assured of general recognition.

11. Germany, Russia and the beginnings of the Paris Peace Conference

The peace conference cast its shadow even before its work had begun. Once it had started the significance of some unsolved questions paled and others were cleared up by the circumstances. The difficult decision of whether the conference should first concern itself with a preliminary peace or a definite armistice or whether it should go on immediately to the final peace settlement does not seem to have been taken in so many words at any time. This issue ceased to be considered because it was in fact overtaken by other decisions and by events. As the work of the conference progressed, as more proposals, recommendations and demands were made and great catalogues were produced it became clear that the objective was to reach a comprehensive and final peace settlement, to be prepared by the technical commissions of the Allies, without leaving room for negotiations with the vanquished enemy.

The military had always been opposed to the idea of a preliminary peace with Germany. Marshal Foch feared that if a definitive peace was delayed the tensions among the Great Powers would be clearly revealed; at the same time, as the armed forces were progressively being demobilised and as this process could not be delayed, the Allies could lose their great military superiority and the most powerful of their enemies could find himself in a more favourable position.

This reasoning was one-sided but not false within the limits of power politics and above all of strategy. The limited and conditional armistice with Germany seemed to the soldiers the most reliable safeguard which they were not prepared to abandon until there was a permanent settlement.

During the negotiations on the extensions of the armistice the Allies produced a batch of additional agreements and contractual obligations on the part of Germany towards France and Britain. These anticipated some of the provisions of the peace treaty. As Germany took no part in the first phases of the peace conference and was merely handed the peace conditions – a procedure which has proved grist to the mill of those who have talked about a 'dictated peace' – it remained outside the conference and therefore in unfavourable circumstances for the continuous negotiations that arose from the armistice agreement. In the course of these negotiations a number of preliminary decisions were made which belong to the sphere of the reparations or the disarmament complex. In the two so-called Trèves agreements of 13 December 1918 and 16 January 1919 all gold reserves of the German Reich and of the Reichsbank and all foreign securities and assets in Germany were blocked. The German negotiators were anxious to achieve the complete lifting of this blockade and of the international restrictions on trade to which Germany was still subject and also to enable Germany to participate freely in international currency transactions. This happened finally only after the signing of the peace treaty. But when the armistice agreement was extended for the last time, on 16 February, Germany was promised supplies of urgently needed food and raw materials and in practice the blockade was lifted shortly afterwards.

The question of Russian participation was raised early on but was soon decided by the growing differences between the Western powers and the Soviet state. At the London meeting of the three Prime Ministers early in December 1918 Lloyd George raised this topic for the first time. He expressed himself in favour of the Bolshevik government being present at the conference table because in his view it had the support of the majority of the Russian people. He may have been motivated by thoughts of the future balance of power on the continent. At any rate he considered it inadvisable not to invite the biggest country of the world to the peace conference. But in this he was alone. He therefore used delaying tactics so that he later got his way with American assistance. However, shortly before the start of the Paris Conference, on 12 and 13 January, the representatives of the five Great Powers – the United States, Britain, France, Italy and Japan – finally adopted the opposite position, the main exponent of which was Clemenceau. On this occasion Lloyd George was forced to move cautiously as in the British Cabinet both Churchill and the Conservative ministers Lord Robert Cecil and Lord Curzon were advocating military intervention against the Bolshevik government. Although prepared to compromise they tied Lloyd George's hands at Paris on the 'Russian question' and this henceforth took second place to the issue of strengthening the states of eastern central Europe and southeast Europe.

For the French, however, the progress of the revolution in Russia created one of the biggest post-war problems. The loss of its ally and main financial partner of the pre-war period, which was what the Tsarist empire had been for a quarter of a century, deprived the French Entente system of its basis. This serious side effect of the Russian revolution cast a shadow over France's great victory over Germany and over the prospects opened up by the new French policy in the Near East. It now became necessary for France to find a completely new basis for its foreign policy. For France the peace conference became – far cry from the biased legend of nationalist German propaganda which saw nothing but schemes for revenge – the vital instrument with which to reestablish its relations with the outside world on a lasting and secure footing.

The most obvious course was undoubtedly to follow up the military association with Britain which had effectively strengthened the links between the two peoples and which was certain to produce lasting results. In fact during the peace conference and later both powers never completely abandoned this natural starting point and for the whole period between the two wars it constituted something like a last and completely reliable safety valve in the relations between them. But subject to this reservation there was no lack of disagreement and tension. Even during the preparation of the armistice conditions the conflicting interests of the soldiers were responsible for serious differences. Foch insisted on strict disarmament and demanded the occupation of the left bank of the Rhine, the bridgeheads included. Sir Douglas Haig and the spokesmen of the British Admiralty concentrated on the surrender of the main part of the German fleet; at the same time they regarded the French demands as exaggerated and unnecessarily harsh. Future differences over policy towards Germany and Europe are discernible here. In the end both military points of view were more or less accepted without limiting each other, in spite of the fact that Haig had the support of Lloyd George, whereas Foch on the French side may have had that of the Foreign Minister, Pichon, but certainly not the Prime Minister's. But the British were handicapped by differences of opinion between Haig and Sir Henry Wilson who – as on previous occasions – had the support of the Conservatives in Lloyd George's Coalition Cabinet and could therefore propagate his ideas and also those of Foch once the British demands had been met.

But over other disputed issues that were discussed between Britain and France before the beginning of the peace conference – the evacuation of Poland by German troops, the return of Haller's Polish army to its homeland and the treatment of Danzig – Balfour's foreign policy was at odds with that of France. Balfour had far more faith in the traditional principle of a European balance of power which did not permit the French to gain the ascendancy than in the ideas of the American President; and it was this principle that came to be regarded by Conservative foreign policy as a tested and reliable guarantee for a secure peace. Once Russia ceased to be among the powers concerned with Near Eastern questions and even more after the defeat of Turkey, Britain set about extending step by step its sphere of influence in the Near East where it acquired a permanent supremacy of which there had been as yet no sign in the secret Near East agreements of the war. It was therefore obvious that although British and French foreign policy could on occasion follow the same course the two countries had widely divergent objectives.

Clemenceau and Pichon now proceeded to base French policy on the security doctrine. This remained important until World War II and in its original and extreme form was influenced by Marshal Foch's military and political ideas which hinged on considerations of strategy, geo-politics and population policy. In its most extreme form the doctrine was disapproved of on the British side by both Lloyd George and Balfour. The fronts had been established by the time the conference began and the differences between Clemenceau and Lloyd George, who had Wilson's support on this, continued through several stages. The essence of this doctrine which was based on the bitter experiences of two German wars was that Europe east of the French frontier must become an area that could be reliably controlled and where no development was allowed that might threaten France. But Clemenceau, unlike other French politicians, various generals and diplomats, never thought of annexing part of Germany for France or even of breaking up Germany. He was one of Germany's greatest and most determined opponents, but he had no wish to destroy Germany and with all his determined and brutal energy in the last resort did only what he regarded as vital in the interests of French politics. And Clemenceau's views on what was essential for his country had nothing in common with the inflated ideas of the French pre-war imperialists.

On the basis of these views Clemenceau and Pichon shaped French east European policy for half a generation. French influence did not extend to the new Russia. From the beginning France therefore pursued a policy which, given the structure of the European order, was obvious and for which the ground had been prepared by older historic associations. With all the means at its disposal it set out to strengthen the Polish state which had arisen between the two former great powers, Germany and Russia, and to ensure with Poland's aid that the *status quo* once established would not be threatened.

Several influential members of the British Cabinet whose opinion the Premier could not ignore shared the French views on Russia. It is less easy to define British policy on the states situated between Germany and Russia. But during the last years of the war a number of British experts and politicians had undoubtedly come to look favourably upon these states. We cannot ignore the testimony of a young member of the British delegation in Paris who says that it was not Germany, Austria, Hungary, Bulgaria or Turkey which several British participants at the conference were primarily interested in: 'It was the thought of the new Serbia, the new Greece, the new Bohemia, the new Poland which made our hearts sing hymns at heaven's gates.'* Mixed up in this hosanna there was certainly also pride in participating in the demiurgic acts which were creating a new continental world of states and in working for a just cause. But it would be wrong to think that on this point there was any close connection between British and French motives.

The course of the civil war in Russia with the formation of counter-revolutionary governments in Siberia, Archangel and 'southern Russia' and the advance of the Kolchak army kept the Russian question alive even after the peace conference had begun. Lloyd George remained opposed to the idea of intervention favoured by the French and in the British Cabinet by Churchill, the Minister of War, and by Lord Milner, the Secretary of State for the Colonies. To Lloyd George the protection and security of Russia's border states were of paramount importance. Both Lloyd George and Wilson expected the Western countries to show growing reluctance at being militarily involved in Russia. Both therefore tried temporarily to stabilise the situation in an acceptable manner. The United States was anxious to clear up foreign policy issues as well as the war debts question and to settle its claims from the days of pre-Bolshevik Russia. Lansing and House with the

* Harold Nicolson, *Peacemaking 1919*, Constable & Co. Ltd.

agreement of Lloyd George and Balfour sent William Bullitt, a member of the American peace delegation in Paris, on a secret mission to Moscow. His instructions were quietly to establish workable contacts which would make it possible to end the embarrassing intervention adventure. More widely known is the appeal made by the representatives of the Great Powers present in Paris on Wilson's initiative to the parties in the Russian civil war. They called upon them to cease fighting and to send representatives to a special conference at Prince Islands in the Sea of Marmara to discuss with the participation of the Allies how to assure peace in southern Russia and how to restore the relations of the Western powers with Russia. What was of the greatest importance to the Allies was that the Soviets should acknowledge the pre-war and wartime debts of the Tsarist empire. The invitation was phrased in such a way that none of Russia's governments could interpret it as *de facto* recognition.

The Soviet government adopted a diplomatically clever position, not of outright rejection but of evasion while its opponents gave a negative reply. But these answers as also Bullett's proposals were overtaken by the double event of the advance of Kolchak's troops and the spread of the revolutionary movement to Central Europe. During the transition to a Communist regime of peoples' commissars in Hungary in March 1919 Southern Germany appeared also to be in the grip of unpredictable developments; and in the central German and Westphalian industrial areas strikes and risings threatened to develop into civil war, while the situation on both sides of Germany's eastern frontier remained overshadowed by military measures.

Collaboration between the Czechs and French had in the first phase of the peace conference led to the drawing of a preliminary border-line that generously met the interests of the new Czechoslovak state, exclusively at the expense of Hungary. When the Allies military mission in Budapest issued an ultimatum demanding the evacuation of the territories allocated to Rumania and Czechoslovakia even before the peace settlement the Hungarian Prime Minister, Count Michael Károlyi, resigned. He did so that his place might be taken by the socialist Garbai with whom he shared the opinion that Hungary's cause could now only be defended with help from the east. The Socialists had previously come to an agreement with the Communists whose leader Béla Kun at once became the leading man in the government of the Hungarian Soviet Republic and who tried to establish a new type of relationship between national Magyar policy and the Communist revolution. The Hungarian Soviet government organised military resistance and quickly struck successful counter-blows against Slovakia and Rumania with the twofold objective of regaining former Hungarian territories and of obtaining a land link with Soviet Russia. This sudden threat to Central Europe through the expansion of revolutionary Bolshevism temporarily caused the Allies great embarrassment and even led them to discuss the possibilities of a military operation.

By comparison the situation in Germany seemed as yet less dangerous. Since the November revolt the Bavarian communist movement and counter-revolutionary groups in Bavaria had been fighting a bitter duel which dominated the political scene completely after the murder of Kurt Eisner, the revolutionary leader. Armed militias were formed in town and country and used by the superior forces of the old order to protect their interests with quasi military means. Munich became the focal point of secret organisations for 'the struggle against revolution'; these had a militant precursor in a secret political order by name of *Thule-Gesellschaft* which had been in existence since the summer of 1918. From November onwards other organisations of a similar kind came into being. These groups were dominated by pan-German and so-called 'patriotic' ideas and spoke and wrote, not only in secret, of a 'German national renewal and purity of race' – whatever that meant. They provided a home for those literary spokesmen of 'folkish' nationalism who later became the propagandists of National Socialism, such as the popular nationalist Bavarian poet Dietrich Eckart, the engineer Gottfried Feder who toyed with economic ideas in a nationalist setting, or the student Alfred Rosenberg, a German from Russia, who had fled from revolutionary Petrograd and had the eccentric ambition of using his autodidactic educational zeal to construct a new German ideology. In these circumstances it was politically not without danger to give official recognition to these secretly armed organisations. The Bavarian government would probably have put up some opposition when Berlin ordered the former commander of the Royal Bavarian infantry regiment, Ritter von Epp, to draw up a Bavarian volunteer corps in Thuringia to protect the frontier in the east, had the pendulum of public opinion not suddenly swung in favour of the communists under the impact of Eisner's assassination. At the beginning of April the Communists assumed control in Munich, prevented the Landtag from sitting, imposed a state of seige, proclaimed a general strike, suppressed the press and established contact with the rulers in Moscow. The counter-revolution immediately mobilised its forces, the Communist dictator-ship started to hit back and the situation moved towards open civil war. Signs that the Communist-dominated Central Council of Soviets in Southern Bavaria was prepared to resist to the utmost led the military authorities in Berlin to intervene and to move in South German troops, who within a few weeks brought the Munich Communist government to a grim end.

In Eastern Germany, particularly in the areas predominantly inhabited by Poles, the first military actions occurred before the beginning of the year, before the withdrawal of German troops from Southern Russia had even been completed. Their purpose was both to offer determined resistance to Bolshevism and to preserve the *status quo ante bellum* on the frontier. There were differing and vague ideas about the political future of these regions. The loss of Alsace-Lorraine had generally been accepted. After all there was no alternative after the US–German exchange of notes of October 1918 and Germany's acceptance of Wilson's Fourteen Points. But the German Foreign Ministry shared the view that it was more serious for East Prussia to be cut off from Germany, and Posen, Upper Silesia and Western Prussia to be detached than for Germany to suffer territorial losses in the west and in the north for which the nation was prepared. The Foreign Ministry was therefore ready to make considerable concessions to Poland and to the Polish population of these regions as long as German sovereignty was not affected. But this was not the view of the Army High Command to whom the government was in the last resort compelled to give a free hand. The problem of an understanding with the Poles did not exist for the military; they regarded the situation in the east exclusively from the standpoint of providing reliable safeguards for the old frontiers. The continuation of the fighting in the Baltic region and the reinforcement of the Polish forces by units of the Haller army which had been equipped by the Entente created an increasingly difficult military situation. In view of Germany's limited resources a peaceful solution would have been desirable and also more advisable than the continuation of the many-sided military test of strength. But as the Polish population in the provinces of Posen and West Prussia presented an increasing military threat the army authorities decided on strict measures against the civilian population and thus placed the German part of the population and the Prussian administration in an extremely difficult position. The surprise appointment in January 1919, unauthorised by the Prussian authorities, of a supreme civil commissar for the whole of the zone occupied by the army on both sides of Germany's eastern frontier was only one of the consequences of the precarious relationship between the civil authorities and the military in the frontier region. But the civil administration also behaved in an inconsistent manner. During the Paris peace negotiations Prussia tried vainly to prevent plebiscites from being held in the eastern territories because it expected no good from them, while the case for them was defended with justified arguments by the Reich Ministry of the Interior. The gradual disintegration of the political administration in the vital areas with a Polish majority in the province of Posen helped of course to create a panicky atmosphere.

The year 1919 in Germany thus became a year of bloodshed in which the newly formed military units played as big a role as the National Assembly which met on 6 February in Weimar, a quiet town which had been almost completely bypassed by the events of the past months. On the domestic front the Reich government gained some elbow room; but this success went together with a new display of military force. Noske was the first Reich Minister of Defence also to head the war ministries of the *Länder*. Under a law passed on 6 March 1919 the Reich President was given power to dissolve the existing army and to set up a temporary *Reichswehr*. A legal basis was thus provided for the reshaping of the armed forces which was already in full swing.

The military command was hard pushed both to fight Bolshevism and to preserve Germany's eastern frontier against the claims of the Poles led by Roman Dmowski and against the Polish population whom he and his nationalist supporters were inciting to rebel. But at that moment the military neither admitted nor envisaged any alternative way of dealing with Russia and Poland. The political and diplomatic efforts and ideas of the Western Powers were apparently ignored.

The Army High Command transferred its headquarters to Kolberg, a move which brought it geographically closer to the centre of the most important military activity. With the collaboration of General von Seeckt, a new headquarters, *Grenzschutz Nord* (Frontier Defence North), was created from the traditional commands of the last army

HQs in the area *Oberost* where it took on the twofold strategic task in the east. Because the army wanted to give military protection to the old frontiers of the Reich and also to suppress by force any opposition in the hinterland it was prepared to stay in the Baltic provinces as far as the Libau (Liepâja) line and if necessary to defend them. For this purpose *Freikorps* were recruited in the Reich and mobile military district commissars were sent to the eastern territory. A minor but perhaps characteristic feature of the recruitment of these volunteers was that they were promised land on which to settle in the former eastern territories of Russia. In a proclamation of 9 January 1919 the Reich government gave its support to all these efforts of a purely military nature and in the eyes of both the German and the non-German public legitimised them without reservation. Officially a stop was put to Seeckt's more extreme plans to recall to the colours age groups which had already been demobilised so as to be in a position to start an offensive against Poland. But such schemes continued to be considered behind the government's back with Reich Commissar Winnig and officials of the Foreign Ministry when – with the slowing down of the Kolchak offensive – new White Russian ventures were being prepared in the south and the north. Under the protection of guns of a British Baltic fleet lying off the Estonian coast General Yudenich moved away from the immediate vicinity of the German sphere of influence to advance on Petrograd.

The Allies, however, on principle avoided direct contact with the German military organisation in the east. This is not surprising in view of the connection between the activities in the Baltic theatre of war and the happenings in the German–Polish frontier regions; from the Allies' point of view it was advisable also for other reasons to keep their distance. The fact that individual commanders of allied army or naval units occasionally broke this rule or adopted an ambiguous attitude does not change the overall picture. There may, however, have been a time when other possibilities were seriously considered. As the revolutionary movement spread to Central Europe and as signs of dissatisfaction became apparent among the British and particularly among the French troops in action against the revolutionary armies in Russia it became imperative for the Allies to change their policy towards Russia because they feared that these soldiers would sow seeds of unrest when they returned home. There was also the hope, nurtured with varying degrees of conviction, of a decisive military success of the White Russian operations, although these were accompanied by happenings for which the politicians assembled in Paris had little sympathy. A war of the Allied powers against Bolshevik rule seemed less on the cards than ever before. But for the time being recognition of the Soviet regime was unthinkable.

In this situation Marshal Foch's staff toyed briefly with the plan of erecting under French command a military cordon against the Red Army with the help of volunteers from Germany and from the European countries sandwiched between East and West. But it was precisely this military vision of an anti-Russian campaign with Allied volunteers that galvanised into action the most determined opponent of any attempt to come to terms with the Soviet government. Clemenceau mobilised the Council of Four where he received the most effective support from the American President. Once the leaders of the Great Powers had agreed to oppose any military schemes of conquest the policy of the Allies towards Russia entered upon a new phase. In April the remaining Allied troops in Russia were gradually withdrawn. No further assistance was given to the White Russians, some of whose units continued to fight until the following year. The new course met with some resistance in the British Cabinet where Churchill insisted successfully for quite a while yet that British troops should remain in the Caucasus within reach of the important Baku oil fields. But with the abandonment of the idea of a military cordon protecting Western and Central Europe from the revolutionary energies of the east the policy of military intervention was also finally buried. It was replaced by the idea of the political *cordon sanitaire* against Soviet Russia's political expansion which had a much longer lease of life and provided an important common interest for French and British diplomacy. But the German military operations in the east were anyway rendered futile by the further course of the Paris Conference and their results, achieved with the sacrifice of human life, were destined to be of no consequence.

Let us now after this necessary digression return to the Paris Peace Conference. The moment has come to examine the conference's organisation which in many respects proved fateful. After a slow start an extremely cumbersome machinery was set up. Twenty-seven nations sent their representatives. As requests and claims were made by all participating states the conference in plenary with its membership of over 1,000 delegates was not a suitable body for serious work. Consequently a hierarchy gradually emerged and the final decisions were increasingly taken at top level.

The *Conseil des Dix*, the council of the heads of government of the four Great Powers, the United States, Britain, France and Italy, together with their foreign ministers and two representatives of Japan was the direct offspring of the Supreme Council of the Allies – the *Conseil Suprême* – which had been set up during the last stages of the war and had met in Paris, without the heads of government. In the course of the conference, on 24 March 1919, after confidential talks on the future of the left bank of the Rhine and on the safeguards against German attacks demanded by France had already begun Wilson suggested a meeting of the heads of government only, a Council of Four, without the foreign ministers and without the representatives of Japan, a country not directly concerned with European events. After ten weeks the conference was thus given its supreme authority which continued to take the final decisions until the signing of the peace treaty with Germany. The Council of Four met almost daily for more than three months and frequently more than once a day; altogether it held 148 meetings. When questions concerning Japan arose Viscount Shinda and Baron Makino, the Japanese diplomats, were invited to attend. But this happened only seven times when purely Far Eastern questions were discussed which had arisen in connection with Admiral Kolchak's campaign and the Japanese occupation of eastern Siberia.

In its discussions of all other points the Council of Four remained confined to the Great Four. For a period of three months it had truly impressive powers, not only when it came to preparing the peace treaties with Germany and the Allies' other enemies but also in connection with every important issue arising out of the pacification of Europe and the events in Russia. It was an international directorate composed of the top political authorities of the world's greatest powers. Italy's inclusion in this group was of greater benefit to the self-esteem of its politicians than to the fulfilment of its ambitions. On the occasions when the Council of Foreign Ministers of the five great powers failed to agree and to reach a final decision the Council of Four acted at the last instance. As this happened frequently the burden of decision-making rested with the Council of Four. It was not until peace had been made with Germany that the place of these two bodies was taken by the council of the heads of delegations of the five great powers.

As the representatives of all Allied and associated states were asked to state their claims bulky packages of subjects for negotiation were produced which had nothing in common but that they affected one or more of the Central Powers. In the course of the conference expert committees were set up composed of two specialists from each of the five great powers who examined in detail various claims and problems. These committees were established on an *ad hoc* basis, without system and only after several weeks. A week after the ceremonial opening of the conference five committees were set up; others followed during February. Towards the end there were fifty-eight committees which held 1,646 meetings in all and which placed their conclusions before the Council of Four. Their activities, which were certainly not subject to continuous co-ordination, were largely concerned with the solution of technical questions and occasionally had a decisive effect on the manner in which the issue was finally handled. The committees' activities therefore decisively influenced some aspects of the contents and formulations of the peace treaties.

Germany's future was decided in the Council of Four after a continuous struggle between Wilson, Clemenceau and Lloyd George. Although Wilson was squarely defeated on a number of important issues, as for example the reparations question, he successfully modified with the support of the British Prime Minister various other major decisions. Together they prevented the left bank of the Rhine and the Saar from being separated for ever from Germany. Lloyd George stopped Germany losing the whole of upper Silesia; and Wilson insisted that East Prussia should remain German. This was achieved by the corridor solution which gave Poland access to the Baltic and brought more than one million Germans under Polish rule, whereas before four million Poles had lived under German rule. But the Polish nationalists had set their sights higher still.

The fact that some problems were indissolubly bound up with each other produced compromise solutions which had the effect of making matters worse for Germany. Clemenceau's main concern was to prevent Germany from regaining its strength in the foreseeable future. The terrible experience of the war which had been fought mainly on French soil and had resulted in frightful destruction naturally gave rise to the conviction that France must never again be attacked by a superior

German force. The destruction of Prussian–German militarism had always been one of Lloyd George's objectives; it was also in line with the views of the American President who in the fourth of his Fourteen Points had asked for the maximum possible disarmament. France's insistence on security could therefore become one of the main principles underlying the peace treaty with Germany.

But the military experts disagreed on how to limit Germany's military strength on a lasting basis; and this controversy was not confined to army circles. From the first preparations for the armistice onwards Foch had stubbornly pursued the goal of permanent military protection for the Rhine line; this was also Clemenceau's aim but he wanted to achieve it by an Allied occupation without annexations. Foch further wanted to replace Germany's professional army, which to him constituted by far the biggest threat, by a short-service force of some hundred thousand men. In his view:

> . . . une armée de métier . . . deviendrait rapidement la citadelle de l'esprit prussien, s'identifierait avec l'Allemagne traditionelle et finirait par dicter ses conditions au gouvernement.

But on this point he met with opposition from Clemenceau and also from Lloyd George who like the Americans was opposed to the French plans for the Rhineland. Lloyd George and Clemenceau both disliked the idea of conscription in Germany. When Foch realised that his views were unacceptable he pressed for a further reduction in the size of the German army thereby, as he thought, removing the last element of danger from what he regarded as an unsatisfactory solution. Step by step therefore – in the end against opposition from Lloyd George – provisions were drawn up and incorporated into the Versailles treaty under which Germany was given a professional army with a twelve-year period of service and a strength which was to be reduced within a given period of 100,000 men. Article 160 of the peace treaty laid down further that the actual numbers of 'the Army of the States constituting Germany' was not to comprise more than seven infantry divisions and three cavalry divisions. Such an army could not and should not be used in war and was to be devoted exclusively 'to the maintenance of order inside Germany and to the control of the frontiers'. These restrictions, together with a general prohibition of preparations for mobilisation and the fact that the manufacture and stocks of arms and ammunition were to be subject to the control of an inter-allied commission, reduced to a minimum the value of the future German army. The prohibition of modern armaments – military aircraft, warships, submarines, heavy artillery and armoured vehicles – the prohibition of a general staff, the minutely detailed list of permitted arms and the restrictions on fortifications together with the dismantlement of several major fortresses under supervision of the inter-allied control commission, all this rendered the future German armed forces all but useless, not only as an offensive weapon but as an effective defensive force among the armies of the European states. The whole of the permitted stocks of artillery ammunition, on the basis of the quantities used during the great offensives of 1918, would have been enough for barely nine hours of fighting.

In view of Germany's military past and even more in view of their effect on its development these clauses constituted the most important basis for future world peace. German foreign policy now faced the alternative of ensuring that a functioning League of Nations guaranteed Germany's freedom of decision if there was no other equally effective international system of alliances or of seeking a revision of the peace conditions which legally was again possible only within the League of Nations. Come what may, the objective of German policy would therefore need to be trusting collaboration with the enemies of the past. But for the time being France was determined not to admit Germany to the League of Nations, while in Britain the Round Table group envisaged the future League of Nations as being confined to the victorious powers with the British Empire playing the leading role.

The full significance of the military clauses was brought home to the German public only in the course of the following year when the extent of the proposed disarmament became known. What attracted the maximum attention from the start was the big complex of reparations commitments. This was true of all countries. An American expert later remarked that the reparations question was responsible for more excitement, more quarrels, more ruthlessness and more delays than any other issue at the Paris Peace Conference. It even took precedence over the difficulties that arose over Poland's western frontier and the future position of Danzig as well as over the controversy over the fate of Germany's territory on the left bank of the Rhine and of the Saar.

As far as Germany was concerned this comment must be both qualified and expanded. At first and for a long time the statement that

Germany was responsible for the war was seen as the worst and most invidious part of the peace conditions and caused great indignation. Although related to the question of the reparations that Germany was made to pay, it went much further. From the start the German public regarded the war guilt issue as a point of honour which added to the reparation burden. In these circumstances the real issues were not always clearly recognised.

In the end the accusation that Germany was responsible for the war was incorporated into the text of the peace treaty in three different places. It is contained first in the preamble in the form of a general and fundamental statement, reappears in connection with the reparations provisions and lastly forms the basis of the treaty's sanctions clauses.

Not one of the leading statesmen at the conference doubted Germany's guilt. The discussions in public and among the jurists of the Allied states rested primarily on four different arguments which were used to prove the guilt theses before any detailed historical investigation had even begun. Germany was condemned for its pre-war policy, its declarations of war on Russia and France, the violation of Belgian neutrality and the decision to wage unrestricted submarine warfare after the *Lusitania* incident. But to note Germany's guilt was one thing, to formulate punitive provisions was another. Two different concepts of 'crimes' emerged. As regards the upshot the British and French points of view were reconcilable; because British case law, the appeal to common law and the view that crimes must be expiated, made it possible to apply a new international law which had not existed when the crime was committed. But the American lawyers were not prepared to accept this line of argument. They upheld the general maxim of *nulla poena sine lege* and the axiom of international law that legal norms must be voluntarily recognised. Even if there were no doubts about Germany's moral guilt and about the need for moral condemnation legal action was not justifiable on the basis of this view. In the war guilt and war crimes committee which was set up by the peace conference and included representatives of several small states – Belgium, Poland, Czechoslovakia, Greece and Rumania – the American point of view found no support. As the committee failed to agree this issue too was settled by the Council of Four. Wilson gave way and it was decided to bring William II before a special Allied court and for this purpose to demand his extradition from the Dutch government, a move which, however, had little prospect of success.

But the war guilt question was linked also with the war crimes issue: Germany was to hand over on demand anyone accused of having committed acts against the 'laws and customs of war'.

In the long term, however, the war guilt thesis was more important than any other issue because on it depended the reparations clauses. To restore the economies of the peoples who had suffered during the war and to pay off their war debts required tremendous financial resources. How to find these was to present a big problem to the victors for a long time to come. In France, but also in Britain where the Dominions helped to form opinion, the view had come to be accepted – as earlier in Germany when victory seemed assured – that the vanquished opponent must be made to make the maximum possible financial restitution. It was the war guilt argument that was now used to give legal justification to the burden imposed upon the enemy.

Some of the concepts involved deserve examination. There was first of all the Anglo-Saxon concept of 'indemnities' to which House referred in his commentary of 29 October 1918 on Wilson's Fourteen Points. Then there was the concept of 'reparations', the meaning of which seemed ambiguous from the outset. As it referred only to damage done by violations of the law its significance – compared with 'indemnities' – was essentially of a qualifying nature. But as the violation of the law was itself treated on a global basis, first with the help of the French concept of *invasion* which was later supplanted by the Anglo-Saxon term 'aggression', the novel concept of reparations was in the end applied on a very wide scale. It was the British Cabinet's view that because economic questions were involved it would be best to hand the matter to the experts; so Lloyd George and Clemenceau agreed early in December 1918 to appoint a commission for 'reparations and indemnities'. This double concept which later disappeared suggests that from the outset the intention was to make global claims.

Although Britain and France reached initial agreement on this point they remained for a long time at loggerheads over the problems arising from it. Two questions in particular led to series of exchanges even after the conclusion of the peace treaties because it had proved impossible to agree on a final solution during the conference. On the one hand the question was what Germany should pay and on the other what it could pay and what form the payment should take. The French Minister of Finance, Louis Lucien Klotz, in his capacity as chairman of the Reparations Commission sought to give the entire reparations issue a broad legal basis by establishing the principle of Germany's integral obligation to make restitution. With the doctrine of compensation for damage done which existed also in German civil law he justified the claim for a restoration of such conditions as would have existed if the damage, that it is to say the war, had not occurred. But a memorandum which Klotz submitted on 3 February 1919 revealed how the legal, political and moral issues were mixed up:

> L'Allemagne doit réparer l'intégralité des dommages qu'elle a causés. C'est le seul moyen de rétablir, . . . comme sanction pour le passé, comme exemple pour l'avenir, elle doit s'acquitter de la totalité de sa dette . . .

Without any doubt this went far beyond the arrangements made through Colonel House between the United States and the Western Powers before the armistice. There was no question that Klotz's ideas were contrary to the letter and to the spirit of Wilson's Fourteen Points.

To start with, the Americans pressed for a definite limitation of the reparations payments by excluding all war costs. Their counter-proposal in the Reparations Commission was based on the pre-armistice exchange of notes and restricted Germany's reparations obligations to two spheres. First there was to be restitution for damage caused by breaches of existing international law. This included the violation of Belgian neutrality but also the illegal treatment of prisoners of war. Then Germany was to pay compensation for damage done to property of the civilian population of its wartime opponents and for illegally inflicted physical damage. The French view was that Germany should be held responsible for all war damage including damage caused indirectly because it was regarded as having started the war which was the general cause of this damage; the Americans on the other hand thought that restitution should be made according to internationally recognised legal principles relating to damage to the property, health and life of the civilian population, that is to say of non-combatants. The French justified their demand for global reparations with the theory of Germany's general responsibility; war as a political tool became a crime of which Germany was found guilty and for which it was held fully responsible. The United States representatives in the Reparations Commission and its three sub-commissions set up in the course of the meetings refused to accept this point of view. From the outset they restricted the reparations demands to observable consequences of violations of the law. For them the issue was one purely of international law, whereas for the French the legal aspects of the question were of functional importance and subordinate to economic considerations.

As the concept of *réparations des dommages* had already found its way into the text of the armistice agreement the French used this fact – not without success – in support of their own thesis. The legal adviser of the American experts, John Foster Dulles, stood up for the exclusion of pure war costs and sought to minimise the significance of the text of the armistice agreement in the face of the French interpretations; in this he had Wilson's explicit support. Against the French, who on this point had the support of the British, the Americans appealed to the spirit of the Fourteen Points and to Lansing's last pre-armistice note. But they met with resistance from the rest of the commission and found themselves completely isolated; in the end the Reparations Commission was able to reach a decision only by adopting Dulles' proposal to lay down distinct categories of damage and to determine Germany's liability separately in each case. On the basis of this compromise the war guilt clause was incorporated into the text of the treaty. At the same time the French and the British were given an excuse to create categories of so-called civil damages which were very widely conceived.

During this controversy Wilson was in America. He instructed the American delegation by telegram to oppose the French demands and authorised them to make public statements. In the period that followed the American point of view was made known with great vigour. In the last resort the United States was motivated by fear that the lack of balance and restraint of the French reparations demands would jeopardise post-war economic reconstruction in general; this would be detrimental to the economic interests of the American banking world which since the war had had a substantial share in the international capital market. Complete satisfaction of France's demands would certainly have allowed the French economy to live for a long time on reparations and would have given it a rate of growth faster than it could have achieved by its own efforts; it would also have led to the economic collapse of Germany or have forced Germany to adopt a policy of export or die. Neither was in the interest of the United States; because either would have jeopardised the economic stability of the world. But Lloyd George, with the support of the South African Prime Minister, Smuts, finally persuaded Wilson to agree against his experts' advice that war damage should extend to gratuities and service pensions arising out of the war. This alone meant that the conference powers would be paid an enormous sum, far in excess of Germany's resources.

In view of this situation the need to limit German reparations payments to a manageable figure became the central theme of the discussions. The French financial expert Louis Loucheur put Germany's reparations capacity at $200 milliard to be paid within fifty years. Earlier, in a speech at Bristol during the election campaign of November 1918, Lloyd George had committed himself to the unfortunate demand of £8 milliard for Britain. And the British expert Lord Cunliffe even went beyond Loucheur's estimates. The American expert Lamont, on the other hand, in his submission put the figure at a total of $52½ milliard at the outside. Thereafter the reparations question was dealt with by a committee of three experts, Norman Davis, Loucheur and Montagu, to whom the Council of Four had entrusted the settlement of the problem. In a memorandum dated 20 March 1919 Davis estimated that 'on a liberal basis' Germany could manage to pay between $10 and $20 milliard in a period of twenty to thirty years and this came very close to the payments which were actually later made. But at the time the figure reached was still close to $30 milliard.

These discussions revealed other even more far-reaching problems lurking in the background: for instance the difficulties of transferring the German payments into other currencies if they were not to be made in gold or foreign exchange only which presupposed the stability of the German mark. But the one and the other were attainable only on the assumption that Germany would earn enough gold or stable foreign currencies by substantial exports of goods or services. This again brought home the need to restore the strength of the German economy as the only way of making sure of reparations payments. Allied to this was the further question of a loan to Germany and agreement on a rate of interest which again presupposed further payments and deliveries. Some experts thus came to realise at an early stage that reparations involved more than a simple transfer of capital to the victorious powers and that they raised a number of important economic issues.

Lloyd George feared that if these complications were made generally known there would be a swing of public opinion in Britain; there was evidence of this already as shown for example by the famous telegram of 8 April 1919 in which 233 MPs called upon the Prime Minister to speed up the recognition of Germany's guilt and to stake a substantial claim for compensation. Lloyd George therefore decided that a change in the British membership of the Reparations Commission was the only means of bringing these arrangements to a speedy conclusion. From then on the British avoided the mention of any figures. For this reason the Commission was able at the end of March to adopt as a basis for discussion the draft proposal of the French Minister of Finance, Klotz, which assumed that there would be no payments ceiling. It led to the appointment of a permanent Reparations Commission with considerable powers whose main task it was to accept, catalogue and add up claims for compensation and to determine the annual German payment on the basis of Germany's economic capacity. But the formulation of the duties of this commission already proved difficult enough for the Council of Four to be asked again to intervene. Wilson did not attend this meeting; he was represented by Colonel House who was somewhat more flexible in his attitudes than the other Americans. He finally abandoned the American point of view in favour of the solution that a global German reparations commitment should be tied to the war guilt theory but that the text of the peace treaty should not go into specific details. The final formulation of the reparations clause was argued over until the text of the peace treaty was handed to the German delegation. In principle the settlement in the end did not exclude the American idea of making Germany's capacity to pay the criterion of the final reparations levels. But because of the activities of the others who in the end included Lloyd George, the formulation was strengthened so as to give the claimants the maximum amount of freedom *vis-à-vis* Germany: Germany was made explicitly to recognise its guilt.

12. The appearance of the German delegation and the Treaty of Versailles

The German public was from the start greatly concerned about what went on during the peace conference in so far as it was told about it. There was widespread hope that the peace conditions would not go beyond the content of Wilson's Fourteen Points as seen in Germany. It was almost impossible for official German foreign policy to influence the negotiations in Paris. The German public nevertheless participated in the world-wide discussion of the war guilt thesis and therefore became involved in the happenings at Paris. The heatedness of the arguments vividly recalled the wartime front lines.

The Germans' own discussion of the guilt question went back to the days of the war. But the uncompromising nature of the theories widely accepted in the Entente countries led on the German side to a defensive attitude which was adopted even by those who wholeheartedly condemned their country's pre-war policy. At the beginning of 1918 Germany's last pre-war ambassador to London, Prince Lichnowsky, created a sensation abroad by violently criticising the policy of the imperial government during the July crisis of 1914. His memorandum, *Meine Londoner Mission*, which was printed and distributed already contained those accusations that later continued to occupy a central position: Germany had encouraged Austra–Hungary to act against Serbia 'although no German interests were involved and we must have been aware of the threat of a world war', Germany had rejected British attempts at mediation, issued a premature ultimatum to Russia and then declared war. These points which related to vital issues of German foreign policy in the July crisis have been subjected to continuous examination down to our day and have again and again led to accusations against the German government of 1914. In Germany they were now raised by a man of whom it was known that he had totally disapproved of the alliance with Austria-Hungary, who before the start of the war had done everything to achieve a rapprochement between Germany and Britain and who in doing so had at times been guided more by his own judgment than by directives of the Foreign Ministry.

The accusations which Lichnowsky made towards the end of the war were a straight continuation of his wartime diplomacy. In Germany his memorandum did not at first have much influence. But to the Entente it was welcome material, although Lichnowsky had firmly disassociated himself from the assertion that the German government had brought about the war intentionally or consciously. He condemned its mistakes and in this context spoke of guilt but had no intention of accepting a guilt theory with legal consequences.

Fundamentally this was also the line taken by the writers of the pacifist left in Germany who wanted to discuss the causes of the war and find out where the responsibility lay, because they hoped that this would clear the air and start a reconciliation between the peoples who had fought each other in the war. In contrast to the violent arguments between the Americans, the British and the French, the Germans started by taking a long cool look at the Empire. The Reich government finally called for the appointment of a neutral commission and urged for all archives of the powers involved to be opened so that the guilt questions might be settled once and for all, but also because it hoped thereby to ward off the accusations and their consequences.

After the start of the Paris Conference Max Weber and ex-Chancellor Prince Max von Baden were responsible for the establishment in Heidelberg of an 'Association for a Policy of Law' at which Prince Max set out the distinct issues that would face a future neutral commission, separating responsibility for the war from responsibility for the prolongation of the war and from violations of international law. The objective to develop procedures for international law and in future to condemn declarations of war without prior arbitration as criminal violations of the law formed a logical goal to those who were refining the concept of war. The practical conclusions to be drawn from Wilson's ideas on peace were thus obvious. But here again some Germans were motivated by the wish to reject the guilt thesis and thus to deprive the Allies of grounds for severer peace conditions. Meanwhile the emphasis shifted both in Germany and abroad to propaganda and other forms of influencing the public and this had its repercussions on the attitude of the German peace delegation and of its leader.

German policy began with an important appointment: at the beginning of December 1918 the German ambassador to Copenhagen, Count Ulrich von Brockdorff-Rantzau, was put in charge of the Foreign Ministry. The Rantzaus belonged to the old aristocracy of

Holstein and had repeatedly played an important part in the history of northern Europe, as commanders and statesmen and as supports of the Danish throne, some of them having also served in Austria and in France. Count Brockdorff-Rantzau was a man who consciously played his historical role. As Ambassador to Copenhagen, as Foreign Minister of the Reich and leader of the German delegation at Versailles and later as ambassador to Moscow (1922–28) he was one of the outstanding makers of German foreign policy between 1914 and 1928. In November Prince Max von Baden would have liked to have seen him as his successor and he would probably have offered Rantzau the office of Chancellor had events given him time to do so. Brockdorff-Rantzau had sufficient backbone and independence to keep his distance from Wilhelminian policy. He was the incarnation of the haughty aristocrat *sans phrase*. Nevertheless he repeatedly established contact in the most open-minded manner with the leaders of German social democracy. In 1915 he had obtained German citizenship for the Russian revolutionary, Parvus. But he also enjoyed the complete confidence of various industrialists. Later in a similar unprejudiced manner he strengthened German relations with Bolshevik Russia and spoke not only of the 'joint interests' but once even of the 'community of fate' of Germany and Soviet Russia. We may well regard Versailles as the decisive stage on this road of Brockdorff-Rantzau's.

To the Council of Peoples' Representatives he made from the outset conditions reminiscent of the attitude adopted in these weeks by the Army High Command. This was because the army – as 'the absolutely vital support of law and order' – the National Assembly, the conclusion of peace and the protection of life and property were seen by many as an indissoluble whole which was in turn regarded as an essential prerequisite for all future policy. Count Brockdorff-Rantzau demanded the right to be consulted also on important domestic issues because he saw in their successful handling the basis for success in foreign policy and from the beginning insisted that he should be empowered to refuse to sign peace conditions that made it impossible for the German people to lead a 'decent existence'. In a major speech which the Foreign Minister made to the Weimar National Assembly on 14 February 1919 he argued that the future peace must be based on the principles of Wilson's Fourteen Points, without additions or alterations: on the League of Nations, the obligation to recognise international arbitration, a general renunciation of armaments, general agreement on the international solution of social questions and the unqualified recognition of the principle of peoples' right to self-determination, to be applied in connection with the union of German-speaking Austria with the German Reich and henceforth in all frontier settlements.

Although Brockdorff-Rantzau certainly exercised a dominating influence on German foreign policy during the six months that he was in office he did not decide it singlehanded. Erzberger, who had conducted the armistice negotiations and the ensuing negotiations, sought increasingly to influence the government's foreign policy. And in addition General Groener emerged as the spokesman of the Army High Command and as the opponent of Brockdorff-Rantzau.

Groener was concerned primarily with the plans of the Allied armies towards the Soviet Union. Of these he learned something between January and May from the head of the information service of the staff of the American supreme commander, Colonel Conger, who secretly established contact with German diplomats and soldiers and who had a number of talks with Brockdorff-Rantzau, Erzberger, Hindenburg and above all Groener, who certainly took a more optimistic view of the prospects of American military diplomacy than was justified. From the German Ministry Conger received a memorandum for transmission to the American President setting out the view that Germany regarded the exchange of notes before the armistice as the legal basis of the future peace and that it would cite the principles of equality and the right of national self-determination in its support. In mid-March Conger visited Kolberg. On this occasion it was primarily military questions that were discussed: the continued presence of German troops in the Baltic region and military action against the Bolsheviks. Groener now felt justified in impressing upon the Foreign Minister his hope that a deepening of the divisions in the enemy coalition might open up more favourable prospects for Germany. Wilson's idea of a League of Nations on the other hand the General viewed with the greatest suspicion; and with regard to Germany's future frontier with Poland, he refused to consider the populations's right of self-determination because to him the loss of Posen was as unbearable for historical and military reasons as the abandonment of western Prussia or of Upper Silesia, whereas the Foreign Ministry was thinking in terms of shorter front lines for the defence of Germany's interests.

At two cabinet meetings at the end of April Brockdorff-Rantzau and Groener presented their views one after the other. The Foreign

Minister expected the Allies to hand over the completed text of a peace treaty which they actually later did. He proposed to respond to this not by rejecting it outright, not by submitting a complete counter-draft, but by preparing detailed comments which would pick holes in the text with the aim of getting better terms on certain points. But this demanded the possibility of negotiations which the leader of the German delegation wanted to conduct in authoritarian fashion on his own responsibility. From the beginning Brockdorff-Rantzau's main aim was to attack the moral foundation of the enemy's war guilt thesis and to return to the legal basis of the pre-armistice agreements. Groener's primary concern on the other hand was to preserve the army on the basis of general conscription. On this point he wanted complete inflexibility on the grounds that it was essential to protect the frontiers in the east and to fight Bolshevism. But Brockdorff-Rantzau refused to be won over to this line. He made it known that in the policy towards Bolshevik Russia he saw common action with the Western powers as the only possibility but did not wish to destroy future opportunities. But he certainly could not accept the strategic position of the army leadership as an essential prerequisite for a future peace.

The German delegation departed in the shadow of an attempt to familiarise both German and non-German opinion with the ideas that the Foreign Ministry regarded as the basis for future peace. At the suggestion of Count Bernstorff, the former ambassador to Washington who was now in charge of the peace bureau of the Foreign Ministry, the public was acquainted with a German proposal which insisted on the League of Nations as an everlasting association in which all members had equal rights. No attempt was made to differentiate to any extent on colonial issues and the introduction of self-administration was envisaged for all colonies. This was the first effort by the Germans to define an area of ideas where it was thought that the opponent could be met. But it quickly became evident that the complicated discussions of the Allied statesmen did not ease the position of the German negotiators and that anything that might encourage them to make counter-proposals was strictly ruled out. The Germans later coined the phrase of the 'dictated peace of Versailles'. It would be more correct to speak of the peace of isolation in which Germany found itself because of its past policy but which was also a reflection of the instability of the coalition of the Allied powers whose strongest common bond was the war against the German Reich.

On the afternoon of 7 May 1919 the peace conditions were handed to the German delegation. For this act the representatives of the Allies had gathered in the great hall of the Trianon Palace at Versailles before the Germans were led in. Already on their journey and during their stay the German delegation were under the impression of unusual measures. Its members were under constant control. This step was apparently motivated by fear of secret contacts which might split the Allies. In the light of Conger's mission and of Groener's proposals such fears do not seem to have been totally unjustified. But Brockdorff-Rantzau's reaction was that of the *grand seigneur* whose pride was deeply wounded; it was a very personal and emotional response, although it may well have been conscious, intended and perhaps even carefully planned in advance.

When the Germans had taken their seats Clemenceau as chairman of the assembly rose to deliver the opening address in which he recalled the events at Versailles in 1871 and the preliminary peace which had ended the Franco–German war on 26 February 1871. Clemenceau spoke of the 'second treaty of Versailles' which seemed to explain the choice of location. The thought of revenge for the defeat of 1871 was therefore certainly present on the French side.

After his speech Clemenceau sat down again while the secretary of the conference handed the bulky text of the peace treaty to the head of the German delegation with the customary courtesies. Brockdorff-Rantzau rose only briefly, sat down again immediately afterwards, placed the text of his speech before him without casting a glance at it and, seated, began without hesitation to deliver his prepared reply. If the leaders of the conference had remained just within the limits of diplomatic form Brockdorff-Rantzau now expressed to the whole assembly in novel form his deep contempt for this act. He had prepared at least three drafts of his speech and chose the most outspoken version which attacked the war guilt verdict of the Allies:

> We know the force of the hatred that confronts us here and we have heard the impassioned call of the victors that we should pay as the vanquished and be punished as criminals. We are asked to say that we alone were responsible for the war; such a confession from my lips would be a lie.

He spoke of Germany's willingness to admit that it had done wrong in the war but immediately went over to the counter-attack by referring in scathing terms to those who had fallen victim to the Allied blockade when there was already an armistice because the French and British – for not very creditable commercial reasons – had not ended the blockade until March, at the insistence of the Americans.

In one respect the response of the German Foreign Minister was certain of success: it caused a great stir. In Germany it was given a mixed reception; among the French and the British public it caused indignation which deprived the factual part of the speech of any effect. Because the Count made a strong impression by the manner of his response he focused attention completely on the war guilt thesis as the point of honour of the peace treaty conditions. He used this point to show up as unjust and as the clear result of the political situation the treatment meted out to Germany by the victors, against which Germany appealed to the higher principles of law which were recognised also by its enemies. Brockdorff-Rantzau even described the exchange of notes of October and November 1918 as a 'treaty' on the peace principles, a claim which was certainly more than disputable in terms of international law. At the same time the German Foreign Minister showed himself willing to examine the bases of the 'pre-peace'. As intended he avoided any clear statement on the acceptance or rejection of the conditions but gave the impression that the Germans would measure them against the peace principles of the American President and treat them accordingly and that the statement of Germany's war guilt had no prospect of being accepted. This must be seen as more than a carefully calculated tactical counter-move.

The Germans were given fifteen days in which to reply during which there were to be no oral negotiations. But it was not until twenty-two days later, on 29 May, that the German counter-proposals with comprehensive comments on the Allied conditions were handed over. In the meantime there was an active exchange of notes during which views were defined and the tone became less conciliatory. The German delegation handed over seventeen notes, some of which took the form of extensive memoranda on various complexes of the peace conditions. The Allied draft resembled a badly arranged book which dealt with a number of very distinct issues which the experts concerned only gradually succeeded in unravelling. The reparations section alone covered eighty-one articles and had been assembled into a set of carefully worked out regulations the full significance of which only emerged on detailed examination. In Articles 231–5 Germany and its allies were described as causing the war and held responsible for all losses and damages incurred by the Allied and Associated Powers. The extent of these damages was to be definitely assessed by the Reparations Commission not later than 1 May 1921 so that on the basis of their investigations a settlement plan could be prepared. In the intervening period, that is in less than two years, Germany was to make a fantastic advance payment of 20 milliard mark in gold.

The reactions to the first news of the conditions handed over at Paris were unanimously negative in Berlin and in Weimar. The Reich government's first comments were on the same lines. Inside the government coalition the most determined opposition to acceptance came now and later from the Democratic Party, whereas the leaders of the Majority Social Democrats subsequently revealed themselves as being at odds with each other over the decisive issue and the *Zentrum* under Erzberger's influence also soon began to react with less unanimity. The depressed helplessness of those days is reflected in the first words of the Prime Minister of the Reich, Scheidemann, that this day they were witnessing 'the nadir of Germany's fate . . . we stand at the graveside of the German people if all the things described here as peace conditions become contractual facts'. With these words he merely gave expression to the feelings of wide sections of the German population to whom the Allied conditions now brought home the full force of the German defeat, so different from the prolonged illusions of victory during the war. Scheidemann's words suggested the answer 'unacceptable', without his explicitly saying either yea or nay; because every reply would only push Germany 'even more hopelessly towards political and national destruction'. But on the basis of a vote of their parliamentary group the Democratic Reich ministers Dernburg, Schiffer and Preuss called upon Scheidemann to reject the peace conditions outright. Erzberger, however, who was strongly opposed to this line, warned against a 'one day success' that would merely create uncertainty.

Scheidemann gave such melodramatic expression to the emotional disturbance of the politicians that it was almost impossible to distinguish clearly between a political sense of reponsibility and the emotional response of deeply patriotic feelings. His speech to the National Assembly in the great hall of Berlin University of 12 May was an eloquent expression of despair and indignation and already contained the basic elements of those judgements that determined subsequent views of the peace in Germany, a peace which Scheidemann even then condemned as a 'plan to murder' the German people. The factual part of his speech was – in spite of all warnings – the statement now formulated more clearly than four days previously: 'In the opinion of the Reich government this treaty is unacceptable.' The coalition partners agreed at any rate that the German delegation must remain at Versailles and depart only with the express consent of the Reich government. A break-off was thus avoided. An official pronouncement to the Allies remained for the time being a matter for the peace delegation while excited discussion on a rejection of the peace treaty and the likely consequences of such an action continued.

It appears that a resumption of military operations was not considered. But the German Foreign Ministry was afraid Bavaria might break away from the Reich if the peace treaty was not signed. The reports which reached Berlin from Ravensburg, to where the Bavarian government had escaped from the revolutionary government, and from Munich, however, amounted clearly to recommendations against accepting the treaty conditions. Although it was thought likely that as a result the French would occupy Bavaria, observers considered that in the last resort such an event would revive Bavarian loyalty to the Reich. Military action against individual parts of Germany seemed anyway not to cause any more fear. Moreover, the Germans assumed that in this way they could for a while pass onto someone else the difficult problem of feeding the population. Another factor which entered was the hope of a renewed strengthening of the population's determination to resist from which a great national counter-movement would one day emerge.

But the link of the eastern provinces with the Reich government really threatened to break when there were moves to use arms to prevent the Poles from taking possession of the regions which they had been promised, if necessary even to separate these provinces from the Reich and to set up an independent German eastern state. But nothing came of these attempts when the military refused to support them.

Against a background of the threat of civil war, the breakaway of the provinces in the east and the fear of more attacks by the Bolshevik forces in the Baltic region, the differences in the Reich government and among the leaders of the coalition parties went on. The fear of the odium associated with the responsibility for signing the peace treaty formed the strongest obstacle on the road of a decision. It was Erzberger who sought to end these discussions in which the arguments of the National Right now prevailed and were generally shared; he pressed for a quick end to the exchange of notes between the Germans and the Allies in Paris and for handing over comprehensive German counter-proposals. As Secretary of State in charge of the German armistice commission he more than anyone else appreciated the problems of the situation and had come to the conclusion that the state of war must be terminated as soon as possible, so that the Reich could get back its freedom to take domestic and foreign policy decisions. In a memorandum to Scheidemann he set out the probable consequences of a refusal to sign the peace conditions without then being able to persuade the majority of the Cabinet to accept his view. The principle by which Erzberger was guided was clear and above the smears later spread by the extreme Right. Because it was in his nature to isolate from other decisions whatever he regarded as the most important issue, he now sought unconditionally to subordinate all else to the need to preserve the unity of the Reich so that its economic and political reconstruction could begin in secure conditions.

But within the *Zentrum* opinions remained divided until they settled for a compromise by which the Germans would agree to sign under protest provided items affecting the honour of the nation were removed. The discussion of the peace treaty thus moved away further still from factual problems and concentrated entirely on points of honour. On the basis of this decision an understanding with the Social Democrats became possible.

The paper war begun by Brockdorff-Rantzau was viewed with increasing displeasure by the Reich government. But as Brockdorff-Rantzau took no notice of the objections which reached him from Berlin a conflict between the leader of the peace delegation and the government became inevitable. After Brockdorff-Rantzau had ignored a formal request of the Reich Cabinet not to transmit any more notes which Berlin heard about only through the press, a quickly arranged meeting between Brockdorff-Rantzau and three members of the Cabinet at Spa – halfway between Berlin and Paris – could do no more than to clear the air for a little while. Having begun an examination of the German documents, part of the Cabinet was, moreover, convinced that a systematic historical investigation of the war guilt question might show Germany in an unfavourable light; it was therefore thought advisable not to regard the war guilt thesis any longer as the central point of German criticism. But this amounted to a disavowal of the manner in which Brockdorff-Rantzau had conducted the negotiations; this the Foreign Minister was not prepared to accept and probably could not accept. He called four experts to Versailles, the historian Hans Delbrück, Max Weber from Heidelberg, Count Montgelas and Felix Mendelssohn, all of whom later assisted with the publication of the German documents concerning the outbreak of the war, so that they would append their names to a memorandum against the war guilt thesis which was prepared specially at Versailles and transmitted by Brockdorff-Rantzau to the Allies on 28 May, contrary to Berlin's strict orders.

One day later the German counter-proposals were handed over as requested by the government in Berlin. They were characterised by a considerable rapprochement to the position of the Allies and accepted both the long-service army of 100,000 men and the renunciation of battleships. They were reconciled to the loss of Alsace-Lorraine – although only after a plebiscite the outcome of which was, however, hardly in doubt. They agreed to the transfer of a stretch of territory to Poland; they wanted to provide the new Polish state with free ports in Danzig, Königsberg and Memel and envisaged a railway treaty which gave it good connections with these ports. Even on the reparations question the German concessions were considerable. In money terms the Germans offered 100 milliard gold mark – a sum that was higher than the American minimum estimates – as interest-free compensation payment. Of special interest among the contributions in kind was the offer to supply coal to France until the complete restoration of the mines destroyed in the war and to help with the rebuilding of the devastated regions of Belgium and Northern France. On the other hand the Germans asked for few Allied concessions. They took the line developed by Count Bernstorff that Germany should as far as possible place itself firmly behind the American principles in so far as there was any chance of benefiting from them. Germany thus made the following demands: its immediate acceptance on equal terms in a League of Nations provided with strong executive authority; full guarantee that the Germans in Austria and Bohemia would be allowed to determine their own fate; neutral commissions to examine the war guilt question with access to all secret archives of the states involved.

The rejection of the German counter-proposals threw Weimar

into a state of complete confusion. But looked at in the larger context they did in some respects achieve modifications of the peace conditions. The future of upper Silesia was to be decided by a plebiscite, whereas before it was simply to have been handed over to Poland. The provisions concerning the Saar were considerably modified by a new formula under which the possibility of a future return of this region to Germany was made dependent on a plebiscite. Other provisions regarded as painful by Germany – the prohibition of a union of German-speaking Austria with the Reich, the occupation of the Rhineland and all disarmament and reparations clauses – remained basically unchanged. The whole was tied up with an ultimatum demanding acceptance or rejection within five days.

The German Foreign Minister's persistent attacks on the Allied thesis that Germany was responsible for the war failed completely. In the end the issue was put even more uncompromisingly in the cover note which accompanied the final treaty text when it was handed to the Germans on 16 June. Once more the decision to accept or reject the Allied conditions hung upon a thread because the demand for a quick reply was coupled with a condemnation of the wartime opponent. There was suddenly almost complete unanimity in the National Assembly from the *Deutschnationale* to the Social Democrats that the verdict of guilty must be rejected in the firmest possible terms; even the Independent Social Democrats were not prepared to accept it. There was no party in the National Assembly prepared voluntarily to agree to the peace terms. Encouraged by the partial success of their tactics the Democrats tried to strengthen the resistance. The situation was complicated by the fact that the majority of the Social Democratic group in the National Assembly no longer supported the majority of their ministers. A break-up of the coalition seemed inevitable when during the night from 18–19 June the Cabinet under the chairmanship of the Reich President proceeded to the vote and the result was found to be a deadlock. Seven ministers voted in favour of signing the treaty and seven against; the Social Democrats were split. Thereupon the Scheidemann government resigned on 20 June.

The next day brought a further indication of the prevailing confusion which upset many people and which was certainly memorable although it had no political significance. The German fleet interned at Scapa Flow under British supervision was scuttled by its crew; it disappeared in the waters of the North Sea on the decision of its commander but without a 'blow being struck'. The creation of Tirpitz was outlived by its creator. In some sense it remained loyal to the laws under which it had served. Its end was as dramatic as its history and as far from 'the noise of battle and the smoke of gunfire' as its birth. In the years to come the nationalists glorified this event. At the end of June 1919 it merely strengthened the national feeling of gloom and did not make it any easier to take the serious political decisions that were required.

In the new government formed by the Social Democrat, Bauer, the Democrats no longer participated and the *Zentrum* did so only with inner reservations, merely because of the inescapable need to assure an acceptance of the peace treaty. But as the Social Democrat, Scheidemann, had left the government the Social Democrat, Erzberger, now became its strongest political force. He took over the Reich Ministry of Finance which because of the reparations problems and their financial and fiscal consequences became the most important of the ministries, while the Social Democrat, Hermann Müller, was entrusted at this difficult hour with the direction of foreign policy. It was he who signed the peace treaty jointly with the *Zentrum* minister, Johannes Bell.

But before this occurred the Germans tried one last escape. On 22 June the new government declared itself ready to accept the peace conditions in a limited form provided they were not linked with a recognition of Germany's war guilt and without agreeing to the demand for a trial of the Kaiser or for the prosecution of German individuals in connection with the conduct of the war. The government statement was approved in the National Assembly by a large majority; only the Independent Social Democrats abstained. The German reply of the same day also listed other reservations which it described as basic to the peace treaty. It rejected all responsibility for the consequences of not being able to comply with the treaty and referred to possible difficulties that could arise from opposition by the population to a separation of the eastern regions. It protested against the seizure of Germany's colonial possessions and called for re-examination of the treaty provisions by the Council of the League of Nations within two years after the signing of the treaty. In the Council the representatives of Germany were to have the same right as the contracting powers.

These reservations went pretty far. It cannot be disputed that they put to a hard test the Allies' determination to keep to their ultimatum.

They explored to the last the possibilities of lessening the severity of the peace treaty. But the Allied statesmen anxious to be ready for any eventuality had asked Foch to prepare plans for military action if Germany rejected the peace terms. It emerged that by now the military possibilities were already limited. A thrust to Berlin and Weimar, with the subsequent occupation of Germany by the Allied forces then still available, Foch regarded as totally out of the question in view of the opposition to be expected and of Germany's military strength at the time. Meanwhile demobilisation had begun and the superiority of the Allied forces in France over the reformed but not yet disarmed German units was no longer as great as six months previously, although it was still sufficient to permit limited operations. An advance along the Main Foch regarded as possible. It could have been linked with the disarmament and special treatment of Southern Germany. In North Germany an operation up to the Weser seemed possible. More ambitious plans would have needed renewed mobilisation so as to exclude any possibility of a military setback. This thought had a disturbing effect on the statesmen of the three Great Powers. They therefore hoped that the Germans would give way and accept the peace terms but did not abandon their determined stand on the demand for global acceptance of their conditions and revealed no sign of weakness.

If Weimar still hoped to gain anything by further delays its illusions were shattered the following day by the Allies' note refusing to extend the ultimatum, thus leaving the Reich government barely twenty-four hours to make its final decision. Under the pressure of this new turn of events there was no time for the National Assembly to protest. But the *Zentrum* group in the assembly was thrown into renewed confusion when the general commanding the Reichswehr, Maercker, announced that if the treaty were signed the officer corps would disassociate itself from the government, thereby jeopardising the preservation of law and order at home; and the Reichswehr Minister, Noske, who had previously been in favour of signing the treaty, now thought it necessary to confirm this depressing news and thus also caused the Social Democratic group to have renewed doubts. It was not until a telegram arrived from General Groener denying the statements of Maercker and Noske that the situation was clarified after renewed intervention by the Reich President. On 23 June the National Assembly resolved by a large majority to authorise the government to sign the peace treaty. In the midst of obscure happenings a decision was thus taken which permitted the inescapable to happen but which did not mean that the Germans accepted the peace terms without qualifications, any more than the Russians had done a year before at Brest-Litovsk.

The Reich Government acted without delay and on the same day signified its readiness to sign the peace treaty. But it made a declaration documenting in the only remaining way that its decision was taken under duress:

> From the latest communication of the Allied and Associated Governments the government of the German Republic has learned with dismay that they are determined to compel Germany by extreme force to accept even those peace conditions that without being of material importance are aimed at depriving the German people of its honour. An act of force does not touch the honour of the German people. After the terrible sufferings of the last years the German people lack the means with which to defend its honour against the outside world. Surrendering to superior force but without retracting its opinion regarding the unheard of injustice of the peace conditions the government of the German republic therefore declares its readiness to accept and sign the peace conditions imposed by the Allied and Associated Governments.

It can be regarded as a tragedy or as one of the famous ironies of history that the effects of this war in the form of the conditions laid down by the Paris Conference hit and burdened not imperial Germany but the new state. It remains impossible to say what would have been the eventual outcome if Germany had not signed the peace treaty. But the situation which confronted the Reich government and the National Assembly must in the last resort be judged only in the light of the ideas which referred to the political shaping of the future. The worst peace treaty was bearable if it created even a trace of real peace and thereby opened a way into the future. It was this situation that Lenin in April 1917 had advocated peace for Russia and finally even became reconciled to the conditions of Brest–Litovsk. In the last resort domestic policy took precedence over foreign policy in Germany even at this decisive hour. In the end the leading men in the government, Erzberger, Noske and David, but also General Groener who finally voted in favour of signing, were motivated by the idea of buying at a high price security both externally and internally. They saw the conclusion of peace as a means of internal consolidation and protection of the Reich, whose unity seemed threatened primarily from within, against disintegration and revolution.

But we are confronted with difficulties as soon as we raise the question of what the aims were for the future. It is difficult to find a common basis in the visions which started from Germany's internal consolidation. We can unreservedly point to a profound dislike of Bolshevism and of revolution. But the split in the government, in the political groups of Weimar and in many an individual's mind was evidence of a feeling of impotent isolation created by the peace conditions; and this deprived the new beginning of German policy of its impetus, even before the Treaty of Versailles was signed. Widespread lack of resolution, lack of generally accepted ideas that might have helped the new political start to surmount the crisis, which was not resolved by the conclusion of the discussions on the Weimar constitution, are symptomatic of a state of great mental and political stress. The attitude and reactions of the political Right and overwhelmingly also of the government parties convey, in spite of general criticism of the Wilhelminian style of government, the impression of a people lastingly stunned by the impact of military defeat and the outcome of the war. There was no group that did not feel bitter about the failure of the hopes of victory, the heavy sacrifices of the war and the peacemaking, the triumph of the enemy or the Kaiser's abdication, the overthrow of the monarchy or the peace terms and all the circumstances surrounding the 'dictated peace of Versailles', the loss of national power, the loss of economic strength and the direct consequences of a war which had become so senseless.

To the future the peace treaty bequeathed an atmosphere of lasting political and mental depression in Central Europe. Given this fact in a Europe in which three out of five great powers had been eliminated – one of them completely while the other two were facing an uncertain fate – and in which ten new states had been created or assumed a totally new shape, any lasting settlement presented a permanent problem with unforeseeable consequences. At the Paris Conference Lloyd George, certainly from the Fontainebleau memorandum of 25 March 1919 onwards, showed increasing opposition to the French expansion of power. He had some success in preventing France from establishing a foothold on German soil on the left bank of the Rhine. But on most issues he was compelled to take account of British opinion which was still dominated by wartime nationalism and which changed only gradually later on. Lloyd George's efforts were also hampered by the necessity not to allow a break to occur with Europe's second great power, France. Then and later British foreign policy was forced by the new situation in Europe into the paradoxical situation of restraining the expansion of French power while always remaining associated, if not allied with France in a sort of West European duumvirate which until the beginning of the Second World War sought to bridge the phase of unconsolidated conditions in international relations. But even the stubborn advocate of the security principle on the French side, Clemenceau, was more than once prepared to make concessions and it was certainly not for personal reasons that he became the most unyielding spokesman of the Allied cause at the Paris negotiations. He had behind him French public opinion which was more afraid of giving way than of alternatives which for the moment lay in the dim and distant future; but he also had to contend with Marshal Foch and Raymond Poincaré, the President of the Republic and for long Clemenceau's bitter political opponent against whom he now supported the nationalist Right and whom six months after the treaty of Versailles he pushed out of French politics.

The ultimate reason why the Anglo-French Entente, regarded as vital by Clemenceau in spite of all differences, was not abandoned from then on was the disappearance from European politics of the United States. It was logical that after the collaboration of the three world powers during the peace conference and after the compromise structure of the peace treaty on the day that the treaty was signed at Versailles a Franco-British and a Franco-American treaty should be concluded which gave France the indispensable compensation for its concessions on the duration of the occupation of the Rhineland. This took the form of a guarantee and the promise of assistance from its partners if Germany were to violate the provisions concerning the demilitarisation of the Rhineland zone. Such a step was to be regarded as a hostile act and to be resisted jointly. The coming into force of the Franco-British treaty was, however, linked with the assumption that it would be preceded by the ratification of an identical treaty between the United States and France. But as this never happened the Franco-British guarantee treaty never came into force either. The National Right in France never forgave Clemenceau this failure. The British Foreign Office was prepared to commit itself to a permanent, legally binding association with France only if the United States remained in Europe. But as this did not happen France – with a declining population and a decreasing armaments potential – was permanently dependent on support from Central Europe and compelled to some extent to take British policy into consideration.

Wilson signed the document of Versailles; but the US Senate refused to ratify it, thereby disowning the President's policy in a manner that was tragic both for him and for Europe. The state of war between Germany and the United States was not ended *de jure* until two years later, after Wilson, who was by then a very sick man, had ceased to be President. America's withdrawal destroyed a substantial part of Wilson's work. His efforts at Paris, later frequently misinterpreted, to meet British and French interests sprang from the desire to achieve the greatest and most important of his aims for which he needed the collaboration of Britain and France. This aim was the permanent assurance of world-wide peace which given continuous American participation could indeed have been of the greatest importance.

Wilson managed to push through the adoption of the statutes of the League of Nations during the peace talks with Germany at the plenary session of the peace conference. They became an integral part of the Treaty of Versailles and compelled the Allied and Associated signatory states, entirely in the spirit of the Fourteen Points, to adhere to the principle of general disarmament, the introduction of arbitration in international disputes and the establishment of a permanent international court; they also condemned secret treaties. No less important was a clause which held out the hope of a possible future revision of even the harshest provisions of the peace treaty. Article XIX stated that the League could 'from time to time advise the reconsideration by Members of the League of Nations of treaties which had become inapplicable, and the consideration of international conditions whose continuance might endanger the peace of the world'. Seen in the light of this provision the League of Nations could therefore become more important than the whole peace treaty. There seems justification in the claim that many difficulties only arose as the result of the prospects opened up by this Article. But in view of the great importance which the League of Nations acquired also in this context the disappearance from the European stage of the United States was a double blow. They left to the European powers and their allies an important instrument of international policy designed to ensure world peace; but they refused to give lasting protection to the principles on which this instrument was based. The United States Senate refused to let the United States join the League of Nations in the same way that it abstained from approving the Treaty of Versailles. Twelve days before the signing at Versailles the storm unleashed by the Republican opposition broke when the President submitted the draft to the Senate for ratification. The Republicans were joined by some of his old supporters whom he had disappointed by his attitude at Paris, by the German-speaking Americans who were opposed to the treatment of their former country, by the Irish Americans because to them the guarantee of territorial integrity embodied in the acts of the League of Nations threatened the aims of the independence movement in the mother country. But the main reason for the rapid growth of the opposition to the treaty lay in the deep-seated view of many Americans that the country should keep out of the complications of European affairs.

13. The new south-eastern and eastern Europe

During the painfully prolonged clarification of the situation in Paris a series of uncontrolled events occurred in south-eastern and eastern Europe which were a direct continuation of the war and were designed to achieve by force a new settlement of the frontiers. Those mainly affected were the losers, Germany, Russia and above all Austria and Hungary. Incidents and finally fighting occurred early in 1919 at Germany's eastern frontier in the Posen region and in western Prussia and later repeatedly in Upper Silesia, the fate of which the peace treaty of Versailles had made dependent on a plebiscite. Almost at the same time Polish troops entered eastern Galicia which had belonged to the Austrian part of the Empire. They crushed the Western Ukranian population, while the Russian part of the eastern Ukraine which in the peace of Brest-Litovsk had obtained a doubtful independence was hard pressed by the Red Army and finally occupied in the summer. But resistance by the supporters of Ukranian autonomy to both Polish and Soviet Russian rule continued for years.

Bitter fighting took place between Czechoslovakia and Communist Hungary at the Slovak–Hungarian frontier where the dividing line had not yet been finally drawn. It was followed by fighting in eastern Hungary when the Rumanians occupied Transylvania.

In the south, in southern Styria, in Carniola and Carinthia the new frontier of southern Slavonia remained in dispute. There were constant incidents in Dalmatia and also on the new south Slav–Italian frontier where a conflict of international significance finally occurred over the Croatian port of Fiume, giving new stimulus to the slogans of Irredentist nationalism. The agitation and actions brought forth by the heightened national sensitivity and the tensions created by the war here took forms which were characteristic of the period of transition. The conflict over Fiume is a good example of the confused political conditions which prevailed in the disputed regions of the former Danube monarchy where the old system had collapsed and nationalities and nationalism were engaged in a bitter feud. In the political history of Italy it became the rallying point of the resurgent Italian nationalism of the post-war era.

The link with the nationalism of the pre-war period becomes visible in the right-wing extremist organisation *Associazione Nazionalista* whose focal point from 1910 onwards had been a number of literary publications, particularly the journal *L'Idea Nazionale,* and from whose midst had emerged the intellectual *avant garde* of Fascism. Some of these men were later rewarded with high honours by the Fascists: the publicist Enrico Corradini, the deputy Luigi Federzone and the economist Alfredo Rocco. Independently of them the renegade socialist, Mussolini, had joined forces with an organisation which on the model of a commando type unit, the *Arditi,* applied the methods of military organisation to the day-to-day political struggle. The élite of the *Associazione Nazionale* produced the political doctrine which Rocco in March 1919 expressed in the formula: national unity for the fight against the world outside. The direct link with war aims advocated by the Italian nationalist Right is evident. Their *Italia oltremare* anticipated the expansion of the Fascist state. Rocco proclaimed an age of 'super imperialism'; the future world powers as he saw them were the United States of North America which he thought would control the whole of South America, Japan which would rule China, but also Germany and Russia which would regain their strength. Italy needed to find a place among these powers. As advocated by the sociologist Vilfredo Pareto this élite pretended to be guiding the people whom it used for its purpose.

One of the first of these actions was the attack on Fiume which before the conclusion of the peace treaty of Trianon was legally in no-man's-land. It had once belonged to the Hungarian part of the Danube monarchy. The city was occupied by Italian as well as by British and French troops and was therefore not in south Slav hands, although there were everlasting rumours about an impending Croat coup. Under the influence of feelings against the Nitti government that pervaded the nationalist opposition a number of incidents occurred in and around Fiume which led the Allied High Command to withdraw the Italian troops completely from the city and to transfer them to Italian Ronchi. Nationalist officers there plotted a coup against Fiume; they turned to Gabriele D'Annunzio who in May 1915 had been the herald of war and who now expressed himself ready to take charge of this coup by which Fiume was finally to become part of Italy.

A day after the peace treaty of St Germain, on 11 September, the coup was staged in the form of a solemn entry into Fiume of several hundred soldiers from Ronchi. Militarily this was an unimportant act. Because it was to be assumed that the French and British occupation troops would not meet this demonstration with force. Politically it was an affront to France and Britain which both powers were forced to accept. For the rest it was a big bluff which gave its perpetrators a noisy triumph.

Official Italy did not support the coup; but it did as little to oppose it as did the Allied occupation troops. This enabled D'Annunzio, until the occupation of the city by regular Italian units, for several months to exercise almost unlimited authority as commandant of the city. He ordered a state of siege and gave Fiume its own constitution which was a model for and an anticipation of the corporative ideas of Fascist Italy. This episode not only revealed the neo-nationalist movement as an association of the dissatisfied, of discontented soldiers and ex-officers, of students and restive *petit bourgeois* who had fought in the war and failed in peace but who remained loyal to certain military habits; it also contributed to the formation of the neo-nationalist doctrine with D'Annunzio's inflammatory rhetoric, which later served as a model for the Fascist dictatorship's propaganda, and with a charter of authoritarian discipline being imposed on the community. Nor should we underestimate the effect of D'Annunzio's attack on the peace treaties. His slogan was 'Versailles', which he used as referring to the whole post-war period and contrasted with the 'profoundly new development' in Fiume. It was in Fiume and 'not in Odessa' that in his view Europe's future had been revealed. Odessa had been evacuated by the Allies in April 1919 and occupied by the Bolsheviks. But D'Annunzio played on the renewed advance of the Slav peoples which he saw as aimed also against Italy even more than on the success of the Red Army and the growing consolidation of Soviet rule. Words such as D'Annunzio used about the Slav peoples of the Balkans the Slav nationalities of the Danube monarchy had previously heard only from anti-Slav and anti-Semitic spokesmen of the Vienna parliament. Even if we ignore the incredible distortion of the facts behind the Fiume story we are left with the impression of great and insurmountable tension between Italy and the southern Slavs over what view to take of the increasing hold which Italian nationalism was acquiring over the state.

Super-nationalism with its new doctrines took root wherever disappointment with the outcome of the war aroused deep feelings and wherever there was indignation about usurping 'robber nations'. But it flourished also in places where the slogan about autonomous self-determination promoted national awareness rather than an intellectual capacity to keep a sense of proportion or a feeling of what is right and proper without which there can be no productive order.

Against the background of these happenings the peace treaties that ended the war for south-east Europe and created a new system of states emerge only as carefully thought-out attempts; while they were undoubtedly based on reasoned argument they proved inadequate in the long run to establish a new order and to harmonise right with might. The peace treaty nearest in time to the Treaty of Versailles was concluded with what little remained of Austria on 10 September 1919 at the Paris suburb of St Germain-en-Laye. It sealed in legally binding form the end of the dual monarchy Austria-Hungary and confined Austria to the vicinity of Vienna and to some Alpine provinces. The peace treaty with Hungary followed later, on 4 June 1920 at the Grand Trianon Palace in Versailles, after the interlude of Communist rule which came to an end in August 1919 and after a period of subsequent internal consolidation.

The provisions of this treaty in many respects resemble important groups of articles of the Treaty of Versailles. By far the most important decision, however, which profoundly affected the fate of southern Europe, was the one which settled the new frontiers. As they were drawn Rumania, the new Czechoslovak state and also the newly established southern Slavonia found themselves with large areas with substantial German and Magyar minorities. This cannot, however, be seen as the vital problem affecting these new states, because the nationalities had long lived side by side and together in many parts of south-eastern Europe. But with the collapse of the dual monarchy and the acceptance of the right of political self-determination new states emerged based on associations of nationalities without being pure nation states; because in this part of Europe with its confusion of peoples there could be no such states.

Even Italy, which was given less than it had hoped for on the basis of the Treaty of London of 1915, received regions occupied by non-Italian people: South Tyrol to the Brenner with over 200,000 German-speaking inhabitants, some of the regions inhabited by Italians, Slovenes and Dalmatians, Friuli and Istria – together with the important ports of Trieste and Fiume and the former Austrian naval port Pula – and in Dalmatia to the city of Zadar and the island of Lagosta.

The substantial share of the remains of the Danube monarchy received by the new 'Kingdom of the Serbs, Croats and Slovenes' which had emerged from Serbia turned into a reality the ancient dream of the 'greater Serb', 'south Slav' or 'Illyrian' state. In 1929 the kingdom officially called itself 'Yugoslavia'. It was given southern Syria, which was inhabited predominantly by Slovenes, and Carniola with the capital Laibach (Ljubljana), which now became the centre of Slovenia, the north-western part of the kingdom. Croatia and Slavonia, Bosnia, the main part of Dalmatia and Hercegovina became the new Croatia with Zagreb as its capital. The old kingdom of Serbia with Belgrade which had survived the war on the side of the Allies, together with a few regions of southern Hungary, Montenegro and former Bulgarian districts in northern Macedonia, remained the core of the new Yugoslav state and controlled the army and the senior civil service. Its domination of the domestic policy of the federal state resulted in repeated conflicts with the other south Slav ethnic groups, particularly with the Croats who were as self-aware as they were restless. But the constitution which the constituent national assembly gave the state on 28 June 1929 recognised only three Yugoslav tribes in whose direction it made a few meaningless bows while dividing the whole kingdom into departments (*oblasti*) with roughly comparable numbers of inhabitants. The men in charge of these departments were given considerable authority and were subject only to control by the government in Belgrade. The federalism of the new state which was based on ethnic differences and historical development was restrained by Belgrade's administrative centralism which later survived only with the help of the dictatorship of the king.

The northern counterpart of the federation under Serb hegemony and Serb centralism was the centrally governed multi–nation state of Czechoslovakia. The fragmented party groups of the ethnically related Czechs and Slovaks who made up barely two-thirds of the entire population together possessed a majority in the Prague parliament and always formed the government. The national and parliamentary opposition groups to which belonged the Catholic Slovak People's Party joined the government only after the election of 1925 when the permanent coalition of the Peasant Party, the Czechoslovak National Socialists, the Peoples' Party and the Republican Party lost its stability and when the support of German and Slovak Agrarians was welcomed by the leading protectionist group of the Peasant Party and their Prime Ministers, Švehla and Udržal.

While Poland received the Austrian part of Galicia, Rumania gained a great mass of territory with the former Austrian Bukovina, the eastern Banate which was part of Hungary and the whole of Transylvania with its many ethnic islands in areas inhabited predominantly by Rumanians or Magyars or Germans. With the Dobrudja it also acquired a former Bulgarian territory with a substantial Bulgarian population. The ruthless Hungarian minorities policy of the past was now replaced by Rumanian centralism which gave the minorities individual rights and freedoms without giving them politically significant autonomy.

When Masaryk wrote in 1918 that in fact every consciously national community strove for its own national state he expressed the nationalistic notion which dominated national consciousness in Germany in the nineteenth century and foreshadowed that path which led to the emergence of a united nation-state. The victorious nationalities of the upheaval in south-eastern and eastern Europe in 1918–19 were agreed in their ultimate desire for statehood. But fundamentally this objective conflicted with the right of self-determination which had been proclaimed by Wilson and had originally sprung from the oppressed peoples' demand for autonomy. In the multi-nation reality of the nationality states of south-eastern and eastern central Europe the idea of the national state led to priority or even hegemony for the predominating nationalities, recreating the autonomy problem in a different form – one might say in reciprocal fashion – because in fact it repeated the relationship between ruling people and national minorities.

The Western Powers and in particular the United States became fully aware of these problems only after the beginning of the Paris Peace Conference and under the impact of developments in the Austro-Hungarian part of the world which was in a state of ferment and where force was the order of the day. Stimulated by Jewish groups and advised by American experts the Western Powers insisted on the protection of minorities as a corrective to the right of self-determination where it was interpreted in a nationalist sense and recognised as such; with great effort they imposed upon the reluctant states of south-eastern and eastern central Europe treaties for the protection of minorities. *De jure* they safeguarded the rights of minorities by guarantees and controls of the League of Nations. But these were artfully evaded and never became effective. The first treaty protecting a minority was signed with Poland on the day of Versailles, 28 June 1919. Further treaties, with Czechoslovakia, Greece, Yugoslavia and Rumania, followed in the autumn of 1919 and in 1920 after the peace treaties of St Germain-en-Laye, Neuilly-sur-Seine and Trianon.

With the treaties of St Germain and Trianon the Allied war front in south-eastern Europe was perpetrated in peacetime. They allocated to Austria and Hungary the role of small states. In an area of less than 100,000 square kilometres they accommodated under 8 million inhabitants and faced three medium sized states, each twice as big with almost double the number of inhabitants and above all with better equipped and numerically significant armies. But Austria and Hungary, in contrast to the substantially enlarged or newly formed states which had emerged from the territories and peoples of the former dual monarchy, did not suffer from permanent internal instability which manifested itself in endless conflicts. Four of these five states later became dictatorships, first Hungary, then Yugoslavia, then Austria and finally Rumania where Fascism and Antisemitism flourished. Only Czechoslovakia remained a parliamentary and democratic state, thanks to the delicate balance in parliament of the Czech parties. It was never possible to achieve a compromise between the confused and conflicting interests of German, Hungarian and Jewish groups, often with south Slav, east Slav or west Slav characteristics and languages; in part they demanded a separate existence and in part they were already fully caught up in the process of integration. If a settlement had been possible it could obviously only have happened through the establishment of an internally balanced territorial and ethnic federal system which Austria-Hungary in its historic hour had failed to create.

If only for economic reasons the states of the new south-eastern Europe stood in need of strong support from outside. To the extent that this coincided with the orientation of their foreign policy a dependence was thus established. Most difficult was the position of the countries which were at a disadvantage both economically and politically: Austria which was in need of imports and Hungary which because of its new frontiers was cut off in several places from its most important natural and traditional sources of supply. In addition Austria and Hungary faced difficult social problems. Vienna and Budapest were cities with millions of inhabitants which had once been centres of the Court with all that this involved, administration, officialdom, army leadership and an active as well as an inactive officer corps. Officials and officers lost their jobs because the state no longer needed their services in such numbers. The old upper class if it could not seek refuge on its own estates was pushed out. In part it displayed extremist psychological reactions to the outcome of the war and the peace negotiations.

In Hungary the minor nobility from which the imperial officialdom and the officer corps had been largely recruited became the standard bearers of a reactionary movement which in response to the short-lived Communist regime joined forces with the old landed aristocracy and set up an authoritarian state. The new Hungarian rulers secretly took ruthless action against Communists and Jews and set up concentration camps, hitherto unknown in Central Europe. Outwardly they strengthened the links with the past. After the consolidation in the autumn of 1919 Hungary continued constitutionally as a kingdom in which the royal authority was exercised not by a monarch but by a regent. The national assembly elected for this post the last commander-in-chief of the Austro–Hungarian navy, Admiral Miklós Horthy von Nagybánya. But the last monarch was unsuccessful in his attempt in the spring and autumn of 1921 to regain the Hungarian crown in several coups in which he was supported by the officer corps which had not been released from its oath of loyalty. He was finally defeated in a bitter battle outside the gates of Budapest. Although the traditional elements benefited from the restoration to power of Hungary's old upper class it proved impossible to bring back the old ruling house. The attempt to do so suffered the same fate as German plans of roughly the same period for the restoration of the monarchy in Bavaria and the union of this state with what remained of Austria.

The new system of states in south-eastern Europe which – without external intervention – contained numerous centres of conflict could achieve stability in domestic and foreign affairs only if these states became sufficiently consolidated to permit them to adopt a more liberal domestic policy. There were beginnings of this. In December 1921 the Austrian Federal Chancellor, Schober, concluded the Treaty of Prague–Lana with Czechoslovakia. Both states mutually guaranteed their territory and promised in case of an attack by a third party on one or the other to preserve neutrality and also not to permit in their state political or military organisations whose activity was directed against the existence or security of the other state. But in spite of the economic arrangements which went with this treaty it remained the only and therefore inadequate attempt – and one of which there was by no means universal approval – to bridge the gulf between the countries that wanted to maintain the *status quo* in the Danube region and the vanquished states which hoped to gain from a revision. The unrealistic 'greater Yugoslav' ideas of Bulgaria's second post-war Prime Minister, Stambulijski, who had signed the peace treaty of Neuilly, were based on a union of southern Slavonia and Bulgaria into a federation of Serbs, Croats, Slovenes and Bulgarians. They acquired significance only during the short period of tension between Britain and Turkey but failed to have any serious influence on the situation; when they came to grief it was not only because of opposition from the 'greater Serb-minded Prime Minister, Pašić'.

The relations of the states of south-eastern Europe with the rest of the continent quickly led to the creation of an alliance system which was designed within the framework of European politics to preserve the situation created by the peace treaties. After the Magyar restoration in what remained of Hungary this little Entente at first brought Czechoslovakia together with Yugoslavia and Rumania. It was the ambition of Take Ionescu, Foreign Minister of Rumania from 1920–21 and then for a short time Prime Minister, of the Czech Foreign Minister Eduard Beneš, and of President Masaryk to draw Poland and Greece into this alliance system. But repeated frontier disputes between Czechoslovakia and Poland prevented lasting co-operation. The alliance was further strained at times by a dispute between Yugoslavia and Rumania over the frontier in the Banate. Greece was uncooperative because it was cultivating good relations with Italy in view of the situation in the eastern Mediterranean and because of its desire to prevent a revision related only to Bulgaria and the peace treaty of Neuilly.

The whole system therefore remained fragmentary, although for years it was important when it came to the collaboration of the three central states of south-eastern Europe on important League of Nations questions. It began in August 1920 with a military alliance between Yugoslavia and Czechoslovakia for the purpose of preventing an attack by Hungary and any move to restore the Habsburg monarchy in Hungary. The alliance proved itself when in March and again in October ex-Emperor Charles tried to seize power in Hungary. In April 1921 Czechoslovakia concluded a military alliance with Rumania, which was followed by an alliance between Rumania and Yugoslavia aimed against Bulgaria.

To start with these alliances were concluded for short periods only, but they survived and were repeatedly renewed and supplemented until they developed into the pact of 1933. But before the Second World War no other projects aimed at large-scale integration in south-eastern and eastern central Europe came to fruition.

To begin with these alliances remained a diplomatic arrangement because it proved impossible to establish closer links given the big ethnic differences between the states concerned. No penetrating association developed; nor was it possible to establish close economic collaboration because to varying degrees these states were all competing with one another. To all three of them the export of timber was important. Yugoslavia and Rumania both exported grain for which there was no market in Czechoslovakia because the Czech Agrarian Party, for years the dominating voice in the government, made sure of high protective tariffs. Yugoslavia and Rumania on the other hand did not offer a sufficient market for the exports of Czechoslovakia on whose territory was situated over two-thirds of the entire industry of the former dual monarchy.

No economic compromise was possible without Hungary and Austria and this moreover presupposed co-operation with the neighbouring economic zones. But the policy of autarchy soon adopted by the members of the Little Entente could only offer limited encouragement to the possibilities of economic development which did in fact exist. But even in the wider context of European politics the Little Entente alliance for the preservation of the *status quo* brought with it many problems. Because of Yugoslavia's position and policy there was increasing tension between the whole system and Italy which began to emerge as the leading power in southern Europe. Rumania's annexation of Bessarabia after the Russian October revolution had been confirmed by the Central Powers in the peace of Bucharest and by the Allies in Paris but was responsible for tension between the Little Entente and Russia. At any rate a substantial strengthening of Italy or a return of Soviet Russia to the ranks of the great powers was likely to present the Little Entente with a serious test.

It was with this prospect in mind that the French adopted the policy of supporting the Little Entente. For France this policy, which it embarked upon as early as the Paris Conference, replaced the military interventionism of the last war years and the first post-war years when all attempts to support the counter-revolutionary forces in the Russian civil war had proved unsuccessful because of their military onesidedness and the lack of co-ordination.

From the autumn of 1919 onwards the history of the Russian civil war is a chronicle of the triumphs of the Red Army. On 1 February 1920 the Estonian government made peace at Dorpat. A few days later the last threat disappeared at the Siberian front when the French General Janin handed Admiral Kolchak, whose army was in a state of total disarray, over to the Bolshevik forces. In March in the south the remnants of Denikin's troops withdrew to the Crimea from where the Baltic General, Wrangell, made a last sally in the summer and for a few months held the border regions of the Sea of Asov. But in November 1920 Wrangell was forced to withdraw his troops from the Crimea and to give up the fight for Russia.

Meanwhile a new and far more serious threat to the Bolshevik state had arisen in the form of a Polish invasion. The provisions of the Treaty of Versailles had not touched upon the Polish frontier in the east. In December 1919 the Supreme Council of the Allies recommended an eastern frontier proposed by Lord Curzon, but the Poles did not agree to this. When the Russo-Polish negotiations over a frontier further to the east collapsed there was a military test of strength. In the autumn of 1919 Polish troops suddenly occupied the Vilna area; this belonged to Lithuania but its frontiers had not yet been internationally agreed and it was bare of troops. Subsequently Polish units penetrated into Bielorussia. In the course of the main thrust which began in January 1920 after the collapse of the armies of Kolchak, Denikin and Yudenich, Polish troops penetrated as far as Daugavpils, Gomel and Kiev.

This advance led to a surprising response from the Russian popula-

tion. For the first time since the revolution the Bolshevik rulers benefited from signs of nationalist emotion. The last supreme commander
of the Tsarist empire, General Brusilov, appealed to all ex-officers to put
themselves at the disposal of the Red Army in its struggle against
Polish aggression. Because of the collapse of the White Russian forces
it was the Red Army which profited from the resurgence of Russian
patriotism; strengthened and consolidated it shortly afterwards
launched a successful counter-attack. Instead of stopping at the Curzon
line it did as Lenin wished and penetrated deep into Poland; in July
1920 General Tukhachevsky reached the eastern suburbs of Warsaw,
Lemberg in the south, and in the north the east Prussian frontier. For
the first time the Red Army of the new Soviet power stood at the
gates of Central Europe. Only a year had passed since the Treaty of
Versailles; the peace treaty with Turkey, the last of the peace treaties
with the Central Powers, remained to be concluded when the unsolved Russian question presented itself to the Allies in a form that
seemed to jeopardise all that they had achieved.

There is no doubt that some members of the Politbureau of the
Bolsheviks pursued ambitious aims. Lenin above all thought of exploiting the unexpectedly favourable circumstances, of advancing further in the hope that the Polish workers would rise, and of carrying
the revolution into Central Europe. There were also those in the Politbureau who advised caution; they included Trotsky and Radek. But
Lenin had his way and experienced the worst defeat since his return
to Russia, which put an end for the time being to Russian expansion into territory of the new border states and confined Russian
history for the next years to internal consolidation of the Bolshevik
system.

It was more than just supply difficulties and manifestations of exhaustion among the Russian army which in mid-August 1920 led to
the 'miracle on the Vistula' and forced the Russians to withdraw.
Joseph Pilsudski, first President and commander-in-chief of Poland,
appreciated that Poland could not stand up to the Russian onslaught
alone and addressed an urgent request for help to the Allies. This led
the French to take immediate tangible steps to help the Poles and in
July French war material reached the Polish front via Germany.
General Weygand, Foch's chief of staff, took a French military mission
to Warsaw, reorganised the Polish resistance and led the counter-
offensive which resulted in the annihilating defeat of the Russians. A

military balance was thus established in the east and the situation became stabilised. In the summer of 1920 the Soviet Union made peace with Lithuania and Latvia and in October also with Finland; it recognised the new states and promised to respect their frontiers. The final eastern peace treaty, concluded with Poland at Riga on 18 March 1921, drew the remainder of Russia's frontiers to the west and – going beyond the Curzon line – brought a broad strip of Bielorussia and the eastern Ukraine into Polish possession. The new Poland obtained only part of what had been the historic kingdom before the partition of 1772; but its newly acquired regions in the east were inhabited predominantly by White Russians and Ukranians so that Poland now also became a multi-nation state with big minorities of Ukranians, Russians, Lithuanians and in the west also of Germans.

In European politics France's effective aid to Poland remained of importance for some time to come. It was the start of a lasting association directed against both Russian and German efforts to revise the position in the east and thus became the cornerstone of the bridge built by French foreign policy to the states of Central Europe and the Little Entente system. Still before the peace of Riga, in February 1921, a Franco-Polish treaty of alliance was concluded. This was the beginning of the military and diplomatic *cordon sanitaire* against the Soviet Union which was extended by alliances between Poland and Rumania and between Czechoslovakia and Rumania, concluded in March and April 1921 respectively. Early in 1924 France signed a treaty of alliance and friendship with Czechoslovakia, thus laying another cornerstone of the pact system which it continued to promote.

The changes in the political map which resulted from the war and the peace treaties in eastern and south-eastern Europe led to the establishment of a system of new small and medium sized states which before the war had been under Tsarist or Habsburg rule. They had been helped to statehood in part by the German policy of encouraging revolution against the Tsarist empire but ultimately only by the assistance rendered by the United States to exile groups. The belt of these states stretched from the Arctic to the Black Sea and the Adriatic and filled the area between the vanquished powers Russia and Germany, dissatisfied Italy and what remained of the Turkish empire. In the north efforts to establish a Baltic League comparable with the Little Entente were unsuccessful. All that was achieved was an alliance in 1923 between Estonia and Latvia which was of no importance. A significant factor was the difference between Poland and Lithuania which the German commander-in-chief in the east had, in effect, intended to cause with the creation of Lithuania; this became insurmountable when Poland annexed the territory of Vilna and represented as great a stumbling block in the East European system of alliances as the differences between Poland and Czechoslovakia after the controversy over the Teschen region. Finland remained interested in keeping on good terms with the Soviet Union, which for the time being guaranteed Finland's independence. Its interest in the affairs of the Baltic states was hardly greater than in the fate of Poland, let alone of the states of south-eastern Europe.

14. The unratified Treaty of Sèvres and the Near East

The Treaty of Sèvres signed on 10 August 1920 was the last of the series of peace treaties concluded by the Allied powers with Germany's allies. Its preparations were the most prolonged and in several respects the most difficult. There was also less to show for these efforts because the treaty never came into force. Of the treaties concluded at various Paris suburbs the Treaty of Sèvres was the one that was least influenced by Wilson's principles and most by pre-war ideas. Its conclusion did not put a brake on the fast-moving events in the Near East, nor did it effectively channel them into paths that were in line with the wishes of its architects.

One of the early and lesser problems of the Allies was the re-shaping of Arabia. The secret partition treaties of the wartime period in so far as they affected the interests of those Great Powers that still had a military presence in the Near East proved more important than might have seemed from the various statements made during the last year of war. Husein, the Sherif of Mecca who had himself proclaimed King of the Hedjaz, together with his sons represented liberated Arabia at the Paris Conference; but he was forced almost at once to accept a curtailment of his sphere of influence. His eldest son, Feisal, played a less than happy role on the Paris diplomatic stage which was unfamiliar ground to him. At the suggestion of his Foreign Office advisers he tried by an agreement with the Zionist leaders to deal with the Palestine problem independently of the Great Powers in such a way as to meet the wishes of the Jews and to gain the Zionists for the Arab cause. The Feisal–Weizmann agreement of January 1919 was the result of the dynastic ideas of Husein's family which tried by concessions to achieve a rapprochement with the leader of Zionism. But with the growth of Jewish settlements Palestine became a crisis area and the presence of a strong protectorate power became justified, indeed inevitable.

In his official capacity in Paris, Feisal was merely the head of the Hedjaz delegation. The French were in possession of large parts of

Syria which under the Sykes–Picot agreement was part of the zone earmarked for them. But the British – at first with Arab troops under the British commander of the Palestine front – had occupied Damascus even before French marines marched into Bierut; and at the last hour of the war Britain recognised the Arabs as allies which entitled them to attend the Paris Peace Conference. But unlike Britain, France had never had any relations with Feisal. It therefore refused to recognise him as spokesman for Syria. Like Palestine, Syria therefore acquired a status that put it outside the influence of the Grand Sherif and his sons.

Circuitously and only at a late stage in its activities did the peace conference come to concern itself with questions of the Near East. It chose the mandate as the legal form for the settlement of the new colonial situations; this took into account the principles expressed in the Fourteen Points and avoided the open annexation of former Turkish territories. Later, however, it was not legal forms but the political interests of the colonial powers that proved decisive. But then Wilson hardly thought in terms of doing away with existing colonies. It was only relatively late and at the instigation of those around him that he concerned himself in detail with the German colonies and developed the idea that the fate of the non-European nations which had freed themselves from their former rulers should be entrusted to the League of Nations. Given Wilson's conception of the League this seemed to offer the best possible protection for the rights of indigenous populations.

Wilson's first idea was that the territories concerned should be administered 'under the mandate of the League' in the interest of the 'backward peoples' and entrusted exclusively to small states. But on this point the South African Prime Minister, Smuts, who agreed with Wilson on some things achieved a change to the advantage of the colonial powers and also of the British Dominions. Other representatives of Britain and of the Dominions were less inclined to make concessions to the President's ideas. The differences between Wilson and the Dominions could only be settled by Smuts' compromise formula by which the League of Nations mandate was safeguarded as a legal structure as Wilson wanted but which in practice also made concessions to his opponents. The mandate would continue until such a time when it would be possible to ascertain the wishes of the population concerning a termination of this state. The development idea was also recognised. But no detailed arrangements were made about the ways and means of the mandate regime. Henceforth, however, there were three kinds of mandate. For the German colonies annexation pure and simple became an accomplished fact, although *de jure* the possibility of terminating this state was not excluded. Another form of mandate was established in Arabia. Following Wilson's suggestion the situation in the Near East, and particularly in Syria, was to be settled by an American commission which would establish the wishes of the population. The relevant clause of the fourth paragraph of Article XXII of the League of Nations Covenant said:

> Certain communities formerly belonging to the Turkish Empire have reached a stage of development where their existence as independent nations can be provisionally recognised subject to the rendering of administrative advice and assistance by a Mandatory until such a time as they are able to stand alone.

This was more or less in line with the known protectorate principle. But another sentence followed: 'The wishes of these communities must be a principal consideration in the selection of the Mandatory.'

The length of the peace conference and the postponement of final settlements in the Near East, the insistence of France and its High Commissioner, Georges Picot, on the withdrawal of British troops from Syria, the attitude of the United States and the dispatch at Wilson's instigation of a commission headed by Henry King and Charles Crane all confirmed the Arab leaders in the determination to take their fate into their own hands and to pursue a line independent from British policy. Although the United States never showed as much interest in the Near East as in Europe and the Far East the Arab leaders recognised that the policy of the American President differed from that of the colonial powers. They believed that their aspirations were being encouraged even when intervention by Wilson came to seem more than doubtful. Feisal prevailed upon the provisional administration in Damascus under Ali Rida Pasha ar-Rikabi to hold elections for a constituent assembly in the whole of Syria under Turkish electoral law; this assembly met on 2 July 1919 as the 'Syrian National Congress' and a few days later was able to submit to the King–Crane commission a resolution rejecting all foreign control.

After Wilson's return to America the two great European colonial powers were left to themselves. On 13 September Lloyd George came to an agreement with Clemenceau on the political partition of Arabia under which 1 November 1919 was fixed for the beginning of the complete evacuation of Syria by British troops. Britain thus fulfilled the promises made to France during the war.

The Arabs immediately set about making the Syrian Congress more radical; this explains why some Arab officers who had served in the Turkish army tried to establish contact with Mustafa Kemal and the new Turkey. But these attempts were frowned upon by Feisal for whom the link with Turkey was broken forever and who hated nothing more than any form of association with that country. At his instigation the Syrian Congress decided in March 1920 to proclaim two independent kingdoms: Syria, consisting of north-western Arabia including Lebanon and Palestine, was to become a constitutional monarchy on the European model under King Feisal; and Iraq, as the territory of Mesopotamia together with Mosul and the surrounding zone was now called, which was to be ruled by Feisal's brother, Abdallah.

But at the conference of San Remo convened in April 1920, after the peace treaties of Versailles, St Germain and Neuilly, to settle outstanding or new problems which cast a shadow on the relations between the Great Powers it was decided to translate into reality the mandate provisions of the Paris Peace Conference. The conference determined which the mandate territories were to be and thereby sealed the fate of the two new kingdoms. In an ultimatum addressed to the government in Damascus the French commander-in-chief called for recognition of the mandatory power. Great Britain, which in San Remo had been given the mandate over Palestine, Jordan and Mesopotamia, displayed no interest in the events in Syria. On 26 July 1920 Damascus was occupied by the French and King Feisal was driven out of the city. This brought to an end the Arab struggle for independence in Syria. In Iraq the revolt continued for several months and tied down a large number of British troops until Winston Churchill, as Lord Milner's successor at the Colonial Office, somewhat changed British policy which had become generally unpopular. Britain now expressed itself ready to recognise two Arab kingdoms within its sphere of influence. Feisal who had been expelled from Syria was recognised on 23 August 1921 as King of Iraq and given a number of prerogatives. His brother Abdallah as the powerless Emir of Transjordan was nominally put in charge of a large but barren, thinly populated and economically poor zone. Like Palestine, Syria and

Lebanon remained under the direct administration of the mandatory powers.

The fate of what remained of Turkey as that of Germany – although in much harsher and more drastic form – was to begin with determined by the armistice conditions. In the sphere of foreign policy the Grand Vizir, Ahmed Tewfik Pasha, undermined attempts at restoration at home by apparently leaning heavily on Britain. His successor, Damad Ferid Pasha, who appeared at the Paris Peace Conference in June 1919 stood for the complete disassociation of the people and its sovereign from the Young Turks, who with their secret treaties had brought Turkey into the war and on to the side of the Central Powers. He maintained that the Ottoman Empire itself was not to blame and could therefore not be treated as an enemy. Ferid recalled that in the past the principle of preserving the balance of power in the eastern Mediterranean had usually, though not always, been behind the British policy of the Sublime Porte. He was prepared to give the Arab parts of the country autonomy under Turkish sovereignty and to make some territorial concessions to the Armenian state which was being established on Russian soil; but in all other respects Ferid demanded the preservation of the *status quo ante bellum* and even proposed to extend Turkey's immediate pre-war territory by asking for the return, from Greece and Bulgaria, of Western Thrace lost in the Balkan war and also of the Aegean islands. But the confidence which Ferid displayed in Paris proved totally unjustified. Clemenceau showered him with irony and brusquely rejected the Turkish proposals. There were no further negotiations and peacemaking was postponed until further notice.

But in the last resort time worked not for but against the Entente. In connection with the growing unrest in India there were demonstrations also in Turkey in the autumn of 1919 in which the Mohammedan population expressed itself in favour of the preservation of the Caliphate in Constantinople; in principle this was granted by the Supreme Council of the Allies. But for the rest the Great Powers disagreed and their differences were complicated further by the demands of the clever Greek Prime Minister, Venizelos, who asked that in return for its participation in the war his country should receive not only the rest of Thrace, which it had in principle already been granted, but also those regions of Asia Minor that were inhabited by Greeks together with the important port of Smyrna which under the secret treaty of Saint Jean de Maurienne of 1917 had been earmarked for Italy.

In support of its claims Italy at the end of April 1919 landed troops on the southern coast of Asia Minor, an act which led the Greek government to occupy Smyrna and much of the surrounding area. The Supreme Council of the Allies saw no way out but to sanction both steps. But Italy was reprimanded and the pride of its politicians hurt. Thereafter Italian foreign policy was aimed at closer relations with Greece and in the Tittoni–Venizelos agreement of 29 July 1919 Italy formally renounced all claims to Smyrna, Rhodes and the Dodecanese and contented itself with a strip on the southern coast of Asia Minor.

After this Italo–Greek arrangement the three Great Powers at San Remo on 24 April 1920 drew up a tripartite agreement in which they prepared the ground for the Treaty of Sèvres by agreeing on three spheres of influence; in some respects these bore a close resemblance to the zones laid down in the secret wartime treaties. The tripartite agreement did not directly involve Greece which had come to terms with Italy; it formally confirmed the Italian sphere of influence as agreed to in the Treaty of Saint Jean de Maurienne and defined the French zone essentially on the lines of the Sykes–Picot agreement but without Kurdistan or Mosul. Moreover, France gave up its claim to a voice in the affairs of Palestine. This French surrender to Britain led to violent reactions in Paris against the Millerand government which was responsible for this development of French Middle Eastern policy. So as to involve the United States in the Near East, America was offered a mandate over Armenia which was, however, rejected by the Senate.

It was against this background that the Turkish government on 10 August 1920 signed the harsh conditions of the Treaty of Sèvres. Turkey was made explicitly to confirm all losses of territory back to the Balkan war and to hand over to Greece eastern Thrace up to the Chatalja line, as well as the islands of Imbros and Tenedos. All that remained of European Turkey was a small strip west of the Straits. Italy was given the Dodecanese islands, which it handed to Greece under the Tittoni–Venizelos agreement. For a period of five years the Smyrna zone remained *de jure* under Turkish sovereignty while *de facto* being under Greek administration. After the expiration of this period a local parliament could ask the League of Nations for final

union with Greece which the Council of the League could then ar-
range after a plebiscite. The fate of the Armenian vilajets was to be
decided finally by Wilson. This was another attempt – once more in
vain – to revive American interest in the partition of the Near East.
But in any case Turkey agreed to recognise a free and independent
Armenia. In the Kurdish region – between Armenia, the Euphrates and
the Iraqi frontier – the population was given the right to apply within
a year to the League of Nations for the separation of Kurdistan from
Turkey. In this eventuality provision was made for the Iraqi part of
Kurdistan to join up with Mosul. Turkey was made to recognise the
settlements in Arabia. The peace treaty described Syria and Mesopotamia as states independent of Turkey, and Palestine as a mandate
territory under indefinite control of a mandatory power whose only
obligation was to carry out the Balfour Declaration.

Constantinople was recognised as the seat of the Sultan and Caliph
and also of the Turkish government, but with the proviso that the
peace treaty must be faithfully adhered to. Noticeable in the Treaty
of Sèvres, as in the peace treaty with Germany, are the extensive safeguards with which the Entente powers sought to compel Turkey to
fulfil its obligations. But they also had certain intentions regarding
the Straits. Free passage for warships and merchant shipping both in
peace and in war was to be assured by a future Straits agreement, by
the total demilitarisation of the surrounding zone and additionally
by reserving to Britain, France and Italy the right to intervene and to
occupy this area including the town of Constantinople itself. Access
to the Black Sea was kept free; but in practice these three powers could
stop anyone at any time from passing through. Above all this affected
Soviet Russia, which was given a vote in the International Straits
Commission but no right of occupation.

Furthermore, the tripartite agreement was built into the peace
treaty. France and Italy were assured of unassailable rights in the
south-west Turkish territory, in the southern coastal zone and in
western Kurdistan: in detail the treaty gave them permanent priority
in the allocation of economic concessions, the right to appoint specialists for the reorganisation of the administration and the police, and
above all the right of military occupation until the terms of the treaty
had been complied with.

The remaining conditions were no less harsh. The army was restricted to a small bodyguard of the Sultan, an insignificant force,

and a gendarmerie of 35,000 men. Turkey lost the right to control its tariff and financial affairs which were to be handled by a finance commission of the three powers, Britain, France and Italy. This body was to be responsible for Turkey's budget, occupation costs, certain types of compensation for war damage to foreign citizens, the raising of loans and guaranteed the current payments of the state to the Ottoman Public Debt, the historic international debt administration of the Sublime Porte. In return the three powers took over and divided between themselves the public debt of the Turkish state.

This peace made Turkey completely dependent politically, economically and in every financial respect on the three Great Powers of Western Europe. The policy of the Sublime Porte had visibly failed. Turkey had not been given protection by Britain so as to put its house in order but had been made to consent to a tripartite division which exposed the country to an uncertain fate.

But on the Turkish domestic scene the picture was in fact very different because the political impetus generated by the Young Turk revolution and the military experiences of the war was by no means spent. In many places local committees had been set up comparable to the soviets of the Russian revolution which spread the protest against the government at Constantinople and against the conditions of the peace treaty among the masses. Large regions had been in open rebellion for months. The east of Anatolia was controlled by the leader of this movement, General Mustafa Kemal, who as long ago as the end of the last century had produced a remarkable and far-sighted political pamphlet; as a young officer he had taken part in the Young Turk revolution and during the war he had distinguished himself as a successful commander at the Dardanelles. This shrewd political leader was severely critical not only of Turkey's involvement with the Central Powers and of the Young Turk leaders but also of the reactions of the post-war governments. In the summer of 1919 the rulers in Constantinople transferred this thorn in their sides to the interior of Anatolia as army inspector thereby giving – although inadvertently – the country's incipient popular movement its leader.

The first programme of the Kemalist movement was drawn up at the congress of east Anatolian vilajets at the end of July and the beginning of August 1919 in Erzurum. It was characterised by both brevity and clarity and made the main aims of the national opposition clear to everyone: the preservation of the eastern provinces for Turkey and national opposition to occupation and intervention; religious minorities were merely to be tolerated in the same way as before. On 4 September 1919 spokesmen from all parts of the country assembled in Sivas and recognised this programme as the basis of the national movement in all Turkey. In the same month the leadership of this opposition under Kemal established itself in Angora, the capital of Anatolia, which later under the name of Ankara became the centre of the new Turkey.

Even before the peace treaty was signed the Allies were calling upon the Turkish government to stop Kemal's activities. As the government's efforts were of no avail the Sultan tried to reach an understanding with the General. He even agreed to form a new government, which reached an agreement with Kemal to the effect that only a Turkish national assembly could decide whether or not to accept the peace treaty. The government thus surrendered the ultimate decision in domestic affairs: it accepted a state of dual government, a situation which again suggests formal comparisons with a certain stage in the development of the Russian revolution. On the basis of these arrangements elections were held for a national assembly which met on 19 January 1920 in Constantinople and a few days later proclaimed the 'National Pact': the demand for freedom and independence for the Turkish parts of the Ottoman Empire as well as for all the territories not occupied by the Allies up to the armistice of Mudros, inviolability of territory and people, free development in political and economic matters and security for the capital. This resolution was transmitted to the Allies but its only result was that on 16 March – under the pretext of this being a temporary step only – they occupied Constantinople. The National Assembly protested and adjourned while the government under Damad Ferid Pasha, newly appointed by the Sultan, outlawed Kemal. But what happened then merely illustrated the governments' total impotence. A Great Turkish National Assembly met on 23 April 1920 in Angora and recognised Kemal's government as the only legitimate government of Turkey. This government then took charge – legislative as well as executive – and installed itself in form of an all-embracing dictatorship on the basis of the legitimisation provided by the national assembly. The government in Constantinople tried several times more, although always without success, to enter into negotiations with the rulers in Angora who completed the revolutionary act of assuming power by proclaiming the law of 29 April 1920 in which they described the government in Constantinople as prisoners of the Allies, refused to recognise the validity of their future orders and proclaimed in advance as null and void any obligations entered into by them. Only legitimate plenipotentiaries of the Turkish people were authorised to make peace. But Turkey would only recognise an honourable peace. The Greeks on Turkish soil were assured of protection but were enjoined explicitly not to take action endangering the safety of Turkey.

Immediately afterwards Kemal's government called upon the Turkish people actively to resist the Allies; they had already begun to do so in various places and had caused considerable embarrassment to the not very strong French forces.

After the signing of the Treaty of Sèvres Kemal started regular war activities. With his reorganised forces he turned first at the end of September against the distant Armenian regions; these he was able to occupy without difficulty and he dealt ruthlessly with the long-suffering population which now became the victim of a merciless Turkish revenge. Almost at the same time the Bolshevik troops began their advance in the Caucasus area, in the course of which they seized the Russian part of Rumania. On 2 December 1920 an official peace treaty was signed between Kemal and the Armenians in which the Armenian government solemnly renounced the rights which it had been granted at Sèvres.

In these circumstances the occupation powers, who were no longer in a position to take large-scale military action against the national movement of five million Turks, found themselves in an extremely difficult situation. The fact that they insisted on the letter of the law of the peace treaty was due in part to the efforts of British diplomacy and the policy of Lloyd George but no less to the influence of the Greek Prime Minister, Venizelos. At the conferences at Hythe and at Spa in 1920 he offered the three Allies – Britain, France and Italy – a Greek offensive against Turkey with the intention of enforcing the Treaty of Sèvres. But with this step Greece embarked on a fateful adventure for which it was to pay dearly and which changed the position in the eastern Mediterranean for ever to the advantage of the new Turkey.

Mustafa Kemal successfully aroused the whole Turkish people and inflicted a succession of devastating defeats on the Greeks. It is true, however, that the situation in Turkey was unique and permits no comparison with any of the other countries defeated in the war. There was no endless discussion of Turkey's domestic problems among the broad mass of the people, who were the most primitive types of farmers and who were by and large illiterate, or even among the numerically small educated élite. There was no communism and social stability was not threatened by internal revolutionary forces, nor were there any longer serious differences of opinion on Turkish war policy. Whereas in Germany the war had led to the worst crisis ever suffered by German national pride and had undermined the Austrian state it was only now that a widespread sense of national awareness developed in Turkey. It was only now that the people became conscious of having a Turkish state independent of the political and religious ruler in Constantinople – in this new war which for the Turkish people became the war of liberation from foreign domination.

Mustafa Kemal's unique attempt to achieve a revision of the consequences of the war and of the peace conditions with the help of a national popular movement and military force was marked by ruthless energy but also by a realistic estimate of the situation and by the complete absence of exaggerated objectives. Mustafa Kemal had no illusions about the defeat which Turkey had suffered and never attempted to restore the shattered Turkish empire together with the conquests of Ottoman history. He was concerned solely with the sovereignty and viability of the Turkish state. Hence the Kemalist programme was brief, clear, simple and convincing to all.

In spite of the definite break with the discredited Young Turk movement Kemal's actions were in some ways a logically thought-out continuation of the Young Turk programme which he adapted to circumstances that were of course completely changed. One main difference was that Kemalism was not concerned with the preservation of the Ottoman Empire and did not take up the many objectives of the Young Turks but consciously used the narrower base of the Turkish state as a great starting point from which to set out upon the national rejuvenation of the Turkish people. The confinement of the Turkish state to Turks only was the most important requirement for the nation's struggle for existence. Part of this was the unreserved renunciation of Arabia and Turkey's explicit confinement to Anatolia and Thrace. But within this framework Kemal did not hesitate to use notorious Young Turk methods of coercion against non-Turkish tribes, Armenians, Greeks and Kurds, in order to 'Turkify' the remains of the state and to establish it as a national state. All this was a brutal and truly realistic contraction of the Young Turk programme but not by any means its negation.

But Kemal benefited also from the fact that the world situation was becoming increasingly favourable to Turkey. With the arrival upon the scene of the liberal Foreign Minister, Count Carlo Sforza, Italy came to adopt a more cautious attitude. Having renounced the Tittoni-Venizelos agreement the Count needed prolonged urging before he agreed to sign the Treaty of Sèvres and he watched the Greek moves without sympathy. But France also showed itself anxious to find a way out of the impasse in the Near East as it had no wish to exchange its cultural influence in that part of the world for a lasting feud with the Islamic nations. Shortly after the fall of Venizelos, who was much liked in France, and the return of King Constantine in December 1920 there was a change also in the French attitude towards Greece, so that in their war against Turkey the Greeks now had only the half-hearted backing of Britain. Lloyd George sought to mediate and to stop a revision of the Treaty of Sèvres now openly advocated also by France. But France feared that a continuation of the Greco-Turkish war and further military successes by the Turks would lead to a revival of the Arab movement in Syria. Moreover, a military defeat of Turkey, where France had had strong military interests since before the war, seemed of little advantage in the long run.

After the Turkish victory at Inonu on 7 January 1921 led to the collapse of the second Greek offensive the Allies invited Turkey to a conference in London with the objective of ending the Greek war and of examining ways and means of revising the Treaty of Sèvres. For the first time this invitation went also to the Great National Assembly at Angora, which was thus recognised *de facto* by the Allies. The London conference of 21 February to 12 March 1921 was attended by two Turkish delegations. One represented the old Turkey of the government of the Sultan in Constantinople and the other the Kemalist government in Angora. But if there were hopes that the two groups might differ they were quickly disappointed; because both delegations had agreed on a joint programme which was in the main explained by Kemal's Foreign Minister, Bekir Sami, and which was based on the principles of the National Pact. It demanded the restoration of Turkey's last pre-war frontier in Europe, the recognition of the eastern frontier on the basis of the Armenian peace treaty and complete independence for Turkey in economic, financial, legal, political and military matters. In return Turkey declared itself ready to recognise the loss of Arabia, to agree to freedom for merchant shipping in Turkish ports and through the Straits, to support the setting-up of the International Straits Commission, to demilitarise the coasts, to protect the minorities and to reorganise the Turkish army with foreign assistance.

This programme no longer had anything in common with the content and spirit of the Treaty of Sèvres; it had also emancipated itself completely from the armistice conditions. It was a programme which wanted to create a new basis for Turkey's existence and which had come to terms with the sad facts of defeat. But Turkey did not yet have its way completely at the London conference and the war with Greece continued. Two years later, however, the main points of this programme were agreed upon in the Treaty of Lausanne which established the relationship between the new Turkey and the outside world. It had been preceded by a period of internal political reform which began in November 1922 with the abrogation of the temporal powers of the Sultan and the dismissal of the last Grand Vizir in Constantinople, Ahmed Tewfik Pasha, and in September 1923 led to the proclamation of the Republic and the election of Mustafa Kemal Pasha as President. In March 1924 Kemal did away also with the spiritual rule of the Sultan and abolished the Caliphate.

The period between the London conference in 1921 and the Treaty of Lausanne saw the ending in October 1922 of the renewed Greco-Turkish war with the armistice of Mudania after the Turks had been very successful militarily and the Greek king Constantine, had fallen for the second time. During this time the united front of the Allies collapsed. First Italy and then France pulled out completely and made bilateral arrangements with Turkey which invalidated the tripartite agreement even before the peace of Lausanne led to a general revision of the Treaty of Sèvres. Lloyd George's determined attempts to maintain the British position and not to question the permanent occupation of the Straits zone in the autumn of 1922, after the collapse of Greece, almost resulted in another war when Turkish and British troops confronted each other at Chanak. But the tension was eased relatively quickly by Soviet Russia's reaction to the threat to peace at the Straits, by France's efforts at conciliation but still more by the opposition of the Dominions which refused to become again militarily involved in Europe. The apparent fiasco of Britain's Near Eastern policy led on

19 October 1922, immediately after the Chanak crisis, to the overthrow of Lloyd George by the Conservatives without whose assistance he could not govern.

Lord Curzon, who remained Foreign Secretary in Bonar Law's Conservative administration, was forced to give in to the changed position in the Mediterranean and to recognise the inevitability of the new situation in which not only France and Italy but also the states of a Balkan bloc, Yugoslavia, Rumania, Greece and Bulgaria, were seeking at France's insistence to establish peace in the Near East. The Soviet Union profited from the crisis of the West European Entente and after its treaty of friendship with Turkey in March 1921 played a more and more active part in the Near East. For Britain Kemalism and the collapse of the Entente in the Near East brought the biggest defeat for the post-war policy of Lloyd George, who was made to pay a bitter price for his uncompromising attitude towards the new forces in the territory of the old Ottoman Empire. But Curzon then managed in months of clever manœuvring, after a temporary interruption of the peace conference at Lausanne, to obtain completely free passage through the Straits in peace and in war, and to preserve the important oil region of Mosul in southern Kurdistan for the mandate territory of Iraq.

15. The 'System of Versailles' – criticism and revision

The peacemakers failed to establish a permanent order. Their work continued the political transformation of the world begun with the war; but they did not find the lasting state of calm for which humanity longed after experiencing to the full the horrors of war and after making such terrible sacrifices. The great movements of the age did not come to a stop.

If one examines the work of the Paris conference one finds errors and mistakes in rich measure and can criticise to one's heart's content. The Swiss historian Leonhard von Muralt described the 'System of Versailles' as the result of 'wrong power politics', power politics that failed to 'take all relevant issues into consideration'. But what in 1919 were 'all relevant issues'? To the present generation some of the Great Four's solutions together with their justifications are beyond comprehension. It has even been said that given the subsequent fate of south-eastern Europe some of the historic reform plans produced in the old Danube monarchy, particularly those put forward shortly before or during the war, would have given better results than the efforts of the peacemakers did.

It is understandable that in Germany in the conditions prevailing in the post-war period the peace treaty was condemned as the 'dictated peace of Versailles' and was judged in the light of Germany's territorial losses and military, financial and economic burdens; but this does not do justice to the real state of affairs. When we look at the general situation in Europe we find problems which regardless of the mistakes that were made and might have been avoided could not in fact have been solved within the framework of a conference; yet it was necessary to solve them within a few months because the desire for peace and the internal unrest among the war-weary nations permitted no postponement or prolonged delay. The fundamental problem which is also at the heart of the more penetrating subsequent criticism of the 'System of Versailles' continued to exist after the conclusion of peace. This was the problem of establishing a sound political equilibrium in Europe not based merely on the distribution of power as it was at the end of the war. Yet how could a new balance of power be achieved while the Western powers were fighting Russia or trying to isolate it and while Russia was threatening to expand westwards? How could there be an equilibrium when a number of new states were emerging at the European periphery of old Russia and others resulting from the break-up of the Danube monarchy, and when their internal situation, their reactions in the international sphere and their economic potential were totally unknown quantities? How could there be an equilibrium if it was impossible for statesmen accurately to take into account the invisible forces of both great and small states that had been irresistibly mobilised by the war? How could there be a lasting settlement that took account of all the elements that would be of importance in a radically changed world? There is a serious lack of logic in all verdicts passed on the peace treaty which ignore the fact that the pre-war policies could not prevent war and which fail to appreciate the essential continuity of the pre-war period, the war, peace-time and the era of revision.

The Paris peacemakers were caught out and mercilessly put right by historical developments just as the German leaders during the war were caught out in their main assumptions and decisions and mercilessly put right by the war. But it was by no means the vanquished alone who suffered; the whole world was affected. The political fates of the great men who met in Paris provide evidence of the internal conflicts and movements, of the disappointments and antagonisms that existed also among the victor nations. Orlando fell even before the end of the peace conference; he was succeeded by seven short-lived governments until three years later the Italian monarchy entered into an alliance with the Fascist dictatorship. Wilson's political career ended shortly after his return from Paris. The rest of his period in office was a trying struggle with his critics, with the indignant and with his own disappointment. Clemenceau's career came to an end shortly afterwards. Lloyd George's fall, which was caused by the unsolved questions of the Near Eastern peace, put an end not only to his historic role as a statesman but also to the era of the Liberal Party.

The historian only does justice to his great legitimate task if he detaches himself from contemporary judgments with their over-dependence on first impressions. There is a wide gap between the real significance of the peace treaties and the subjective verdict passed on them. Yet both were undoubtedly of great political importance.

Many Germans saw the results of the Paris peace negotiations as a millstone round the neck of the Weimar Republic. After a second world war which ended in total capitulation the outcome of the First World War does not in retrospect seem nearly so terrible. The treaty, however harsh and humiliating some of its provisions were felt to be, promised the German state opportunities which it managed to seize. But after the hopes which the German public had harboured for so long the awakening was terrible and the memory of it was never forgotten. In the end public opinion in Germany – in spite of some differences of opinion about the enemy and his motives – was unanimous in rejecting the treaty. It is certainly no exaggeration to say that on no other political issue has there been a like degree of unanimity; the literature on the subject, at different levels, is endless.

But hostile comment on 'Versailles' was by no means confined to the vanquished. It was not long before critics also became vocal in the Allied countries. In France the nationalist criticism of the inter-war period gradually came to be accepted. It began by seeing the Treaty of Versailles essentially as a success for the policy of Clemenceau, Foch and Poincaré but eventually accepted the verdict of Jacques Bainville, who found that from the French point of view also serious mistakes had been made. Germany was preserved but Europe was broken up; the balance of power in Europe which might have acted as a counterweight to a united Germany was not restored; the small European states to the east of Germany forced France permanently to maintain a strong army for their support. In this sense Bainville was probably right when he said that the Treaty of Versailles was too severe towards Germany in view of its inherent weakness and too weak in view of its severity. In Italy the Liberal, Francesco Nitti, who had replaced Orlando a few days before the Versailles treaty was signed became the spokesman of the view that Versailles was the worst solution: Clemenceau's peace achieved with Wilson's methods had in fact created a 'peaceless Europe'.

From the British there came a warning about unreasonable peace conditions as early as 25 March 1919 when Lloyd George said in his Fontainbleau memorandum:

There is a consideration in favour of a long-sighted peace which influences me even more than the desire to leave no causes justifying a fresh outbreak thirty years hence. There is one element in the present condition of nations which differentiates it from the situation as it was in 1815. In the Napoleonic war the countries were equally exhausted, but the revolutionary spirit had spent its force in the country of its birth, and Germany had satisfied legitimate popular demands for the time being by a series of economic changes which were inspired by courage, foresight and high statesmanship. The situation is very different now. The revolution is still in its infancy. The supreme figures of the Terror are still in command in Russia. The whole of Europe is filled with the spirit of revolution. There is everywhere a deep sense not only of discontent, but of anger and revolt amongst the workmen against pre-war conditions. The whole existing order in its political, social and economic aspects is questioned by the masses of the population from one end of Europe to the other. In some countries, like Germany and Russia, the unrest takes the form of open rebellion; in others, like France, Great Britain and Italy, it takes the shape of strikes and of general disinclination to settle down to work – symptoms which are just as much concerned with the desire for political and social change as with wage demands. Much of this unrest is unhealthy. We shall never make a lasting peace by attempting to restore the conditions of 1914.

Among the public the mood began to change during the summer of 1919; leading Labour politicians who were beginning to emerge as the opposition and soon also Liberals protested against the Versailles treaty. Gradually a mood came to prevail in Britain which can be described as 'bad conscience' and which, reinforced by pacifist tendencies, exerted a profound and lasting influence in subsequent years. Mainly responsible for this was the first devastating condemnation of the economic clauses of the peace treaty. This condemnation which caused a world-wide sensation was the work of a member of the British peace delegation in Paris, an economist who with his critical appreciation of the peace conditions and of the subsequent reparations policy laid the basis for his future reputation as one of the century's greatest economists. The year 1919 was not yet out when John Maynard Keynes produced his epoch-making *Economic Consequences of the*

Peace. Although the book of a scholar and intended primarily as a basis for economic reflections it was violently critical – in part it could hardly have been more so – of the behaviour of the American President. This is not to say that Keynes did not appreciate the greatness and importance of Wilson's personality and his determination to ensure the acceptance of his principles at Paris. Keynes' picture of the conference and some of his character studies of the statesmen involved have dated and are highly subjective. The book's claim to fame lies in the fact that although it at once produced a storm of criticism it demanded respect as a great piece of writing, and that as regards the economic effects of the treaty Keynes' prophecies were soon proved right in several respects.

The book caused a sensation in Germany. It gave support to the German revisionist efforts by stressing the cumulative effect of the economic clauses of the treaty: the strain on Germany's industry and budget, the unilateral benefits given to its trading partners, the confiscation of its capital investments abroad and the fact that it was barred from the world markets leading inevitably to mass unemployment, to a general decline and to moral collapse. But above all Keynes felt it necessary to utter a clear warning for the future: the Central Powers represented the greatest concentration of peoples in the heart of Europe. If through humiliation and starvation they were driven to despair and into the arms of communism this vast mass of people would drag the rest of the continent with it into the abyss. This was the important political message of Keynes' book. Its economic significance lay in the refutation of the principles underlying the reparations provisions. At the same time it contained a devastating criticism of Wilson's mistakes, of Clemenceau's ruthlessness and of his 'Carthaginian peace'. The book came out at a time of growing anti-Wilson feeling in the United States and provided fresh ammunition for it.

In fact the wartime friend–enemy approach lived on in the minds of many people. Reference was made to the 'enemy' after 1918 in almost the same tone as during the war. This was primarily due to the continued existence of nationalism. But it was also the result of the political conditions in Europe where the new order was based on friend–enemy relations which were broken down only slowly and reluctantly and which were by no means overcome by the early efforts of the League of Nations. The prolonged effects as well as the complexity of the consequences of the peace treaties created new tensions and conflicts and gave new food to deeply rooted national differences.

The plebiscites provided for in the Versailles treaty in the territories disputed between Germany and Poland – in upper Silesia, southeastern Prussia and western Prussia east of the Vistula – degenerated in part into nationality clashes which were fought by both sides with as much bitterness as ruthlessness. Relations between Germany and Poland remained delicate; from the beginning they were overshadowed by the closeness of the relationship between the French and the Poles which weighed down the scales in favour of the Poles also during the risings in upper Silesia. The question of sentencing the men accused of war crimes remained an issue for some time before it receded into the background almost without any result having been achieved. The French occupation of the Rhineland was felt as a particularly onerous burden because military ideas and reparations policies went openly together and the French Commander-in-Chief, Mangin, unreservedly supported even the most questionable Rhenish separatism. But it was above all the never ceasing discussion of Germany's reparations obligations that became one of the main issues of European foreign policy and caused more than one serious difference in Franco-German relations until the situation was stabilised in 1924. Lastly Germany's exclusion from the League of Nations was felt for years as a restriction and a political slur which deprived Germany of hope for a better future. For years to come almost all these issues affected not only the relations between Germany and its ex-enemies but also caused differences and tensions among the victors.

In these circumstances all forces in Germany virtually without exception pressed from the start for a revision of the legal obligations arising out of the Versailles treaty. But the ways and means of doing this differed considerably. Official foreign policy in the first years after the war concentrated primarily on fulfilling Germany's inescapable obligations while at the same time seeking short-term and long-term relief and the prospect of revision; indeed it achieved the goal of German membership of the League of Nations. But the road did not, as Count Bernstorff had envisaged, lead via the League of Nations to a rapprochement with the West, but on the contrary the rapprochement with the Western Powers led Germany into the League of Nations.

The German protest against Versailles never ceased and in Germany the revision of the peace treaty seemed of greater importance than all else. Versailles cast its shadow over German policy at home and abroad and with the force of a compulsive idea this policy was guided into the channels of nationalistic reaction. A considerable, if not exactly measurable contribution to the growing radicalism of the nationalist Right was made by the determined accusation against the peace treaty which concentrated primarily on the national 'point of honour', the war guilt verdict. The wartime discrimination led to the discrediting of Germany also after the peace treaty and in the last resort affected only the Weimar Republic on which it imposed a heavy burden.

It was not long after the conclusion of peace that there was a curious development concerning the proposal to investigate the guilt questions, first made by Prince Max von Baden and then taken up by the Reich government. Shortly after the coming into force of the Weimar constitution the National Assembly appointed a parliamentary investigation committee whose task it was to follow trial procedure and to examine a given number of problems from three particular aspects. The first two questions were 'whether faith was kept in dealings between the various political authorities, between the Reich leadership itself, between the political and the military leaders and with the representatives of the people or those who spoke for them'; and 'whether in the military and economic direction of the war methods were ordered to be used or tolerated that were contrary to international law or cruel and harsh beyond military and economic necessity'; but the greatest importance was at first attached to the sub-committee examining the question of 'whether opportunities had arisen during the war for the initiation of peace talks and whether such opportunities had been sufficiently explored'. The evidence submitted put the respected wartime leaders, Hindenburg and Ludendorff, in the position of having to refute the accusation that by insisting on submarine warfare they had provoked the United States' entry into the war and had thus been responsible for Germany's defeat. In practice, however, the verdict was passed by the nationalistic press and by the public which was kept in a state of excitement by the press; they did not allow its respected generals to be found guilty. Simultaneously two legends were born and before the year 1919 was out they began to confuse the issues: the Wilson legend which claimed that from the outset Wilson had been determined to join in the war, a claim that was said to be confirmed by the peace of Versailles which no longer had anything in common with a peace of the Fourteen Points; and the 'stab in the back' legend according to which the German army would have been victorious had it not been 'stabbed in the back' by revolt at home. It was not the army that had failed; the Army High Command had acted correctly. The collapse was entirely the fault of the 'German revolution'. Thanks to these legends and to their gradual and successful dissemination the Field-Marshal's reputation survived unscathed and before long it was suggested that he should become a candidate for the office of Reich President with the constitutional prerogatives of a 'substitute Kaiser'.

In history the 'relentless struggle against capitalism and imperialism', for which Brockdorff-Rantzau had meant to ask in a speech against the Versailles document which he never came to make, became not the affair of the vanquished nations of the First World War but of the peoples of Asia and Africa who were allied with the Entente powers and dependent on them or ruled by them. British rule in India experienced its most serious tests in the years immediately after the war and found it impossible not to fall back occasionally on the oldest methods of colonial policy. The crisis came when the country's two great parties rejected as inadequate by the standards of self-government the new 'dyarchy' established as a result of the reforms of the Viceroy, Lord Chelmsford. The epidemics and poor harvests of 1918 contributed to the general feeling of discontent and raised feelings to fever pitch. With the impression of the events in Russia in mind the British administration in India was afraid of a revolutionary explosion. It took Draconic steps, ordered arrests and set up concentration camps. Under emergency regulations, the Rowlatt Acts of 18 March 1919, political agitators could be interned without trial. But the effect of these measures was double edged. It increased the fear of British rule but it also consolidated the Indian national movement. In answer to the challenge presented by the British measures the Indians, stimulated by Gandhi, offered passive resistance but in the end open rebellion also broke out in parts of northern India. On 13 April 1919 there was the bloodbath of Amritsar. After an attempt on his life the British general in command ordered fire to be opened without warning on an unarmed crowd in the centre of the town. 379 dead and 1,209 injured was the sad balance of that terrible day.

Like the Indians the Mohammedan peoples of the European colonies and protectorates in Asia Minor and North Africa – under French as well as under British rule – were no longer immune to the economic developments, social problems and political ideas of the times; they too longed for independence. The confidence of the coloured peoples in the European powers had suffered a heavy blow. Lord Milner's reign at the Colonial Office during which post-war colonial policies were carried out with pre-war means, but in the awareness that Britain had gained a military victory over its enemies, was criticised also at home. Colonel Lawrence's view that old men were robbing the nation of its victory began to spread and led Churchill, as Milner's successor, to moderate some of the earlier policies. But this did not affect the fate of Arabia to any extent.

In the south of the Arabian peninsula Ibn Saud had meanwhile continued his wars of conquest. With the exception of the Yemen he seized all Arab principalities between Kuwait, the Persian Gulf and the Red Sea. In 1924 his soldiers occupied the holy cities of Mecca and Medina and brought to an end the short-lived rule of the Hedjaz King, Husein, and his youngest son Ali. Arabia had now acquired its new political shape. Arab nationalism was no more extinct than Jewish hopes for a national state in Palestine. But the way to political unity in Arabia, the objective of secret nationalist circles since the end of the nineteenth century, was blocked because of the policy of the west European colonial powers but also because of internal antagonisms in Arabia which prevented unity because of religious differences, differences between the western influenced national movement and the traditional old Arab forms of rule, differences between urban and agrarian society and the culture and modes of life of the nomadic tribes.

The Near East remained a 'storm centre of world politics'; and the main burden in this dissatisfied area was borne by Britain. In the period to come the Arab claim to self-determination produced broad movements that were not dominated by individual families and were not focused on the idea of national Arab unity. Britain was forced to bear also the burden of the clashes between Jews and Arabs, between settlers from all parts of the world who cultivated the land and the Arab sheiks who ruled it and who had exchanged Turkish overlordship for British domination.

The unpredictable developments in eastern Europe had been a nightmare to the peace conference. It was here that there were now the first perceptible signs of Russia's return to the circle of Great Powers. Having suffered by far the heaviest losses in the war it was only natural that it should take Russia considerable time to make an economic recovery and to return to the position of a great power on the continent.

Although Russia had been forced to give up its claim to large regions occupied by foreign nationalities, once the disintegration crisis was over it still found itself in possession of the great European part of the old empire with most of the Ukraine and the whole of its Asiatic possessions. It became a federate state and after an unparalleled process of centralisation came to be politically controlled by the Council of People's Commissars and the Politbureau of the Central Committee of the Communist Party of the Soviet Union. The leadership was supported by an all-embracing party organisation which reached into every sector of public life and into many private spheres. The entire organisation of the state offered the first perfect picture of a totalitarian system in the twentieth century.

As late as the beginning of 1921 the economic life of the Soviet Union was close to collapse. The country's economy, socialised, centralised and planned from November 1917 onwards, was adversely affected by clumsy directives of the Supreme Council of National Economy and the large number of committees under it with dictatorial powers. Drastic methods in the countryside had led to the first serious clashes between the Bolshevik government and the rural population and in the agrarian zone of the Ukraine had repeatedly given new impetus to the partisan movement even after the civil war. Refusals to fulfil delivery targets, black market activities and shortages deprived the industry of its qualified labour force and led to a noticeable lack of consumer goods of all kinds. Shortages, unemployment, a catastrophic food situation, sabotage, refusals by the peasants to cultivate the land and moves among the rural population to band together were characteristic of the disturbed situation in Russia. The Petrograd strikes in February and the brutally suppressed rising of the Kronstadt soldiers and sailors in March 1921 showed that discontent was beginning to undermine the fortresses of Bolshevik power. On the other hand it was true that in the last phases of the war, and particularly in the campaign against Poland, a new patriotism had begun to emerge and that the long sequence of military happenings had made a powerful instrument of the Red Army of the civil war with its nucleus of deserters from the Tsarist army. This was the doing of both ex-Tsarist officers and of communist party agitators interested in military affairs who jointly created a new type of force. From the point of view of military equipment, however, the Red Army did not yet measure up fully to modern army standards.

After the suppression of the Kronstadt rising military problems took second place to the urgent need to provide more food. Lenin now initiated a memorable change. The new era in Bolshevik economic policy which Lenin proclaimed and quickly popularised opened with the granting of immediate assistance to the peasants, the transition to free trade in agricultural products, the substitution of taxes in kind for the requisitioning of surpluses; private enterprise and in some spheres even foreign capital investment were now permitted. Socialisation remained confined to basic materials and heavy industry. Later some smaller enterprises were even denationalised and peasants were allowed to acquire property. The Bolshevik government had the courage but also the strength to make a complete change on a scale hitherto undreamt of and in the shortest possible time did away with the primitive and disastrous consequences of socialisation. But at the backs of the Soviet rulers' minds was the ambitious objective not merely to resolve the country's acute economic difficulties but to initiate a large-scale modernisation of the entire Russian economy which would permit the Soviet Union to join the ranks of the great industrial states. The Soviet government was the first to think in terms of industrial development; this was to some extent suggested by the totalitarian basis of its political power and had been shown by the cruel empiricism of the crisis winter of 1920–21 as the only way out. The government now pursued a strategy of capital accumulation and with the same ruthlessness with which it had previously pursued its policy of socialisation initiated a comprehensive process of nationalisation made attractive to masses with the catchphrase about 'electrification'.

Less rigid co-ordination and the tremendous speeding up of economic activities was accompanied by a consolidation of political power. The removal of the Mensheviks and Social Revolutionaries and the first great show trials of leading members of these parties were followed by the progressive disappearance of independent trade union organisations and their transformation into organs of the Bolshevik party. The New Economic Policy of limited economic liberalisation was followed by permanent centralisation in state and party. The political police (the Cheka which after 1922 was renamed the GPU) adopted the working methods and bad habits of the Tsarist Okhrana and played an oppressive role in domestic life. But with the improvements in economic conditions there came a tremendous increase in the population and the number of farms grew. Together with this general recovery of the broad mass of the Russian people went a gradual change in the Soviet Union's position in the international sphere.

After the low point at the end of 1918 brought about by the cessation of relations with the warring parties of both sides the Soviet Union's first objective was to re-establish contact with the international constellation. This it succeeded in doing only gradually and step by step.

At the beginning Bolshevik Russia did not do much more than influence the communist parties of the other countries and it was difficult to gauge correctly how effective this was. So as to consolidate this influence and to ensure that it lasted the founding congress of the new Third International (Comintern) in Moscow in March 1919 realised Lenin's idea of creating an organisation of revolutionaries of all countries and of rendering all possible assistance to attempts at revolt in Central Europe. The Moscow International was joined by the communist parties of Germany, Austria and of the countries of south-eastern Europe and before long also by the Italian communists, the Norwegian workers' party and the communists of Sweden, Holland and Britain. In Germany the controversy over membership of the Third International led to a split in the Independent Social Democrat Party, the majority of which in 1920 joined the German Communist Party. A similar split rent the French socialists and their trade union movement. And, when the Executive Committee of the International insisted on the exclusion of the party's right wing, the Italian socialists also split in January 1921.

Under the Comintern statutes the International's main political activity was controlled by the executive committee which had extremely close links with the Russian Bolsheviks; thereby the Politbureau of the Central Committee of the Communist Party of the Soviet Union in practice became the headquarters of international communism. Binding directives went out from Moscow to all organisations affiliated to the International, but they were not as a rule allowed to enter into direct contact with one another.

The programme of the Third International was based on the principles derived from Marx and Engels by the first 'International Workers Association' of 1864. The proclaimed aims were the same: 'overthrow of capitalism, the establishment of the dictatorship of the proletariat for the realisation of socialism, this first step towards communist leadership'. But the struggle of the International was henceforth to be directed not only against capitalism but also against 'the aristocracy of the workers corrupted by capitalism', against 'trade union and co-operative leaders' and against 'centrists and defenders of democracy' and whatever else came under this heading. Nor was it to be confined to the objective of seizing control in the industrial countries. An important place was given in both the programme and the statutes of the Third International to political activity in economically backward and 'oppressed countries' which were to collaborate in the overthrow of the imperialist powers. The statutes said: 'For the complete success of the world revolution it is necessary for these two forces to collaborate', i.e. there must be an alliance between internationally organised communism and colonial and semi-colonial anti-imperialist emancipation movements.

Even if the Soviet Union had had nothing more than this instrument which it began to create while still involved in the Russo-Polish war it would probably before long have managed once more to become a factor in international politics. But in addition to the Third International there were two other elements of Russian strength which worked towards the same end: the numerically strong and well-prepared Red Army which gradually also acquired every form of modern equipment, which was always well fed and easily recruited; also trade with the Soviet Union because the beginning of NEP and the period of electrification had led to an enormous Russian demand for industrial goods and equipment.

These two factors held considerable attraction for Germany and the second also for the industrial states of western Europe. Other elements also entered, not least the impact of Russo-Turkish relations during the period of Turkish recovery even though German revision policy attempted to involve Russia, a country with which Germany had no common interests at home or abroad but which like Germany was for the time being excluded from the League of Nations. 'In my view the misfortune of Versailles can be corrected from Moscow,' Brockdorff-Rantzeau is alleged to have said before his resignation as Foreign Minister at the end of June 1919 – three years before he himself went to Moscow as Germany's first post-war ambassador. But while there was hope of improving the situation by a rapprochement with the Western Powers, official German foreign policy tried to avoid being suspected of dealings with the Soviet Union without, however, taking any action about the Reichswehr's secret links with the East. At the same time German foreign policy was not above taking advantage of East–West tensions in Europe. Relations were complicated however – as was everything that happened in the eastern half of Europe and in Asia Minor – by the existence of new states in eastern and south-eastern Europe.

Although most of these young states maintained proportionally enormous armies, in contravention of the spirit of disarmament, they could not deal with the internal and external tensions with which they were confronted and lacked adequate foundations. Therefore from the start they were forced for political and economic reasons to seek the protection of the Great Powers. Wilson had wanted to bring them into the League of Nations so that they would not be driven into the arms of Bolshevik Russia, but this association had not solved their problems. It was not long before these states were drawn into the sphere of influence of the Western Powers, particularly of France. However in the long run the French influence did not last.

A front of revisionist states was first established by Fascist Italy; its activities were directed against Greece and Yugoslavia and it sought to exploit the gaps in the pact system of the Little Entente. The first stages of this policy are marked by the pacts of friendship signed in November 1926 with Albania – a small country but one to which Italy had always paid considerable attention – and in the following year with Hungary. Although as a result relations between Yugoslavia and France became even closer, a pact of friendship between these two states did not grow into an alliance as the French did not wish openly to clash with Italy; and in the last resort its relations with the Great Powers were more important to France than anything else. In the long run this became one of the serious weaknesses of the system. The alliances of the small powers with each other and with the big powers lacked firm foundations and from a geographical and a historical point of view proved only interludes in the life of a Europe which had not yet acquired its permanent shape.

In the long term the problem of revision created more conflicts and opportunities for conflict on the continent than the conciliatory efforts of the League of Nations could contend with. After the peace treaties the balance of power was no longer what it had been before the war; but the differences remained and no compromise was found that could have stabilised Europe's internal situation. For a rapprochement between the states of Europe it would have been necessary permanently to take into account the plurality of forces and interests concerned. But this was unthinkable from the national point of view of each country.

In summing up we cannot ignore the fact that intelligent people must have seen the new dangers of which there were signs early on and that they should have taken them as a warning. The greatest of all threats was certainly that of blind nationalism; this had survived the war amazingly well and before long re-emerged with new force. It was therefore essential if Europe was to be restored to health that a sharp distinction should be made between nationalism and principles of flexible revision and that nationalism should be firmly resisted wherever it opposed revision.

Today there is probably less criticism of the Treaty of Versailles as such than of the whole system which emerged from the peace treaties of the years 1919–20 and which could only have been adapted to changed conditions by a permanent revision of the original criteria. In the last resort the fate of the 'system of Versailles' depended on the League of Nations and on whether or not use was made of the provisions for revision. It was unfortunate that after the failure of the British and American guarantee the nationalist Right in France criticised Clemenceau's policy in almost the same way as Wilson's policy was criticised in America. This was the belated revenge on the part of those whose more extreme and ruthless ideas had been rejected by Clemenceau; as a result French foreign policy was for too long forced to defend itself against criticism from the Right. In these circumstances Briand's attempts to find a reasonable compromise deserve particular appreciation.

Some of Germany's wartime enemies have continued to believe to the present day that the Treaty of Versailles was basically constructive and an important historic 'monument' which, as André François-Poncet has said, 'gives evidence of great intellectual power'. We must respect this opinion. In fact the 'system of Versailles' failed not because the treaties were worthless, not because mistakes were made, but primarily because there was no timely or far-sighted attempt to revise these treaties and to continue the necessarily unfinished work of the Paris Peace Conference. As it was the criteria established were obstinately adhered to even when the belief in their usefulness and viability had begun to vanish.

Bibliography

GENERAL

Chambers, F. P., Grant, C. and Bayley, C., *The Age of Conflict*, 4th ed. New York 1962.

Crouzet, M., *L'époque contemporaine à la recherche d'une civilisation nouvelle*, 3rd ed., Paris 1961.

Grant, A. J. and Temperley, H., *Europe in the Nineteenth and Twentieth Centuries*, 6th ed. (revised and edited by Julian M. Penson), London 1952.

Halecki, O., *The Limits and Divisions of European History*, London 1950.

Kohn, H., *The Twentieth Century*, New York 1949.

Langsam, W. C., *The World since 1914*, New York 1936.

Pannikkar, K. M., *Asia and Western Dominance*, London 1959.

Renouvin, P., *Les crises du XXe I: De 1914 à 1929*, Paris 1957.

Renouvin, P., *La crise européenne et la première guerre mondiale*, 4th ed., Paris 1962.

Taylor, A. J. P., *The Struggle for Mastery in Europe, 1848-1918*, Oxford 1954.

WAR AIMS, PROMOTION OF REVOLUTION AND PEACE MOVES

Birnbaum, K. E., *Peace Moves and U-Boat Warfare*, Stockholm 1958.

Epstein, K., 'The Development of German-Austrian War Aims', *Journal of Central European Affairs*, 1957.

Epstein, K., 'German War Aims in the First World War', *War Politics*, 1962.

Fischer, F., *Germany's Aims in the First World War*, London 1967.

Gatzke, H. W., *Germany's Drive to the West*, Baltimore 1950.

Gottlieb, W. W., *Studies in Secret Diplomacy during the First World War*, London 1957.

Guinn, P., *British Strategy and Politics, 1914-18*, Oxford 1965.

Hanak, H., *Great Britain and Austria-Hungary during the First World War*, London 1962.

Hoffmann, M., *Der Krieg der versäumten Gelegenheiten*, Munich 1923.

Mende, D., 'Die nicht bewältigte Vergangenheit des Ersten Weltkrieges', *Europa Archiv.*, 1963.

Ritter, G., *Staatskunst und Kriegshandwerk*, Vol. 3: *Die Tragödie der Staatskunst, Bethmann Hollweg als Kriegskanzler*, Munich 1964.

Scherer, A. and Grunewald, J. (eds.), *L'Allemagne et les problèmes de la paix pendant la première guerre mondiale*, Documents, 2 vols, Paris 1967.

237

Smith, C. J., *The Russian Struggle for Power*, New York 1956.

Steglich, W., *Bündnissicherung oder Verständigungsfrieden*, Göttingen 1958.

Steglich, W., *Die Friedenspolitik der Mittelmächte*, Vol. I, Wiesbaden 1964.

Stein, L., *The Balfour Declaration*, New York 1961.

Taylor, A. J. P., *The War Aims of the Allies: essays presented to Sir Lewis Namier*, London/New York 1956.

Taylor, A. J. P., *English History 1914–1945*, Oxford 1965.

BIOGRAPHIES AND MEMOIRS

Bethmann Hollweg, T. Von, *Betrachtungen zum Weltkriege*, 2 vols, Berlin 1919/21.

Buchanan, Sir George, *My Mission to Russia*, Vol. II, London 1923.

Churchill, W. S., *The World Crisis*, Vols II–IV, London 1925–27.

Epstein, K., *Matthias Erzberger and the Dilemma of German Democracy*, Princeton, N.J. 1959.

Erzberger, M., *Erlebnisse im Weltkrieg*, Stuttgart/Berlin 1920.

Lloyd George, D., *War Memoirs*, 6 vols, London 1933–36.

Ludendorff, E., *My War Memoirs 1914–1918*, 2 vols, London 1920.

Müller, G. A. von, *Regierte der Kaiser?*, Göttingen 1959.

Naumann, V., *Profile*, Munich/Leipzig 1925.

Naumann, V., *Dokumente und Argumente*, Berlin 1928.

Poincaré, R., *Au service de la France*, Vols IX–X, Paris 1932/38.

Pomiankowski, J., *Der Zusammenbruch des Ottomanischen Reiches*, Zürich/Leipzig/Vienna 1928.

SOCIALISM IN THE WAR

Auclair, M., *La vie de Jean Jaurès*, Paris 1954.

Bernstein, E., *Die Internationale der Arbeiterklasse und der europäische Krieg*, Tübingen 1915.

Bonomi, I., *Leonida Bissolati e il movimento socialista in Italia*, Rome 1945.

Borkenau, F., *European Communism*, London 1953.

Braunthal, J., *History of the International*, Vol. 2, London 1966–67.

Cole, G. D. H., *A Short History of the British Working Class Movement, 1789–1947*, London 1948.

Cole, G. D. H., *A History of Socialist Thought*, Vol. IV: *Communism and Social Democracy, 1914–31*, London 1958.

Drachkovitch, M. M., *De Karl Marx à Leon Blum. La crise de la social-démocratie*, Geneva 1954.

Elwood, R. C., 'Lenin and the Social Democratic School for Underground Party Workers 1909–11', *Political Science Quarterly*, Vol. LXXXI, 1966.

Fainsod, M., *International Socialism and the World War*, Harvard 1935.

Bibliography

Gay, P., *The Dilemma of Democratic Socialism, E. Bernstein's Challenge to Marx*, New York 1952.

Haimson, L. H., *The Russian Marxists and the Origin of Bolshevism*, Harvard 1955.

History of the Communist Party of the Soviet Union, Foreign Language Publication House, Moscow.

Joll, J., *The Second International*, London 1955.

Kotowski, G., *Friedrich Ebert*, Vol. I (1871–1917), Wiesbaden 1963.

Landauer, C., *European Socialism*, 2 Vols, Berkeley 1959.

Lefranc, G., *Histoire des doctrines sociales dans l'Europe contemporaine*, Paris 1960.

Montreuil, J., *Histoire du mouvement ouvrier en France*, Paris 1945.

Prélot, M., *L'évolution politique du socialisme français*, Paris 1939.

Rosenberg, A., *Geschichte des Bolschewismus, Neuausgabe*, Frankfurt a. M. 1966. First edition translated as *A History of Bolshevism*, London 1934.

Rosmer, A., *Le mouvement ouvrier pendant la guerre*, 2 vols, Paris 1936/59.

Schorske, L. E., *German Social Democracy*, New York 1955.

Sturmthal, A., *The Tragedy of European Labour*, London 1944.

Webb, S. and B., *History of Trade Unionism*, London 1920.

Ziebura, G., *Léon Blum*, Vol. I, Berlin 1963.

NATIONALISM AND SOCIALISM

d'Andrea, U., *Corradini el il nazionalismo*, Rome/Milan 1928.

Graziadei, A., *Idealità socialiste e interessi nazionali nel conflitto mondiale*, 2nd ed., Rome 1918.

Rossi, A., *The Rise of Italian Fascism*, London 1938.

Snell, J. L., 'Socialist Unions and Patriotism in Germany', *American Historical Review*, 1953/54.

AUSTRIA-HUNGARY AND ITS NATIONALITIES IN THE WAR

Bauer, O., *Die Nationalitätenfrage und die Sozialdemokratie*, Vienna 1907.

Hantsch, H., *Die Nationalitätenfrage im alten Österreich*, Vienna 1953.

Hantsch, H., *Die Geschichte Österreichs*, Vol. II, 3rd ed., Graz 1962.

Jászi, O., *The Dissolution of the Habsburg Monarchy*, Phoenix Ed., 1961.

Kann, R. A., 'Count Ottokar Czernin and Archduke Francis Ferdinand', *Journal of Central European Affairs*, 1956.

Kann, R. A., *The Multinational Empire. Nationalism and national reform in the Habsburg monarchy, 1848–1918*, 2 vols, New York 1950.

Macartney, C. A., *The Habsburg Empire 1790–1918*, London 1969.

Mamatey, V. S., 'The United States and the Dissolution of Austria-Hungary', *Journal of Central European Affairs*, 1950.
Mamatey, V. S., *The United States and Eastern Central Europe*, Princeton, N.J. 1954.
May, A. J., *The Passing of the Habsburg Monarchy*, 2 vols, Philadelphia 1966.
Seton-Watson, R. W., *History of the Czechs and Slovaks*, London 1944.
Sweet, P., *Germany, Austria-Hungary and Mitteleuropa, Festschrift for Heinrich Benedikt*, Vienna 1957.
Taylor, A. J. P., *The Habsburg Monarchy*, London 1947.
Zeman, Z. A. D., *The Break-up of the Habsburg Empire, 1914–1918*, London 1961.

BIOGRAPHIES AND MEMOIRS

Beneš, E., *Memoirs*, London 1954.
Masaryk, T. G., *The Making of a State, Memories and Observations, 1914–18*, London 1927.

THE RUSSIAN REVOLUTION AND THE GREAT POWERS

Adams, A. E., *Bolsheviks in the Ukraine, the Second Campaign*, New Haven/London 1963.
Bradley, J., *Allied Intervention in Russia*, London 1968.
Carr, E. H., *The Bolshevik Revolution*, 3 vols, London 1950–53.
Chamberlin, W. H., *The Russian Revolution*, 2 vols, London 1935.
Fischer, L., *The Soviets in World Affairs*, Vol. I, Princeton, N.J. 1951.
Fleming, P., *The Fate of Admiral Kolchak*, New York 1963.
Freund, G., *The Unholy Alliance*, London/New York 1957.
Kennan, G. F., *Soviet-American Relations, 1917–20*, 2 vols, London 1956–58.
Mayer, A. J., *Politics and Diplomacy of Peacemaking*, London 1968.
Reshetar, J. S., *The Ukranian Revolution*, Princeton, N.J. 1952.
Schapiro, L., *The Origin of the Communist Autocracy*, London 1955.
Seton-Watson, H., *The Russian Empire, 1801–1917*, Oxford 1967.
Silverlight, J., *The Victor's Dilemma*, London 1970.
Thompson, J. M., *Russia, Bolshevism and the Versailles Peace*, Princeton, N.J. 1967.
Ullman, R. H., *Intervention and the War*, Vol. I: *Anglo-Soviet Relations, 1917–21*. Vol. II: *Britain and the Russian Civil War*, Princeton, N.J. 1961–68.
Warth, R. D., *The Allies and the Russian Revolution*, Durham, N.C. 1954.
Wheeler Bennett, J. W., *Brest-Litovsk, the Forgotten Peace*, London 1963.

Bibliography

BIOGRAPHIES AND MEMOIRS

Deutscher, I., *The Prophet Unarmed: Trotsky, 1921–29*, London 1959.
Fischer, L., *The Life of Lenin*, London 1965.
Lenin, V. I., *Collected Works*, Moscow 1965–69.
Sukhanov, N. N., *The Russian Revolution, 1917, a personal record* (ed. J. Carmichael), London 1955.
Trotsky, L., *Lenin*, London 1925.
Trotsky, L., *My Life, the Rise and Fall of a Dictator*, London 1930.
Trotsky, L., *History of the Russian Revolution*, London 1932–33.
Ulam, A. B., *Lenin and the Bolsheviks*, London 1966.

DOCUMENTS

Degras, J. (ed.), *Soviet Documents on Foreign Policy*, Vol. I, London 1952.
Gankin, O. H. and Fisher, H. H. (eds.), *The Bolsheviks and the World War*, Stanford, Cal. 1940.

THE UNITED STATES AND THE WAR

Bailey, T. A., *The Policy of the United States towards the Neutrals, 1917–1918*, Baltimore 1942.
Bemis, S. F., *A Diplomatic History of the United States*, 4th ed., New York 1961.
Duroselle, J.-B., *De Wilson à Roosevelt*, Paris 1960.
Gelfand, E., *The Inquiry*, New Haven/London 1963.
Gorer, G., *The American People*, 2nd ed., New York 1964.
Hofstadter, R., *The American Political Tradition and the Men who Made it*, New York 1948.
Leopold, R. W., *The Growth of American Foreign Policy*, New York 1962.
Link, A. S. and Catton, W. B., *American Epoch*, 2nd ed., New York 1963.
May, E. R., *The World War and American Isolation*, Harvard 1959.
Mayer, A. J., *Political Origins of the New Diplomacy*, New Haven, Conn. 1959.
Morison, S. E. and Commager, H. S., *The Growth of the American Republic*, Vol. II, 3rd ed., New York 1942.
Osgood, R. E., *Ideals and Self-Interest in America's Foreign Relations*, Chicago 1953.
Schlesinger, A. M. Sr., *The Birth of the Nation*, London 1969.
Seymour, C., *American Diplomacy During the World War*, Baltimore 1934.
Soule, G., *Economic History of the United States*, Vol. VIII: *Prosperity Decade*, New York 1962.

Trask, D. F., *The United States in the Supreme War Council*, Middletown, Conn. 1961.

Trefousse, H. L., *Germany and American Neutrality*, New York 1957.

WILSON

Baker, R. S. and Dodd, W. E. (eds.), *The Public Papers of Woodrow Wilson*, 6 vols, New York 1925–27.

Baker, R. S., *Woodrow Wilson, Life and Letters*, 8 vols, New York 1927.

Bailey, T. A., *Wilson and the Peace Makers*, 2 vols, New York 1947.

Curry, R. W., *Woodrow Wilson and Far Eastern Policy, 1913–1921*, New York 1957.

George, A. L. and J. L., *Woodrow Wilson and Colonel House*, New York 1956.

Gerson, L. L., *Woodrow Wilson and the Rebirth of Poland, 1914–1920*, New Haven 1953.

Hoover, H. C., *The Ordeal of Woodrow Wilson*, London 1958.

Link, A. S., *Wilson, The Diplomatist*, Baltimore 1957.

Link, A. S., *Wilson, A Biography*, 5 vols, Princeton, N.J. 1947–65.

Seymour, C. (ed.), *Intimate Papers of Colonel House*, 4 vols, Boston/New York 1926–28.

Snell, J. L., 'Wilson on Germany and the Fourteen Points', *Journal of Modern History*, 1954.

DOCUMENTS

United States Department of State, Papers relating to the Foreign Relations of the United States, *The Lansing Papers*, 2 vols, Washington 1939:
  1917, The World War, Supplements 1 and 2, 3 vols, Washington 1931–32.
  1918, The World War, Supplements 1 and 2, 3 vols, Washington 1933.
  1918, Russia, 3 vols, Washington 1931–32.

Paris Peace Conference, 13 vols, Washington 1942–47.

Scott, J. B. (ed.), *Official Statements of War Aims and Peace Proposals*, Washington 1921.

ENTENTE

Bourget, I. M., *Gouvernement et Commandement*, Paris 1930.

Bruntz, G. B., *Allied Propaganda and the Collapse of the German Empire in 1918*, Stanford, Calif. 1938.

Chambers, F. W., *The War Behind the War*, London 1939.

Bibliography

Cooper-Willis, I., *England's Holy War*, London 1928.
Daalder, H., *Cabinet Reform in Britain*, Stanford, Calif. 1963.
Hirst, F. W., *The Consequences of the War to Great Britain*, London 1934.
Judd, D., *Balfour and the British Empire*, London 1968.
Watt, D. C., *Personalities and Policies. Studies in the Formulation of British Foreign Policy in the Twentieth Century*, London 1965.

BIOGRAPHIES AND MEMOIRS

Beaverbrook, Lord, *Men and Power*, London 1956.
Beaverbrook, Lord, *The Decline and Fall of Lloyd George*, London 1963.
Butler, J. R. M., *Lord Lothian (Philip Kerr)*, London 1960.
Clemenceau, G., *Grandeur and Misery of Victory*, London 1930.
Falls, C., *Marchal Foch*, London 1939.
Foch, F., *Memoirs*, London 1931.
Hancock, W. K., *Smuts*, 2 vols, Cambridge 1962/70.
Mowat, C. L., *Lloyd George*, Oxford 1964.
McCormick, G. O., *The Mask of Merlin, A Critical Study of D. Lloyd George*, London 1963.
Shane, L., *Mark Sykes*, London 1923.
Trevelyan, G. M., *Grey of Fallodon*, London/New York 1937.
Young, K., *Arthur James Balfour*, London 1963.

MILITARY TURNING POINT, REFORM AND REVOLUTION IN GERMANY

Armeson, R. B., *Total Warfare and Compulsory Labor in Germany*, The Hague 1964.
Carsten, F. L., *The Reichswehr and Politics*, Oxford 1966.
Craig, G., *The Politics of the Prussian Army*, Oxford 1955.
Gordon, H. G., *The Reichswehr and the German Republic 1919–26*, Princeton, N.J. 1957.
Groener-Geyer, D., *General Groener*, Frankfurt a. M. 1955.
Mitchell, A., *Revolution in Bavaria*, Princeton, N.J. 1965.
Rosenberg, A., *Entstehung und Geschichte der Deutschen Republik*, new ed., Frankfurt a. M. 1955. First edition translated as *The Birth of the German Republic, 1871–1918*, London 1931.
Rosenberg, A., *A History of the German Republic*, London 1936.
Ryder, A. J., *The German Revolution of 1918*, Cambridge 1967.
Spindler, A., *Der Handelskrieg mit U-Booten*, 4 vols, Berlin 1932–64.
Waldman, E., *The Spartacist Uprising*, Milwaukee 1958.

BIOGRAPHIES, MEMOIRS AND PERSONAL ACCOUNTS

Baden, Prince Max von, *The Memoirs of Prince Max of Baden*, London 1928.

Bernstein, E., *Die deutsche Revolution*, Berlin 1921.

Delbrück, C. von, *Die Wirtschaftliche Mobilmachung in Deutschland*, Munich 1924.

Groener, W., *Lebenserinnerungen*, Göttingen 1957.

Helfferich, K., *Der Weltkrieg*, 3 vols, Berlin 1919.

Heuss, T., *Friedrich Naumann*, Stuttgart/Tübingen 1949.

Müller, H., *Die Novemberrevolution*, Berlin 1928.

Noske, G., *Von Kiel bis Kapp*, Berlin 1920.

Scheidemann, P., *Der Zusammenbruch*, Berlin 1924.

Scheidemann, P., *Memoirs of a Social Democrat*, London 1929.

END OF THE WAR AND PEACE TREATIES

Almond, N. and Lutz, R. H., *The Treaty of St Germain*, Stanford, Calif. 1935.

Burnett, P. M., *Reparations at the Paris Peace Conference from the Standpoint of the American Delegation*, 2 vols, New York 1940.

Craig, G. A. and Gilbert, F. (eds.), *The Diplomats*, Princeton, N.J. 1953.

Hankey, Lord, *The Supreme Control at the Paris Peace Conference*, London 1963.

House, E. M. and Seymour, C. (eds.), *What Really Happened at Paris*, London 1921.

Mantoux, P., *Les délibérations du Conseil des Quatre*, 2 vols, Paris 1955.

Marhefka, E. et al. (eds.), *Der Waffenstillstand*, 3 vols, Berlin 1928.

McCallum, R. B., *Public Opinion and the Last Peace*, London 1944.

Mermeix (pseud. G. Terril), *Les négotiations secrètes et les quatre armistices*, Paris 1919.

Noble, G. B., *Policies and Opinions at Paris*, New York 1935.

Rudin, H. R., *Armistice*, New Haven, Conn. 1944.

Seymour, C., *Geography, Justice and Politics at the Paris Peace Conference*, New York 1951.

Temperley, H. W. V., *A History of the Peace Conference*, 6 vols, London 1920–24.

Woodward, E. L. and Butler, R. (eds.), *Documents on British Foreign Policy, First Series, 1919–39*, Vols I–VIII, London 1947–62.

INDIVIDUAL PROBLEMS

Albrecht-Carrié, R., *Italy at the Paris Peace Conference*, New York 1938.

Benoist-Méchin, J., *Histoire de l'armée allemande depuis l'armistice*, Paris 1936.

Deák, F., *Hungary at the Paris Peace Conference. The Diplomatic History of the Treaty of Trianon*, New York 1942.

Dickmann, F., *Die Kriegsschuldfrage auf der Friedenskonferenz von Paris*, 1919, Munich 1964.

Low, A. D., 'The Soviet–Hungarian Republic and the Paris Peace Conference', *Transactions of the American Philosophical Society*, Philadelphia 1963.

Luckau, A. M., *The German Delegation at the Paris Peace Conference*, New York 1941.

Marston, F. S., *The Peace Conference, Organisation and Procedure*, New York 1944.

Nelson, H. J., *Land and Power, British and Allied Policy on Germany's Frontiers*, London/Toronto 1963.

Tillman, S. P., *Anglo-American Relations at the Paris Peace Conference*, Princeton, N.J. 1961.

Wright, Q., *Mandates under the League of Nations*, Chicago 1930.

MEMOIRS AND PERSONAL ACCOUNTS

Barthou, L., *Le traité de paix*, Paris 1919.

Baruch, B. M., *The Making of the Reparation and Economic Section of the Treaty*, New York 1920.

Baruch, B. M., *The Public Years*, New York 1960.

Bethlen, Count S., *The Treaty of Trianon and European Peace*, London 1934.

Brockdorff-Rantzau, Count U. von, *Dokumente*, Charlottenburg 1925.

Lloyd George, D., *The Truth about the Peace Treaties*, 2 vols, London 1938.

Nicolson, H., *Peacemaking, 1919*, London 1964.

Nitti, F., *Rivelazioni dramatis personae*, Naples 1948.

Orlando, V. E., *Memorie*, Milan 1960.

Tardieu, A., *The Truth about the Treaty*, London 1921.

CRITICISM

Bainville, J., *Les Conséquences politiques de la paix*, Paris 1920.

Herzfeld, H., 'Nach vierzig Jahren, die Pariser Friedensschlüsse', *Polit. Studien*, 1959.

Keynes, J. M., *The Economic Consequences of the Peace*, London 1919.

Mantoux, E., *The Carthaginian Peace*, London 1946.

Wüest, W., *Der Vertrag von Versailles in Licht und Schatten der Kritik*, Zürich 1962.

THE NEAR AND MIDDLE EAST

Anderson, M. S., *The Eastern Question 1774–1923*, London 1966.

Antonius, C., *The Arab Awakening*, New York 1946.

Beer, G. L., *African Questions at the Peace Conference*, New York 1923.
Cummings, H. H., *Franco–British Rivalry in the Postwar Near East*, New York 1938.
De Novo, J. A., *American Interests and Policies in the Middle East*, Minneapolis 1963.
Evans, L., *United States Policy and the Partition of Turkey*, Baltimore 1965.
Gibb, H. A. and Bowen, H., *Islamic Society and the West*, New York 1951.
Gouilly, A., *L'Islam dans l'Afrique occidentale française*, Paris 1952.
Hourani, A. H., *Arabic Thought in the Liberal Age, 1798–1939*, Oxford 1967.
Howard, H. N., *The King–Crane Commission*, Beirut 1963.
Kedourie, E., *Britain and the Middle East*, London 1956.
Luke, Sir Horace, *The Making of Modern Turkey*, London 1936.
Monroe, E., *Britain's Moment in the Middle East*, London 1963.
Nevakivi, J., *Britain, France and the Arab Middle East, 1914-20*, London 1968.
Zeine, Z. N., *The Struggle for Arab Independence*, Beirut 1960.

BIOGRAPHIES, MEMOIRS AND PERSONAL ACCOUNTS

Garnett, D. (ed.), *The Letters of T. E. Lawrence*, London 1938.
Lawrence, T. E., *The Seven Pillars of Wisdom*, Oxford 1925.
Meinertzhagen, R., *Middle East Diary 1917–1956*, London 1959.
Nicolson, H., *Curzon, the Last Phase*, London 1934.
Weizmann, C., *Trial and Error*, London 1949.

EUROPE AFTER THE PEACE TREATIES

Baumont, M., *La Faillite de la paix*, 2 vols, Paris 1951.
Carr, E. H., *The Twenty Years' Crisis*, London 1946.

EAST

Angress, W. T., *Stillborn Revolution, the Communist Bid for Power in Germany*, Princeton, N.J. 1963.
Carr, E. H., *German-Soviet Relations Between the Two World Wars, 1919–1939*, London 1951.
Debicki, R., *Foreign Policy of Poland*, London 1963.
Eudin, J. and Fisher, H. H., *Soviet Russia and the West 1920-27, a Documentary Survey*, Stanford, Calif. 1957.
Glaser, K., *Czecho-Slovakia, a Critical History*, Caldwell, Id. 1961.
Hulse, J. W., *The Forming of the Communist International*, Stanford, Calif. 1964.
Kennan, G. F., *Russia and the West under Lenin and Stalin*, London 1961.

Korbel, J., *Poland between East and West*, Princeton, N.J. 1963.

Macartney, C. A. and Palmer, A. W., *Independent Eastern Europe*, London 1962.

Pipes, R., *The Formation of the Soviet Union, Communism and Nationalism 1917–23*, Harvard 1964.

Roos, H., *A History of Modern Poland*, London 1966.

Rosenbaum, K., *Community of Fate, German–Soviet Diplomatic Relations 1922–25*, Syracuse, N.Y. 1965.

Szinai, M. and Szücs, L., *The Confidential Papers of Admiral Horthy*, Budapest 1965.

WEST

Bonn, M. J., *Das Schicksal des deutschen Kapitalismus*, Berlin 1930.

Hankey, Lord, *Diplomacy by Conference*, London 1946.

Jordan, W. M., *Great Britain, France and the German Problem, 1918–1939*, London 1943.

Morley, F., *The Society of Nations*, Washington 1932.

Nolte, E., *Three Faces of Fascism: Action française, Italian Fascism, National Socialism*, London 1965.

Nolte, E., *Die Krise des liberalen Systems und die faschistischen Bewegungen*, Munich 1966.

Salvemini, G., *The Fascist Dictatorship in Italy*, New York 1927.

Walters, F. P., *A History of the League of Nations*, 2 vols, London 1941.

Wolfers, A., *Britain and France Between Two Wars*, New York 1940.

Zimmern, A., *The League of Nations and the Rule of Law*, London 1936.

Index

PACE UNIVERSITY LIBRARY
New York, NY   10038
Telephone 285-3332

TO THE BORROWER:

The use of this book is governed by rules established in the broad interest of the university
community. It is your responsibility to know these
rules. Please inquire at the circulation desk.